PENGUIN BOOKS

THE APPLE AND THE TREE

Marina Mahathir is a writer, women's rights and HIV/AIDS activist. She served as the President of the Malaysian AIDS Council for twelve years from 1993-2005 and was a member of numerous international and regional committees on HIV/AIDS.

From 2010-16, she served on the Board of Sisters in Islam, which advocates for justice and equality for Muslim women, and remains a member of the Finance and Fundraising Committee.

Marina has written a column in a local English-language daily for more than twenty years, and writes and speaks regularly on current issues particularly where it relates to gender, human rights and religion. She is active on Twitter (@netraKL) and Facebook and has authored three compilations of her newspaper columns, *In Liberal Doses* (1997), *Telling It Straight* (2012), and *Dancing on Thin Ice* (2015).

In 2010, Marina was named the UN Person of the Year by the United Nations in Malaysia. On the 100th anniversary of International Women's Day in 2011, Marina was one of only two Malaysian women named to WomenDeliver.org's list of 100 Most Inspiring People Delivering for Girls and Women. In 2016, Marina received France's highest award, the Chevalier de la Legion D'Honneur in recognition of her work in HIV and women's rights. This is in addition to receiving the Dato Paduka Mahkota Selangor (DPMS) from the Sultan of Selangor in 1997 which carries the title 'Datin Paduka'.

Marina's abiding interest in education especially for young women has led her to be appointed to the board of the Asian University for Women in Bangladesh. In 1997 she received an Honorary degree from Universiti Sains Malaysia for her work in HIV/AIDS education, in 2014 from Wawasan Open University, Penang for her work in human rights and in 2018 she received an Honorary Doctorate from her alma mater, the University of Sussex, UK. Previously she also co-produced an award-winning TV programme for young women, 3R–Respect, Relax, Respond which ran for ten years on TV3.

Marina's latest venture is a website for women travellers in Asia and the Middle East, Zafigo.com and ZafigoX, an event on women and travel that features inspiring women who have faced challenges and barriers while travelling and overcome them.

In 2019, Marina completed with Distinction a Master's Degree in Biography and Creative Non-fiction from the University of East Anglia, UK.

ADVANCE PRAISE FOR *THE APPLE AND THE TREE*

Marina Mahathir is among the very few children of political leaders who has carved out a distinguished career for themselves, balancing her own commitments to human rights with maintaining close ties to her family. *The Apple and the Tree* is a remarkable account of her life, complete with extraordinary insights into the complex politics of Malaysia and the global struggles against HIV in which she has been a central voice. Reading it made me proud to be her friend.

—Prof Dennis Altman, former President, AIDS Society of
Asia & the Pacific

Marina is no ordinary daughter of an ordinary Prime Minister. By her father's admission she's 'argumentative, stubborn and opinionated'. This book is not just about being the daughter of Tun Dr Mahathir Mohamad but more so about the special bond that defines the father-daughter relationship. She was not just a chronicler of events big and small, tumultuous or otherwise during her father's involvement in politics but a keen but critical observer of the history of the nation. Her lucid style and eloquence coupled with her uncompromising positions on issues make this book fabulously readable. A true gem indeed.

—Tan Sri Johan Jaaffar, senior journalist, former Chairman,
Media Prima Berhad

The Apple and the Tree is a riveting autobiography of a woman, writer and activist, a mother and a daughter to the most important political figure in modern Malaysia. Marina takes us deep into the heart of some of the most important and contentious issues in recent history, sharing her principles and motivation for advocating for women, people with HIV and the importance of the creative arts. At once a gripping insider's account of the most dramatic years in Malaysia's recent history, it is also a story of becoming. Marina is an inspiration to us all.

—Jean MacNeil, author, Professor of Creative Writing,
University of East Anglia

For the first time, Marina Mahathir shares in full her formative experiences as the daughter of Dr. Mahathir—physician, politician, prime minister, and one of the great figures of the twentieth and twenty-first centuries. Born on the eve of Independence, she traces a nation's journey from Malaya to Malaysia with her parallel emergence into a formidable social activist and holds to account our conscience and actions in a rapidly changing and often troubled world. In this book, she reveals the ideas and imagination—many of them born in her own home—behind major events and provides an honest examination of the first Mahathir era, his return to power thirty-seven years after becoming Malaysia's leader, as well as her foray into frontline politics in the historic 2018 election. *The Apple and the Tree* is an excellent account of an exceptional life in extraordinary times.

—James Chau, international broadcaster, host of *The China Current*

Marina Mahathir's book is a glimpse into history, both an intimate glimpse into the world of family and a thoughtful exploration of her beloved country, Malaysia, and its extraordinary political turns. A valuable and poignant record.

—Fatima Bhutto, author

In this memoir, Marina has found this very difficult balance when talking about this always special relationship between father and daughter. My respect for both has only increased.

—Dr Peter Piot, former Executive Director, UNAIDS, former Director, London School of Hygiene & Tropical Medicine

Marina Mahathir writes a charmingly low-key presentation of her life story—and what we read is an important historical document.

In the annals of autobiography, this book is not the only first-person recount of living with a famous father. But Mahathir Mohamad is not just a famous father; he is a Malaysian icon, a controversial hero in the normally boring parliamentary politics, a leader who brought major changes in the country's history (the latest when he was in his nineties!).

And Marina is not only a daughter—his daughter. A columnist and a TV producer, she is an adept chronicler. She says she has an 'impostor syndrome', a lingering sense of insecurity under the shadow of a political superstar, but this book betrays a genuine gift of percipience. It is a testimony that goes beyond the personal.

—Goenawan Mohamad, poet, essayist, founder of Indonesia's *Tempo* magazine

THE APPLE AND THE TREE

Life as Dr Mahathir's Daughter

[signature] 8/11/23

Marina Mahathir

PENGUIN BOOKS

An imprint of Penguin Random House

PENGUIN BOOKS

USA | Canada | UK | Ireland | Australia
New Zealand | India | South Africa | China | Southeast Asia

Penguin Books is part of the Penguin Random House group of companies
whose addresses can be found at global.penguinrandomhouse.com

Published by Penguin Random House SEA Pte Ltd
9, Changi South Street 3, Level 08-01,
Singapore 486361

First published in Penguin Books by Penguin Random House SEA 2021

Copyright © Marina Mahathir 2021

ISBN 9789815017175

Typeset in Adobe Caslon Pro by Manipal Technologies Limited, Manipal

www.penguin.sg

To my parents under whose nurturing embrace I blossomed,
To Tara, for being my steadfast tree,
And to Ineza, Haga and Shasha, my apples.

Contents

Part 3: The Sabbatical (2003-2018)

Part 4: The Return (2011-2018)

Part 5: The End? (2020)

Prologue

Whenever I have reason to tell off my younger daughter Shasha, for being too mouthy, or sloppy, she always comes back to me with the words, 'apple' and 'tree'. It is a code for that adage 'the apple doesn't fall far from the tree'. Everything she is, comes from me. Everything, in short, is my fault.

I may be the apple to my father's tree, but I like to think of our life journeys as two trains running on railroad tracks so close to each other that passing carriages scrape against each other. Of course, Dad's track is thirty-two years longer than mine. He picked up his chief engineer and steward, Mum, in 1956 and then four more passengers with her in the next eight years. Later, another three were added. As we grew up, we got on our trains, all going independently of each other, only meeting at the rail yard when something happens.

Undoubtedly, the trajectory of his journey has been far higher and more distinguished than mine. But we have run alongside each other, his Orient Express to my Keretapi Tanah Melayu, sometimes reaching a junction and stopping to allow the other, usually his more magnificent one, to pass. Our trains ultimately are from the same company and are heading towards the same destination, even though sometimes our paths diverge in big and small ways. There are many mountain-crossing bridges and tunnels along the way, the scenery can be breathtaking and sometimes dark and foreboding. But we chug along in tandem, tooting to different songs, until we come to the station at the end although neither of us knows when we will get there.

Much like the *angsana* tree in the Alor Setar garden of my childhood, my father looms large in my life. So much of what I am today, from my laser beam focus on causes I support, to the discipline that even surprises me, to my impatience at those who are too slow to understand what I'm saying, even my occasional sarcastic snipe, I know they all came from him. Despite all that, I was, and perhaps still am, the little sapling trying to grow out of his umbrella-like shadow, watching, observing and sometimes pushing back so that I may breathe and branch out on my own.

This is the story of the journey that I have taken in my life as my father's daughter. Although much of it will feature him, it's not his story. While he was crafting his, and that of millions of Malaysians, I was trying to write my own with ink-stained fingers on whatever paper was handed over to me. I would be the first to say that being the apple of Dad's giant tree is a life of privilege, at least when viewed from the outside. But branching out from under those leafy branches has its costs.

This is my story, viewed from behind, alongside and sometimes opposite that of Dad's. I am striving to tell it without blowing anybody's horn but with sincerity and honesty, with my truths and nobody else's.

Enjoy the ride.

Part 1

The Beginning (1957-1979)

1

My Beginnings

To understand my story, we have to go back to the beginning.

I was born in Alor Setar, in the northern state of Kedah, over 400 kilometres from Kuala Lumpur, in June 1957, just a few months before Merdeka. My parents had married the year before, long after they had first met at medical school in Singapore after World War II. Dad, the dashing young man from the north of the Peninsula, had been a star student and graduated earlier than Mum, a quiet woman from a strict Kuala Lumpur family who struggled with her books. Their romance is the stuff of legend in our family; how she had many suitors but only he used the excuse of offering tuition in her worst subjects to get close to her. Mum has never been shy about recounting how, over a game of Scrabble, Dad expressed his feelings for her by spelling out with the tiles, 'I Love You'. Although both their families knew of their relationship, there was no question of marrying before graduation. Mum had been brought up by a father, my grandpa Haji Mohd Ali, who believed very much in girls' education and had refused to allow the couple to marry until his daughter finished university. Mum was diligent but struggled to pass her exams and it took another two years after Dad had graduated and done his housemanship before she earned her medical degree and could finally marry her young man.

Mum left a big city, her parents and a family of ten siblings to move to a much smaller, more provincial town. But there she fell into the warm embrace of another big family, albeit one that was much older than hers. Dad was the youngest in a family of nine and some of his oldest siblings were already married with grown-up children, who themselves had children. He was also the only one to go to university to do a lengthy medical degree, a course much delayed by the war. My parents thus not only married late, as compared to most of their contemporaries, they also started the family in their early thirties. I grew up with cousins, some of them old enough to pass off as my parents, and nieces and nephews who were my age or older than me.

Still, Dad and his wife and family were enveloped in a lot of love. Especially, as the youngest, he was very close to his mother and his three older sisters. Photographs of my first birthday show a chubby-cheeked baby, sitting on Mum's lap in front of a table laden with cake. Next to us was a young long-chinned Dad, his hair slicked back as always, smiling with what I hope was pride. Surrounding us were various aunts, cousins and friends so close that we considered them family as well. My childhood was filled with these family occasions; *kenduris* at my grandparents', party picnics in our big garden with Tom and Jerry cartoon films that Dad would screen in our garage. We had so many relatives in Alor Setar that until I went to school, there was almost no need to invite anyone else to our parties. Mum would organize these birthdays, with food, cake and games, for each one of my brothers and I, until after four children, she decided it was easier to just have one big party a year even though our actual birth dates were spread out over several months. We protested—or at least Mirzan and I, the two elder ones did—but in the face of maternal power, had to give in. It did mean a big bang of an annual party with one birthday cake for me and another that the boys had to share. I was particularly proud of my cake one year that featured a doll with a wide skirt made entirely of icing. As for games, my parents were always looking for something new besides the traditional egg and spoon race. Dad once returned from America around 1966 with a new toy: two tubes made of green and red hard plastic containing little marbles on one end. The idea was to shake the tubes and make the marbles descend to the other end through a series of holes just big enough to allow one marble to drop through at a time. It made for a very exciting, somewhat noisy, relay when our party guests were organized into two teams to see who shook their tubes fastest.

In our little town of Alor Setar, Jalan Maxwell was a middle-class enclave of government houses—quarters, as they were called—provided to the top civil servants in our state. Our home, number 929, was a large two-storey brick bungalow surrounded on three sides by an expansive garden, easily two acres in all, similar to the other houses on our side of the street. The design of the house was so standard government-style that my aunt Jameah lived in an identical one in Ipoh because her husband was also a civil servant. You can still see similar ones dotted around Kuala Lumpur, now mostly falling into ruin.

We were surrounded by doctors and bureaucrats, many of whom had children who became my playmates. On our left was Dr Rose Wong, a colleague of Mum's at the General Hospital. Across the road were several large wooden bungalows built in the tropical style with large verandas, raised above the ground on cement stilts to mimic traditional Malay houses and to allow ventilation. My childhood best friend, Ann Wong, no relation to Dr Rose, lived in one of those. Next to them was the home of the Chief Education Officer, in charge of all the schools in the state. Further down the road was the home of the Chief Dental Officer and various other department heads in the Kedah Civil Service, including the home of the Chief Police Officer.

On our right, beyond a tall hedge at the end of a long driveway, was a brick house with green trimmings in the middle of a neatly manicured garden that would not have been out of place in England. In the house lived a mysterious English man, whom we never saw. Apparently, he had no family either because there were no children who played in that garden or were invited to our parties.

When I look back at those days as an adult, a striking fact hits me. As a child, it had not occurred to me that most of the top civil servants who were our neighbours were non-Malays, something that would be rare these days. I was friends with the children of the Wongs, the Ongs, the Foos, the Nayagams, the Ritchies, the Sodhys, the Sidhus and the Vergheses because they all went to school with me, or were the offspring of my parents' friends and colleagues, with little thought of our differences at all. We went to each other's parties and festive occasions without fussing over whether, like today, we needed to worry about the food served or not. Our street was safe enough that we could walk to each other's homes and would always be welcomed. Over time, our neighbours were transferred to other states and I lost touch with most of those childhood playmates although I did discover some of them in adulthood. Only our family remained a constant on that street for a decade, as successive neighbours came and went.

* * *

We lived at 929 Jalan Maxwell because of Mum, not Dad. Our parents both started their careers as doctors in the late 1950s in the Malayan health system but after a few years, Dad decided to leave public service to become the first Malay private practitioner in Alor Setar, mainly because it freed him to enter politics, his long-time passion. Mum stayed on in government service, eventually transferring from the Alor Setar General Hospital to become the first woman head of Public Health in the state. It was her employment in the government health service that entitled her to housing and how we came to live in the brick house with the big garden.

As children, we knew how lucky we were to live in such a house. In an era when many people still lived in traditional wooden houses, to live in a brick one, *rumah batu*, even one that was provided by the government, meant that you were well-off. That idea was so ingrained in my child's mind that when, as a student, I visited English villages where houses were all made of brick or stone, I was momentarily confused. I had equated 'village' with 'poor' and 'wooden houses', and had not realized until much later that wealthy English people did not all want to live in cities.

The houses on our side of the street had two large bedrooms upstairs with two ensuite bathrooms, and a separate living room, dining room and kitchen downstairs. At the back of the house were the servants' quarters, bathroom and laundry area. The servants' rooms had no beds. Instead, they had large wooden platforms called *pangkin* that served as work areas by day and, with mattresses rolled out, beds at night.

Houses in those days were designed for the humid tropical climate. Verandas and air vents were common, and air-conditioning was rare. This also meant that fans and mosquito nets became necessary and those openings which provided good cross-ventilation also allowed unwanted visitors entry into the house. Looking up at the rectangular vent high up near my bedroom ceiling one day, I was horrified to discover that what I took for a sash that someone, perhaps a naughty brother, may have thrown up there was in fact a snake. My Indiana Jones-like aversion to snakes, that has lasted to this day, probably stemmed from that incident.

We were also one of the few houses in town that actually had a telephone. The black Bakelite telephone, with the number '556', sat on Dad's desk in the hallway. To make a call, you simply picked it up and an operator would ask which number you wanted to be connected to. My most vivid memory of that telephone was the time my brother Mokhzani's kindergarten called up to inform us he had fallen and broken his arm. Tok Chah, the nanny who replaced our first nanny Chik after she got married, had answered that call and promptly started wailing at the news, frightening us all.

Our household was quite big. Besides my parents and us four children, there was also a nanny, a cook, a driver and a gardener. Unlike the mothers of most of my friends, my mother worked every day at the hospital. She had to rely on help at home to make sure we were ready every morning, had our breakfasts and were sent to school on time. In those days, we could find household help among locals and we spent a good part of our days at home with them. Yet my brothers and I never felt we were deprived of our parents' attention. We lived in an era in the 1960s when parents could still return home for lunch and finished work at four in the afternoon with plenty of time to bundle us in the car and go for drives to nearby parks.

But so unusual was it then for Malay women to work, especially in professions like medicine, that sometimes I found myself facing comments from other children that I did not understand. Mum had taken me to visit a friend of hers one day, a homemaker with many daughters. While the mothers had tea inside the house, I went outside with the girls who then proceeded to tell me that I was a very deprived child because my mother was not at home 'spoonfeeding' me. For the rest of the day confusion reigned in my head as I wondered if Mum was failing in her mothering. Eventually I must have concluded that I liked things as they were, because Mum was too fierce a mother to have around all day.

For us children, the garden was the jewel in the crown of our home, two vast expanses of green on either side of the house. We spent many hours playing catch with each other, running its entire length and breadth. A large angsana tree was home to a makeshift tree house and a tire hung from its sturdy branch was a favourite swing. Once, after days of heavy rain, the entire garden flooded and became a massive lake surrounding the house. My Uncle Hassan, whom I called Baba, the husband of Dad's sister Rafeah, decided this was only another opportunity to play and to our delight, brought over a toy battery-powered boat that he sailed all over the garden lake.

Behind our house was a small vegetable plot, producing mostly long beans, and beyond the wire fence, were padi fields, ubiquitous in Kedah state which produced almost all the rice for the country. Farmers ploughed those fields with bulky horned buffaloes and in the dry season, we had to watch out for them grazing in the fields if we ever snuck through our fence to take a walk. Traversing the fields was a railway line and we could time our day by the Malayan Railways trains as they headed towards or returned from Thailand only an hour north.

* * *

Our childhood routine at Jalan Maxwell was simple: school in the mornings, home for lunch and perhaps a nap. In the afternoons, after a shower, a change into fresh clothes and tea, we children were let out into the garden for a few hours of play.

There we would find our greatest treasure, Pak Hashim, our gardener. While he mowed and trimmed and kept the garden in order, Pak Hashim would regale us with stories, mostly Malay folk tales involving Sang Kancil, the mousedeer who could outwit bigger predators in the Malayan jungle. We would trail him around the garden, listening open-mouthed to his tales of the mousedeer's wit and cunning, complete with sound effects and dramatics. When he came to the end of his repertoire, we would make him repeat old stories, each time marvelling anew at Sang Kancil's exploits.

Our favourite tale was the one where Sang Kancil outwitted a river full of crocodiles by pretending he was the Royal Animal Census-Taker. By making the crocodiles line up in the river, he crossed to the other bank by knocking each reptile on the head as he counted them— one, two, three, bop! And once he reached the other side, Sang Kancil promptly disappeared, laughing at the angry crocodiles he had fooled! This finale never failed to send us into peals of laughter.

I went to a Catholic girls' school, St. Nicholas' Convent, Monday to Friday and had Saturday and Sunday off. My brothers, however, went to Iskandar School which followed the local work week with Friday and Saturday as the weekend. This meant that I had to go to school on Fridays while everyone else was at home, and then was at home on Sundays when everyone else was at school or work. As the only girl in the family, I quite enjoyed these mismatched days. It meant that instead of our driver, Dad could drive me to and from school in his dark blue fin-tailed Pontiac on Fridays, which gave us both precious time with each other. On Sundays, I loved the idea that I could lay in bed as my brothers rushed to get ready for school.

My parents sent me to St. Nicholas' because it was a good school. At the time, few Muslim parents placed their daughters in the Convent school because there was an unfounded fear that nuns teaching there would convert us to Christianity. In fact, missionary schools for girls and boys in Malaysia were known not just for accepting children from all faith backgrounds but also for teaching in English and for high academic achievements by their students.

I started at St. Nicholas' at the tender age of four, when it was rare for any local parent to send their children to school so young. I spent three years in kindergarten in all. With my two oldest friends, Saw Bee and Saraswathi, we threaded pictures on cards, learnt our ABCs, sang nursery rhymes and as with little children everywhere, we picked up English as easily as breathing. Oddly, I have a memory of Dad asking me when I would speak the language, even though I cannot remember a time when I did not.

In my first kindergarten year at least, my nanny, Chik, would turn up at recess every day with a tiffin carrier of fried rice or *laksa* so that I would not spend any money at the tuck shop. Not that I had any to spend. I was given no pocket money until I was about eight, bringing food in sweaty Tupperware containers every day from home. Mum had insisted on this because there was a cholera epidemic at the time in our state and she did not want to risk us becoming infected through contaminated water. Eventually, I made a successful plea to be given some pocket money after the epidemic was over because I felt so left out when my friends bought junk food for snacks. My daily pocket money was twenty sen, with which I could buy a whole plate of steaming *laksa* as well as a drink.

St. Nicholas' had a kindergarten, primary school and secondary school in the same location. After kindergarten, I graduated to Primary School and was placed in Standard One A, the very first class you would see on the left after you entered the school compound, facing the wooden double-storey building with the large cross on top where Reverend Mother and the nuns lived. I am certain my interest in fashion began then because my class teacher was Miss Ong Eng Eng, a young, slim Chinese woman who wore bright orange flared skirts and white shirts, and high-heeled shoes, her hair a bouffant in the prevailing style of the Sixties. In Standard Two, my class teacher was Miss Chew, with a short bob circling her round face, glasses and a friendly demeanour that ensured that when she left the school two years later, our entire class spent her farewell party sobbing.

St. Nicholas' Primary School was ruled by the one and only Miss Millicent Sibert, or as we pronounced it, 'Missy Bert'. Miss Sibert came from a Penang Eurasian family. Her most distinguishing feature was her size. Due to a hormonal problem, Miss Sibert had a wide girth and seemed like a giant to St. Nicholas' petite students, especially those like me in Standard One and Two. She ranged around the school in floral dresses, men's sandals and long hair framing a face that had traces of a five o'clock shadow. Her voice was actually sweetly feminine but because she was so stern, she terrified all the littlest girls. She came to school every day in a trishaw driven laboriously by a skinny Chinese man. On one of those mornings, as she arrived at school, we heard a loud bang in front of the school gates. One of the trishaw's tires had burst, presumably finally giving up on the weight it had to bear every day. It was all we could do to hide our giggles at Missy Bert's humiliation.

Millicent Sibert was a music teacher. She played the piano at assembly in the school canteen every day, when everyone except the Muslim girls was obliged to recite the Lord's Prayer. It has to be said that none of us Muslims was deaf; to this day I can still recite the prayer as well as my Islamic ones. During music periods, she would teach us to recognize notes and practice singing scales. Eventually, when I was about seven, Mum decided that my brother Mirzan and I should learn to play the piano and Missy Bert would come to our house once a week to give us lessons. That was when I learnt Millicent was as gentle as her name.

Millicent taught me the piano for about three or four years. Mirzan dropped out early; I don't think he was particularly interested in it. When it came time for piano exams, she would pack all her students, about five of us, in her car and drive us to Penang, the nearest examination centre, where we would stay at her family home, a simple one-storey house on Green Lane. In between practicing and preparing for the theory and practical exams, we five had the run of the house, jumping up and down on beds and having pillow fights. Missy Bert never once complained about the noise or the mess we left. Our trips with the very scary school principal were, in fact, the most fun we had.

Sadly, I couldn't keep my enthusiasm for the piano for longer than three years and dropped out after Grade Three. I never practiced enough and found learning music theory tedious. Still, I grappled with telling my parents I wanted to stop because I knew that the shiny upright piano, with the chip on its cover where I once dropped a heavy metronome, had been expensive. Finally, in a flood of tears, at about age nine, I confessed I didn't want to do it anymore and my parents resigned themselves to not forcing me to continue.

As with many childhood follies, in hindsight, looking at my now-stiff fingers, I regretted that decision.

* * *

Chik, whose real name was Fatimah, was my second mother. In the old Malay tradition, she was a distant relative or a family friend—I never figured out the real relationship—who came to live with us to help Mum care for us children. As was typical of people in northern Malaya, Chik's family was descended from Muslim migrants from India. Her mother whom we called *Achi* or sister in Tamil was a heavy-set white-haired and toothless woman with billowing breasts, who made a living buying gold jewellery from traditional jewellers and selling them to the many relatives and friends she had. When Achi wasn't visiting us or some other relative, she lived in a half-finished wooden house on stilts in the town of Changloon, a stone's throw from the Thai border, with her only son, Radzi. Mum and Dad treated her with the utmost respect and we children adored this additional grandmother who would let us snuggle on her lap as she sat cross-legged on the floor chatting with Mum and her daughter Chik or her younger daughter Asmah who also lived with us for a while. It was in our home that she finally passed away many years later at a great old age.

As the first-born, I was under Chik's care the longest. She made sure I was dressed and fed and went to school but could not help with homework as she did not speak English. Mum and Dad went to work every day, so I spent the most time after school with Chik and we grew very close. Perhaps she also indulged me rather too much. To my mother's frustration, I didn't like to eat anything except boiled rice, fried fish and *sambal belacan*, a dish with very little nutrition, but which Chik would make for me every day. Whenever I protested at having to down cod liver oil or take any medicine, she gave up easily. In the afternoons I would lie on her lap and doze, as she read the newspapers. Or I would sit by her side to watch as she dotted a large white sheet with a flour mixture that became *bedak sejuk*, cold powder, when dried. To use, you wetted two or three dots with water, turning them into a paste that you patted on the face to keep the skin cool. Occasionally, especially when my parents were away, she would take me with her to see Hindi movies at the Empire Theatre or to the hairdresser's when she wanted to perm her hair, in those days a long and laborious process. When my parents went on a three-month-long trip to Europe when I was about five, it was Chik who was in charge of the three of us, along with another nanny, supervised occasionally by Dad's older sisters. Mum and Dad returned from their holiday to find Mirzan and I hiding shyly from them, and the one-year-old Mokhzani in hospital, his right leg in a cast. This was not Chik's fault; Jani, as we called him, was just a rambunctious boy who managed to slip on his own pee and fall.

When I was nine, the day came when Chik had to get married. A divorced businessman from Penang, of Arab origin, asked for her hand and seeing a better future than being a nanny with us, she accepted. Mum organized a simple marriage solemnization in our house, with me as flower girl sitting next to her as Chik sat demurely on a large cushion on the floor, dressed in a simple *songket* dress and a white shawl on her head. The next day we all drove to Penang to meet her new family, which included a daughter from her husband's first marriage. It was only then that it hit me that I was to lose the second mother I had known since infancy and our separation was tearful and traumatic. There was never a replacement for Chik in my life but despite living far away, we always kept in touch with her. Chik went on to have two sons and a daughter, all of whom are close to us, and she was the first person outside our immediate family Mum told when I was getting married. Every once in a while, she would come to KL to stay with us and we would visit her in Penang. About ten years ago, Mum took us all to visit her in hospital where she lay ridden with cancer, the last time we would see her.

* * *

We lived in the house at Jalan Maxwell for ten years. When Mum got a different job, as head of the Rural Health Training Center in Jitra, an even smaller town twelve miles away, we had to move. Having never lived anywhere else all my life, I spent my first night in Jitra, my face buried in my pillow sobbing, missing my old bedroom. Not that we were slumming it in our new home, a long one-storey house with two bedrooms and a garden that faced a dusty lane leading to a dam, part of the Muda irrigation project. Rubber trees just outside our fence threw their seeds into the garden and we would collect those to play with. The house was at one corner of the large compound of the training centre that also included hostels for the trainees and housing for the other staff working there. We made friends with the other children in the compound who came to our birthday parties and taught my brothers to play a ball game called *solé*, where players stood in a row behind each other and threw balls over their shoulders in a complicated manoeuvre. By some unwritten rule, it was a boys' game so I was left to watch on the sidelines. We had a small playground and enough paved roads around the buildings where we could ride our bicycles safely especially after work hours when few outside cars entered the area. It was there that I learnt to ride a two-wheel bicycle, becoming so confident that one afternoon I rounded a corner so fast that, unable to brake, I crashed into the grassy bank of a drain. By some miracle, I only injured my pride.

For two years, from 1967 to 1969, we lived in Jitra, travelling half an hour every weekday to go to school in Alor Setar; my sister Melinda, who came to live with us in 1968, and I to St. Nicholas', and Mirzan and Mokhzani to Iskandar School. Mukhriz was still a toddler. By then we had a new driver, Pak Kamil, a large man with a greasy curl on his forehead and a high squeaky voice due to vocal chords damaged by a childhood illness. Even more incongruously, he sometimes drove us in Mum's little yellow Fiat 500, a bubble car with only two doors, obliging us to climb over the front seats to get to the back. When Pak Kamil first came to work for us, it was all that we, and our friends, could do not to giggle every time he said something. He looked like a baby elephant with the voice of a mouse. But he was a kind man, with children of his own, and tolerated our many foibles as he drove us to and fro.

In early 1969 our journey was cut by half when we moved into the house that Dad built at Titi Gajah, near the airport at Kepala Batas, literally the end of the paved road. The house was a very modern split-level design, inspired by something Dad had seen in one of his favourite magazines, and translated into real life by Baharuddin Kassim, one of the architects of Masjid Negara. The main part of the house stood on elevated ground, with a large front garden that faced padi fields and a back garden bordered by a river. Anyone driving up from Alor Setar to the airport would probably be surprised to see our house there, so modern amidst our neighbours' more traditional, half-brick half-wooden *kampung* houses with neat compounds.

My parents called the house Pondok Maharizan or Maharizan Hut. The hut description was an attempt at being modest in the Kedah way, where people rarely named their houses. Maharizan was a combination of most of our names—Ma for Mahathir and Marina, ha for Hasmah, riz for Mukhriz and zan for both Mirzan and Mokhzani.

As big as the house seemed, it didn't have many bedrooms. Melinda and I slept in one room while my three brothers all piled into another, with a shared bathroom in between. My parents had a large master bedroom with their own ensuite bathroom. One of their room's features was a closet invented by Dad. It opened on two sides so that our helpers could place clean towels in it from outside the room while Mum and Dad could access those from the inside. Dad also had a study on the same floor, filled with bookshelves that I used to climb to get at his many books, some so old and dusty that silverfish would scurry when I opened them.

Down on the mezzanine level was a large living room, a dining room and a family room, really a small corner with the piano, TV and a breakfast bar. Next to the dining room was another of Dad's ideas: a dumb waiter, a contraption that allowed our helpers to load trays of food from the kitchen at the 'basement' level below and crank it up to the first floor. This saved them from precariously balancing the same trays up and down the spiral staircase from the kitchen. At the same level as the front door was a guest room and powder room and our kids' study room, complete with desks for each of us where we were expected to sit at and do our homework. Next to it was a door that led to the garage. I can't remember how many times I've dashed out of our car into the house straight to the powder room to relieve myself after the longish ride home. Down a small flight of stairs, before we got to the kitchen, was what we called a basement, really a large room which housed a ping pong table and Dad's workbench for his occasional brass or carpentry work and whatever boxes that had nowhere else to be placed.

Due to these 'innovations', the rumour spread around Alor Setar that we had a space-age house with a lot of gadgets a la the TV cartoon programme *The Jetsons*. The rumour even reached the Sultan's palace at Anak Bukit so one night my parents entertained the late Sultan Abdul Halim and Sultanah Bahiyah to dinner to show them around the house. They may have found the house very low-tech after all but I do remember them remarking on the giant Elvis Presley poster on my cupboard wall.

* * *

Dad first entered politics when we lived in Jalan Maxwell. Or rather, that was when he stood for elections as an UMNO candidate. I suppose he must have discussed this with Mum—he once corrected a woman politician who said men were lucky because they need not get permission from their wives when they wanted to enter politics—but nobody explained any of this to us, his children. All we knew was that in 1964, after winning his first elections, he was away at his maiden Parliament session when my brother Mukhriz was born. I was only seven and in Standard One so I didn't really know what being a Member of Parliament meant. He would take the night train from Bukit Mertajam to KL and stay there throughout the session, which would take several weeks, and then come home. He was no longer just a doctor like before, when I would pop in and visit him at his clinic, Maha Klinik, in Pekan Melayu near the Kedah River.

By 1969 when he stood for re-election, we had just moved to Pondok Maharizan and were still settling in while he was out campaigning. The morning after election day, he woke me up in my new pink room with the flowery wallpaper.

'Did you win?' I asked sleepily.

'No' he said, smiling.

I was puzzled. I knew he worked hard in his constituency, Kota Setar Selatan, visiting it very often. I couldn't understand how he could have lost, at the time to the PAS candidate Haji Yusof Rawa. Haji Yusof, Mum told us, was a distant cousin of hers, which confused me even more. How could family oppose each other in politics? Almost 50 years later, Mujahid Yusof Rawa, Haji Yusof's son, joined Dad's Pakatan Harapan Cabinet as Minister of Religion and we were finally on the same side.

In 1969, Dad took his loss with equanimity, didn't seem too disheartened by it, at least it was not obvious to me. He hid from me and my brothers what we only learnt later: he had been very upset and disappointed by his loss, and that disappointment had set him on course to clash with his party bosses who he felt did not see what was happening on the ground. His was not the only loss that the Alliance, the precursor to Barisan Nasional, suffered in 1969, but Dad thought the leadership should have seen it coming.

A strange thing happened however after he lost in that election. Even though we had nothing to celebrate, we were suddenly inundated with visitors at home, mostly his former constituents who came to see him to commiserate. Every night a busload or two of people would arrive at Pondok Maharizan, men, women and even children. My siblings and I would watch agog as these strangers wandered all over the house, only just stopping short of our bedrooms. As odd as our house looked in front of the padi fields of Titi Gajah, it must have seemed like a spaceship to the folks from Dad's former constituency, a rural agricultural area some twenty-five kilometres away. Mum strove to be hospitable and provided food and drink to all who came. But every night, so many visitors arrived that feeding them became so onerous that finally, all we could offer was bread and curry. I kept wondering what it was like at the winner's house if this was what happened if you lose. At that time, I had no idea that these visits meant something special about Dad.

That period also coincided with the rainy season. One night it rained so heavily that every single gap in our new roof yielded to the onslaught, causing a waterfall to pour into the house and flood our stairs down to the basement. Buckets and brooms were deployed to sweep away the waters, before yet another busload of sympathizers arrived. Our first weeks in that new house seemed to be a blur of people and water all over it. Fancy was not a word I would have applied to it.

1969 was of course the year of events that significantly changed Malaysia. I was not quite twelve but became aware of riots in Kuala Lumpur after the elections, from newspapers and TV and of course through overhearing adults talking. In Alor Setar, there was no violence as far as I knew but the news from KL still made everyone tense. My recollections of that time are dim except that my parents did not seem to be around. My Dad was in fact on his way by car to Kuala Lumpur to discuss his position in UMNO then and was made to turn back when he got to Tanjung Malim at the border of Selangor. He had clashed with the Prime Minister Tunku Abdul Rahman, the President of UMNO, and so was in deep trouble and his political future was uncertain.

But I was not to know this because my parents never talked to us about any of this. Their good friends, Dr and Mrs Panikkar, came over to the house to check on us children and to ensure that we had enough food in case there was a curfew. Otherwise, I was oblivious to what the Emergency then really meant. Perhaps school was closed for a while, which was much welcomed by us kids. Whatever it was, my parents tried to make sure that none of the tension or fear seeped into us.

But nobody is untouched by politics, not even little children. We picked up on things and tried to interpret them with our own limited knowledge. I had a vague inkling that there was a lot of news about Dad then, but I was never sure what it was about. Absorbed in their politics, adults sometimes forget that children are not deaf nor insensitive to nuances. In 1969, I noticed comings and goings in the house, with a stream of visitors coming, in cars, not buses, to talk to Dad. I heard words like 'letter', 'Tunku unhappy' and other bewildering snatches of conversation that nobody explained to us. All I felt, as the eldest of my father's children, was a growing sense of unease although I did not truly know what was causing it. Dad was away in KL a lot and I thought this was odd because he had lost his seat in Parliament and did not have to attend sessions in the Dewan Rakyat anymore.

On 12 July 1969, Mum's 43rd birthday and only two days after his 44th, Dad was fired from his position on the UMNO Supreme Council. I forget how we learnt about this but we didn't know the significance of it. Nor did we realize that it was the precursor of worse things to come.

None of these troubles were really conveyed to us children at the time. As with his loss in Kota Setar Selatan, he merely shrugged his shoulders and made light of it when he told us the bare bones of what happened. We were clueless as to what it really meant. Perhaps we only thought that Dad would just go back to his clinic and would be around much more. We could go on drives and picnics, to *makan angin* again.

I was sitting on the high stool in our breakfast-cum-TV room a few months later on 27 September watching the news when the newsreader announced that Dad had been expelled from UMNO. Having been unaware of the events leading up to this, about the letter that Dad wrote to the Tunku accusing him of not having the welfare of the Malay community at heart, I was shocked and promptly burst into tears. I was certain that it meant that Dad had done something terribly wrong and was going to jail, a prospect that was terrifying to a sheltered twelve-year-old. Mum had to calm and soothe me, assuring me that Dad would be fine, that he did not really mind being expelled and was probably at a party with his friends in KL.

How Mum lied to protect us! That day remains an unpleasant memory for me. It showed how futile it was to put children in a cocoon and hide the truth from them. They can feel what is happening; things need to be truthfully explained to them. This was why in 1998, when my daughter Ineza told me that Nurul Ilham Anwar had spent all day crying at the back of their class at school, I felt instant empathy for her and her siblings. Almost thirty years before, I had been through the same ordeal, although at that time Dad was never accused of any crime nor went to court and jail. But I knew how confusing and disconcerting these political events can be to a child regardless of their gravity.

It was also the first time that I became aware of Dad's involvement in politics, that he was an active participant whose words and actions could sometimes get him in trouble. The world of politics had been remote before this: his constituency was far away, Parliament was even further and his absences were mitigated by the gifts he brought home from KL, including sometimes a cousin or two who would come along for a holiday. But this was different and serious. This was my first inkling of a chaotic grown-up world and somehow, like it or not, it would affect me too.

2

Me, the Impostor

I often have a dream where I am all dressed up in glamorous clothes, my hair and makeup professionally done. When I'm ready, I step into my car and my driver takes me to whatever event I'm invited to. Halfway there, I suddenly realize I'd forgotten my shoes. I'm still wearing the slippers I wear at home.

I think it means I have an impostor syndrome—the feeling that I'm not quite up to the mark, don't quite qualify to do or be where I am. It is a syndrome I suffer from greatly, even now in my sixties. Some may call it false modesty but actually it is a form of inferiority complex, of feeling that I'll never be good enough at anything.

The syndrome manifests itself every time I am asked to speak at a forum of academics or experts. My academic achievements had, for most of my life, been unimpressive. I received a Lower Second for my bachelor's degree in International Relations and only recently, at the age of sixty-two, I obtained my Masters in Biography and Creative Non-Fiction. I actually got a distinction for the latter but inside my head, I'm always qualifying that by noting that I had barely scraped in with the minimum marks to achieve it. Faced with people with a string of degrees to their name, I feel out of place, even when assured that it is my long experience working for various causes, principally in HIV and women's rights, that matters. I suppose it's that old Asian trait of valuing paper qualifications above all else that makes me cower before those with more illustrious academic achievements.

I don't know where it comes from, this constant feeling of not being good enough nor qualified enough to be among some luminaries. Perhaps it comes from being from Kedah, where people are unassuming and reticent, not given to any form of boasting. Our state, after all, was called the Rice Bowl of Malaysia, the most basic of all our needs, and the sight of our chequered patterns of padi fields, so calm and green, also lent us our other name, Darul Aman, Land of Peace. Perhaps also, it comes from having parents who always downplayed our achievements in the hope of spurring us to greater heights.

One afternoon, when I was a gangly fourteen-or fifteen-year-old, I sat with Dad after tea on the stone chair in our garden in Titi Gajah. It was a habit of ours to sit outside in the evenings, after Mum and Dad had returned from work, to enjoy the breeze wafting from the padi fields opposite our house, Pondok Maharizan.

The view of those fields was bisected by a large Angsana tree that grew just outside our gate by the main road leading to the airfield at Kepala Batas. We could time the seasons going by, by watching those padi fields, from the farmers ploughing them with their large black buffaloes, to the women bent over planting the rice saplings, to the rainwater that covered the fields until they turned into a large shimmering lake, to the harvest and dry season that followed. This was the lifeblood of our home state, and living in Titi Gajah, even in a modern house like ours, underscored that fact just by the changing scenes in front of us every day.

On that day, amidst the usual chatter about school and anything else that came to mind, I had a question for Dad. He was my go-to encyclopaedia and dictionary, even though I could have looked up the Collier's he had in his study. He read so widely and knew many things, including the meaning of many English words and idioms. He always said, observing the way people wrote in books, was the best way to learn the language. I always thought he was a better person to ask about English than my own teachers. Besides, it was another excuse to talk to him.

'What does mediocre mean, Daddy?' I was a bespectacled bookworm and must have found the word in one of the many books I had read. I would normally try and figure out the meanings of words through the context they were used in. But this word eluded me. Or perhaps, I just wanted to test Dad.

'It means not particularly good at anything,' he replied, looking at me with the smirk that was his trademark. I should have known that there had to be something more to that answer, but I was a self-absorbed teenager and had yet to acquire insights into other people, even those close to me.

'Oh,' I said, making a note to use it in the next essay I needed to write for English class at school. Which was why I was wholly unprepared for his next words.

'Like you.'

Like most Asian parents, mine tended not to gush over us. To be fair, they didn't make us feel hopeless, useless, or stupid either. Until that moment sitting in our garden with Dad, I had felt fairly confident that while I was no genius, I was OK. Being called mediocre, not particularly good at anything, was a bit of a shock but it put things in perspective for me. If I had no real talent for anything, what exactly was I good at?

Dad had always strived never to be mediocre at anything he did. On finding that he could not read everything he needed to do his job as a Parliamentarian, he taught himself speed-reading. After a trip to Europe with Mum where he found the French language delightful, he set about ordering books and records to learn how to speak it. Many years later when I married a Frenchman, Dad had ample opportunity to exercise his French but shyness and a lack of practice proved too great a barrier. When he saw the beautiful bamboo-fringed river behind our house, he bought plans from one of his magazines and, with the help of Pak Arshad, our neighbour, built boats to cruise on it. The first was called Marina 1. Clearly, Dad did not believe in doing anything in half-measures.

This abhorrence of mediocrity extended to his children and as the eldest, I felt it most. No red marks in our report cards were ever tolerated, even when my first was because I owned up to a mistake my teacher had made in marking my papers. To be called mediocre stung a great deal even though I probably did not deserve it. I had been in the top three in my class for a number of years in primary school, and in the Lower Certificate of Education exams, I had scored three As in all the required subjects to enter the science stream, English, Mathematics and Science. True, I had quit piano early. I was not a natural athlete and swimming lessons, spent at the Kedah Club pool on humid Saturday mornings, proved too arduous and I gave up after just a few lessons. I was no shining star and rarely won prizes or was especially praised at Speech Day in school, not the sort to get up and beguile everyone by reciting poetry by heart as one of my classmates did. There was little to distinguish me in and out of school. That made me, in Dad's estimation, mediocre.

* * *

As a teenager with my nose perpetually in a story book, I read all of Enid Blyton's books, from *The Famous Five* adventures to the boarding school series of *Malory Towers* and St. Clare's. They were not Harry Porter books by a long shot but once you picked one up, you got hooked and had to read the rest. At the time, I did not find it odd to read about White children going off to Africa for exciting adventures, adventures that involved very few people native to those countries. Or to wear blazers and knee socks as your uniform, have midnight feasts in your dorms and play all sorts of pranks on your schoolmates or teachers.

As I entered my first year of secondary school in 1969, I had the opportunity to enroll in Tunku Kurshiah College (TKC) in Seremban. I was excited, imagining myself going on a Blytonesque adventure just like the girls at St. Clare's. But my hopes were dashed when the TKC school board abruptly decided to stop taking in girls at Form One and instead focus on the Upper Secondary classes.

I stayed on at St. Nicholas' Convent, the school I had been in since kindergarten with all my familiar friends and teachers. Secondary school proved to be much more difficult than primary school and I struggled with my subjects, slipping down the class rankings at every exam. Still, at fifteen, after my Lower Certificate of Education results qualified me to go to TKC again, my parents broached the idea once more.

In the intervening years, I had grown from an excitable bookworm to a moody teenager, obsessed with pop music and TV shows like the Partridge Family featuring the long-lashed David Cassidy. I had lost my enthusiasm for boarding school and looked for excuses not to go. Desperate for ideas, I told my parents that I did not want to go to a school that only accepted Malay girls, after spending my entire life in a Catholic school with Chinese, Indian and Eurasian girls.

Dad's face darkened. I don't think he wanted me to go to TKC just because it only took in Malay girls but because it was a very good school. It had been established as the girls' equivalent of the Malay College Kuala Kangsar, an elite boys' boarding school in the mould of Eton and had a very strict selection process based entirely on academic achievement. My parents probably felt I would do better in a more structured environment with proper study hours and more discipline.

But Dad took my excuse as highly insulting, as if going to a school with just my community was a step down. He was so angry that he stalked off upstairs to his room and left it to Mum to persuade me. That didn't turn out to be so difficult. Mum knew TKC very well, having served on its Board of Governors for a number of years. She knew its history and had known many people who had gone there. Its academic record was excellent, but it also did well in extra-curricular activities such as music and drama. Then she unveiled her secret weapon: my best friend Fadzilah, whose parents had transferred out of Alor Setar, was also going there.

I wound up spending two years at TKC in the Fourth and Fifth Forms, a seminal period for me because it opened my eyes to a wider world than the town I grew up in. Although ostensibly it only admitted Malay girls, I was not prepared to discover the huge diversity of the Malay community. Back in Alor Setar, while I had friends from all communities, we had not noticed our differences very much because our entire frame of reference had always been our little hometown. We went to the same bookshops to get our school supplies, to the same Post Office to post letters and ate ice *kacang* at the same stalls. Our religious and cultural differences were sources of curiosity rather than detraction. We had no problems going to each other's homes and festivals.

But at TKC I met girls who seemed very foreign to me at first because they came from the other side of the country. Having grown up speaking my northern dialect with its flat ahs, my first encounter with the Kelantanese dialect, for example, and what sounded like a nasally distortion of every word, might as well have been a meeting with an alien. I understood nothing of what they said.

TKC brought together girls from all walks of life, from the KL sophisticates to the loud Johorians, from girls who were natural-born leaders to the ones who were so introverted we hardly heard their voices.

The main positive impact of TKC however was on my perception of my own community. At St. Nicholas, there were no more than seven or eight Malay girls in a class. Not many of us topped the exams and so over the years, it seeped into my brain that Malays could only achieve so much in school. It never occurred to me that the home background was an important factor in how well any child did in school; whether parents prioritized education, read at home, exposed their children to a diverse range of ideas. In primary school, thanks to Mum's strictness about studying, I was almost always in the Top Three in class. But everyone attributed that to the fact that my parents were doctors. They were clever, so I must be clever too. That made me an aberration, not the norm. Worse, that so-called cleverness eroded when I got to secondary school. This did not help that nagging feeling in my head that maybe I was not as smart as everyone thought I was.

When I got to TKC, I was shocked to discover girls—Malay girls— who had scored seven or eight As in their exams. I had not known it was possible for anyone, let alone girls from my community, to get that many distinctions in their studies. Somehow you could pick out those super-bright girls because they seemed to sparkle as they walked the corridors to class. To top it all, they could also sing, play music, dance, act and run fast. I had never met girls like that.

My stint in TKC may not have been the happiest two years of my life, for other reasons, but it certainly de-coupled any stereotypes I had about race and achievement. I saw that a person's ethnicity, and gender for that matter, had little to do with achievement. What mattered more were the opportunities they were given and what they did with them. Hard work mattered most. I knew many of my TKC schoolmates came from very humble backgrounds but because of the education they received there and the toil they put in, they went on to become high achievers in government, academia, business and politics.

But my impostor syndrome followed me to TKC. My three As were the minimum to get into the school; I had qualified fair and square. But I was marked by some facts I could not escape. First, I had arrived two weeks late. While undergoing the mandatory health check-up before enrolling, the doctor had found a cyst in my ovaries, a balloon-like growth that gave me debilitating period pain. I had to have surgery to take it out and so did not show up in time for the orientation weeks at my new school. Unbeknownst to me, in my absence, the school principal had announced the reason why I was late at assembly and had asked for prayers for my successful surgery. It was well-intentioned but it cast an unnecessary spotlight on me.

The other factor was that I was the daughter of a famous man. In 1972 when I entered TKC, Dad was technically still out of UMNO. But he had resolutely not joined any other party, remaining loyal to his former party in spirit. My schoolmates, all smart girls, knew who he was and so there was a natural curiosity about me and my family. Most of my friends were polite and kind, but a few seemed to begrudge me my DNA as if it was the only thing that earned me a place there.

Any boarding school full of teenage girls is bound to have lots of dramas. Everyone came with their own emotional baggage, some of which they offloaded onto their classmates. TKC was a very competitive place. If we weren't competing for high marks in class, we were going for Best Dorm, Best House, Best Class, Best Team, Best Choir, Best Play and everything else that could pit us against each other. It fostered team spirit in most things and for that, competitiveness was beneficial. But academic achievement is a solitary enterprise. Nobody can put things in your brain but yourself, nobody can sit your exams for you.

I spent a lot of the time believing I was not up to the mark in that high-octane place. I was not stupid, but I believed I was because I never topped my class, except in English. Instead, I hovered somewhere in the middle, in the land of mediocrity. This was reinforced by some seemingly concerned remarks. 'Oh Ina, I was *so* worried about you in the Chemistry paper!' Ergo, you can't possibly pass that, you dumb girl.

Dad would sometimes come and visit, an event that would cause some sensation at school. In the Seventies, Dad was handsome with fashionable sideburns framing his face. He would arrive in his friend the late Tunku Abdullah's red Alfa Romeo sports car that he drove from KL up to Tun Fatimah House, where my dorm was located. I knew when I greeted him that lots of girly eyes were peeking out from the windows above. We would walk holding hands across the campus to the canteen to have a drink, giggling all the way. Such public displays of affection were rare among my friends' families, so it was an endless source of fascination.

But having a famous father did not sit well with some people. One dorm mate, who had lost her father when she was young, reduced me to tears for simply having not just a living one, but one who was constantly in the newspapers. She would snipe at me at every chance, 'Oh it's ok for you, you still have a father!' I don't recall other classmates suffering the same, so it felt as if I was being specifically picked on. 'Were your achievements more valid if you did it without parents?' I puzzled. At sixteen, already insecure in that competitive environment, it only deepened that impostor syndrome I felt then and have never quite been able to shake off even now.

Today, despite having spent three decades as a newspaper columnist, HIV and women's rights activist, TV and movie producer and now the founder of a website on travel for women, I still have a nagging feeling that I have not done enough and whatever I have done, is not really good enough. I have sat on numerous panels both locally and internationally, given many speeches even at the United Nations, and other big forums. My work has been recognized by several honorary doctorates including from my alma mater, the University of Sussex, as well as the Legion d'Honneur from the French government. Yet I cannot escape that nagging feeling that I don't really deserve to sit with my fellow panellists, that I wish I had known the things they knew or been as articulate as they. My standards for myself are never met, perhaps because they are too high and striving to be as far away from mediocrity as possible.

Or perhaps it is the legacy of living under so large a shadow as Dad's.

3

Culture Shock in California

I finished my Malaysian Certificate of Examinations at TKC at the end of 1973. In those days, long before instant communications over the internet, our exam papers were marked in England. Marking the several thousand students who sat for those exams took about three months. From concluding my last paper at the end of November until the results came back in March, I faced a long holiday from school.

Some of my friends in Alor Setar were using that time in productive ways. Some were taking shorthand and stenography classes, which I should have done as well if I had looked ahead a little more. All I could think of was to relax after two intense years of study at TKC and had no plans at all. However, my parents did.

* * *

In the year I was fifteen, before I went to TKC, my family had hosted an American girl, Lauren Hesse, under the American Field Service student exchange programme. The AFS, which began during World War I as an ambulance service, allowed secondary school students from all over the world to visit the US for a year, while American high schoolers could choose to spend a summer abroad. I'm not sure how we decided to do this but my parents, always keen that their children got to know people from other countries and vice versa, must have come up with the idea. We applied, were subsequently interviewed by a Malaysian former exchange student from the programme, and were told that we would be the host family for Lauren for three months during the summer of 1971.

Lauren was the second in an unusually large American family of five girls and one boy. Their father, Frederick W. Hesse, Jr, was a senior executive at TRW, a company that made parts for the rockets in the American space programme. Their mother Betty, a big blonde woman originally from South Carolina, was a homemaker. I could hardly contain my excitement. The very idea of hosting someone from faraway California was for me almost beyond imagination. Was she going to be like those cheery blonde girls on TV programmes like *The Brady Bunch*?

I remember too well the day that Lauren arrived at our home because it was also the day that my uncle Ghani died. Uncle Ghani, whom we called Pak Ngah, or Middle Uncle, because he was married to my father's middle sister Habsah, had been a jovial man who never tired of finding ways to entertain his nephews and nieces. He worked at my father's clinic and we saw a lot of him at family gatherings and outings, always smiling, always amusing. He and my aunt had no children of their own, so they had adopted Kalthom, a girl several years older than me, and Roslan, the son of my uncle Mashahor, just a year my senior. I was close to both of them; we were playmates from childhood.

But in that year, 1971, Uncle Ghani was ill with cancer although I had no idea how long he had had it. By the time I became aware of his illness, it was probably well along. I visited him in the hospital once and although he was pale and thin, he still had that smile that I knew so well. Despite feeling weak, lying there in his narrow hospital bed, he only wanted to talk about how I was doing in school rather than about himself and his illness. I had not realized just how seriously ill he was until that morning, the morning that Lauren arrived, when we got news that Uncle Ghani had died. I had woken up excited to greet Lauren but instead found myself in tears of shock, as I had not anticipated my uncle's death at all.

Lauren thus entered a household that was engulfed in sadness and her first Malaysian cultural experience was a funeral. We found her a bright blue traditional *baju kurung* to wear because we had nothing more sombre that would fit her, one that was a bit too short for her long legs and took her along with us to Uncle Ghani's house in the middle of Alor Setar for the funeral rituals.

Although Muslim burials take place very quickly because tradition dictates that the dead must be buried within twenty-four hours, that hot and humid day seemed to stretch interminably. I was caught between grieving for my beloved uncle and impatience, wanting to properly induct my new 'sister' into our family and Malaysian life. Lauren too must have been bewildered by this total plunge into a very different cultural milieu, surrounded by strangers, so soon after arriving in Malaysia. I worried that she was exhausted from her long flight, and perhaps bored by the lengthy rituals, the cleaning of the body, the lengthy prayers, the farewell kisses by members of the family.

Lauren later recalled that she had not truly understood that it was a funeral for my uncle. She had accompanied us and had been introduced to so many of our extended family that she struggled to remember who anyone was. It was sweltering and Lauren had to sit on the floor for long periods like the rest of us, as prayers were recited, and visitors streamed in to pay their respects. When she got tired, she leaned over on her side, propping her head on her hands, much to my consternation. I was anxious for her not to make a bad impression on my relatives but as it turned out, my worry was totally unwarranted. There was so much going on that the mourners barely noticed this lanky American girl in their midst.

Despite that inauspicious beginning, Lauren's stay in Malaysia became the foundation of a lifelong friendship. She immersed herself in our life and routines, following me to school every day. St. Nicholas' Convent initially had some doubts about accepting Lauren as a student for those short months. When we had first gotten news that Lauren was coming to stay with us, Mum had spoken to the school principal, a nun called Reverend Mother Rita. Reverend Mother Rita's first reaction had shocked and disappointed me: we have nothing to offer her, she said. My mother got off the phone and told me this startling bit of information and I promptly burst into tears, disappointed and angry at the discouraging reaction from the school.

Somehow Mum, who did not become a doctor by giving up easily, must have prevailed over Reverend Mother Rita and Lauren was allowed to attend school, where she was the object of much curiosity. In our little town and school, we had only ever had one White student in the past; Stephanie, an English girl whose father was an engineer seconded to the Kedah state government. Stephanie was quite plain but what struck us most was the way her navy-blue ribbon stood out on her long blonde ponytail. The ribbons we wore, usually regulation navy, black or white to go with our dark blue school pinafores, never contrasted with our black hair the way hers did.

Lauren was therefore only the second White student St. Nicholas' ever had. She was seventeen at the time, tall and rangy, her long face freckled across her nose and cheeks, framed by reddish-brown straight hair. To us, she was an exotic creature with some strange habits. She would dance in the garden when it rained and didn't come down with a cold as our mothers always warned we would. Her mannerisms sometimes seemed crude and rough compared to our polite, gentle and extremely hesitant ways. She had a habit of crushing up her Malaysian ringgit notes, rather than respectfully smoothing them out before keeping them in her wallet. When she had read a letter or anything on a piece of paper, she would simply throw them over her shoulder carelessly, a shocking act to those of us who had been taught to care for and preserve any document that we received. That summer she was reading Herman Hesse's *Siddhartha* and pronounced it a great book although I could not understand it at all, being still engrossed in Enid Blyton's boarding school novels. When I said I was thinking of re-decorating my room, she took me seriously and persuaded my parents to get us sandpaper so we could manually sand down the shellack from the sliding doors of my closet, in order to paint a picture of a dreamy long-haired woman we had found in *Seventeen* magazine onto them. Needless to say, our artistic venture lasted only until it dawned upon us that sandpapering the varnish off those doors was really a tiresome business.

At school, because I was younger than her, Lauren was put in a class above me and therefore had her own friends, which made me a little jealous. Unlike the reticent local girls, brought up to never bring attention to themselves, she was outgoing and full of ideas on things to do.

There was another American exchange student, Martha, who was staying with a family in Perlis, the next state over from ours. One week Martha came to stay with us and the two of them put on a sketch at school depicting the reactions of Malaysians in our small provincial towns towards them. 'Aiya, look at her, why her face so long!' Martha pointed at Lauren, pretending to be a gawking local. We all found it hilarious because we knew this was true. These teenage American girls were treated like circus curiosities and locals had no qualms about staring and pointing.

Despite these quirks, Lauren and I became close, talking well into the night about all the things we wanted to do in our lives as well as the typical everyday things that teenage girls worried about. As the eldest in the family, I had no older siblings to confide in. The closest I had to a big sister was my cousin Siti Aishah who lived with my grandparents in KL and who I only saw during the holidays. Lauren was only two years older than me, but she seemed far more worldly than my sheltered self. She had views that seemed far more sophisticated than I had the imagination for.

As an Asian child, I had a limited idea of what careers were possible in the future. All I knew was that I had to go to school, pass exam after exam and then go to a university where there were more exams. Lauren was thinking about writing poetry, a career I could not even fathom. I knew I loved writing but I did not know what I would do with it. It may well have been Lauren who first planted the seed of the idea of becoming a journalist in me.

Lauren's parents and mine, first by correspondence and then by actual visits, also became good friends. Fred and Betty Hesse came to visit us in Alor Setar about a year later and they found a lot of interests in common with my parents, from interior decoration to music to the global issues at the time. It must have been during those long conversations at our home that both sets of parents came to agree that in 1973, during my long post-exam holidays, I would stay with the Hesses in California on our own private exchange programme.

* * *

My long journey to Los Angeles began in early December 1973, just as the end-of-year school holidays began. I packed my few warm clothes, lots of presents for each member of Lauren's family and a traditional Malay outfit, the baju kurung. People who had gone on such exchange programmes told me that they sometimes had to do presentations on Malaysia and dressing up in our national costume was a good idea. If you couldn't think of what to say, at least you could talk about what you're wearing.

Before I left, barely able to keep still at the thought of going to 'Hollywood', Dad sat with me one cool evening on that hard stone bench in our garden after we'd had our usual afternoon tea. He told me that he was sending me off to stay with the Hesses because he believed that this was a great opportunity for me to learn about another culture. He and my mother were also well-travelled. They had been on a three-month trip to Europe when we were little and had made many friends from Denmark and the US along the way. However, he said, as fascinating as other countries can be, I should still remember who I was and where I came from. The Hesses are very nice people, he said, but they have their own culture, their own way of doing things and these might be different from the way we did things here in Malaysia. We watched a lot of American TV programmes then, mostly musical programmes like *The Andy Williams Show* or action shows like *Mission Impossible* and almost all our impressions of America came from television. It was either sugary pop songs or guns. I listened to Dad and nodded obediently but I had no idea what sort of cultural differences I would face. I suspect neither did he.

Looking back, I didn't know how privileged I was to have had that opportunity to travel at such a young age. Travel, to my parents, was part of education; they believed it was important for us to see how people in other nations lived. In some cases, they were better off, in others they were not. Our very first trip to a foreign country was to southern Thailand, a short drive from our home in Jitra. We marvelled at a people who seemed similar to us but had a different accent. Another year we went 'abroad'; we flew to Medan in Sumatra and visited tourist sites like Lake Toba as well as some of Mum's relatives on her father's side. During one school holiday when I was in TKC, as a reward for doing well in my Lower Certificate of Examinations, Dad took me—and only me—on a trip to Hong Kong where we rode the Star ferry across the harbour and to Japan where I had my first taste of that bitter green tea that a kimono-clad woman served me. But I had never travelled on my own anywhere before.

My first solo trip, with the two hundred dollars spending money Dad gave me, departed from the old Subang airport in Kuala Lumpur and the anxiety it provoked in me must have been the reason why, on reaching Bahrain for a short refuelling stop, I got off on the hot tarmac and felt faint. I faced the prospect of either blacking out right there, an experience too embarrassing to contemplate, or emboldening myself to ask the stranger walking nearest to me if I could take his arm. That was how a balding American man found this 16-year-old Malay girl hanging on to him under that blistering Middle Eastern sun. Who knows what the other passengers thought of this? But it was my first lesson in finding the courage to ask for help from people I didn't know.

My journey to America went via London where I was to stay a week with my cousin Siti Aishah who was working there. It was my first experience of winter and I marvelled at the 'smoke' that came out of my mouth when I breathed out and having to wear lip balm to keep my lips moist. Clad in my cousin's coat, she showed me all the typical tourist sights of London—Buckingham Palace, Hyde Park, Tower Bridge, the Houses of Parliament—but my favourite was Oxford Street, especially Selfridges department store where I loved looking at the displays of clothes and jewellery, all of which I found glamorous but beyond my means. Besides, my luggage was already full of presents for the Hesses.

I finally left for Los Angeles a week later. The sight of that sprawling city from the air at night was breath-taking, with a carpet of thousands of twinkling lights laid out below us. I truly felt, in my wide-eyed way, that I had arrived at the land of the stars, and that I would meet as many of those movie celestial beings as there were lights down there. Surely all I had to do was to walk down Sunset Boulevard—what a lovely name for a street!—and there they would all be!

Betty Hesse, with her blonde pixie haircut and her soft fleshy body, was at the airport waiting for me. Lauren had by then gone to the University of California at Santa Cruz and was not yet home for the holidays. Betty greeted me with bad news: Fred Hesse was ill with cancer. Fearful that my visit would be cancelled, the Hesses had not

informed my parents beforehand but now that I was in Los Angeles, I
had to be told. I was shocked; I had met Fred only when they visited us
in Alor Setar but had warmed to his friendly open nature immediately.
We went from the airport straight to the hospital to visit Fred who
seemed reasonably well, sitting up in bed and smiling. In a few days
he was discharged so that he could spend Christmas at home with his
family, but he was confined to bed and we had to always be quiet around
the sprawling ranch-style house that they lived in.

* * *

The nameless new cultural experiences Dad had told me about occurred
soon after I arrived, although he could not have anticipated any of them.

My California Christmas was the first 'real' one I had ever
celebrated, my family not being Christian. Apart from snow, we had
the full works just like on TV; the tree with those many colourfully-
wrapped presents under it, the tinsel, the carols, that funny drink called
eggnog. And mistletoe. The large Hesse family home housed not only
Betty and Fred, three out of their five daughters and their son, Fritz,
but also a nephew, Roy, and his friend, Ned, two young men in their
twenties, with long lank hair and a daily uniform of flannel shirts and
jeans. I don't know what occupied them but the Hesses were generous
people who housed and fed them for as long as they needed.

That Christmas, the Hesse children decided that they would
introduce me to one particular American tradition. I was standing under
an arch leading from the hall into the living room, unaware that there
was a little sprig of mistletoe hung above me. Ned advanced on me, lips
puckered, arms outstretched to embrace me. I shrieked and wriggled
out of the way, my eyes wide with shock, the Hesses falling about in
hysterics. Apart from my parents and grandparents, I had never kissed
anyone or had any stranger kiss me. Kissing between the opposite sexes
was something that we only giggled about; back in Malaysia kissing
scenes were cut out from Western movies and TV programmes. Was
this the cultural difference Dad was talking about?

For the rest of the Christmas season, I kept a sharp eye out for
mistletoe all over the house and at their friends' houses. I didn't want to

be thought a prude but at that time I had never even held hands with any boys, let alone kiss them. The thought of being randomly embraced because of a little berry branch seemed, in the slang of the day, too gross.

* * *

It is January 1974, and I am climbing with Leslie, Lauren's younger sister, up to the top of the bluff, looking down onto the beach and the shimmery Pacific Ocean. It is sunny as days in California often are but for me, a girl from the tropics, it is still far too chilly. To cope with this unfamiliar weather—I had never associated sun with coldness before—I am wearing a turtlenecked navy-coloured body suit, with vertical ribbing all the way round the body and buttons that you fastened at your crotch, so that the top is tight and flush against your skin and will not ride up no matter how much you stretched your arms. This is worn with blue jeans, another garment I am not familiar with. Betty had taken me shopping to buy my first pair of Levi's. I am so petite that we could not find a pair that would fit me well enough so we bought the smallest pair we could find, still very loose on me, with the idea that once we got home, we would run it in the washing machine several times in order to shrink it. Perhaps we should have washed it while I was wearing them. Although that pair did shrink somewhat, there remained a gap at my lower back that could only be closed with a belt. I still looked like a child strapped into an older brother's jeans.

That day, Leslie and I had driven to Abalone Cove, some miles from her house in Palos Verdes, not so much to swim—I don't remember that we brought swimsuits—but to simply have some peace and quiet away from her large and boisterous family. Perhaps Leslie, only a week older than me, had wanted a smoke without the risk of being caught by her mother and had decided that taking me sightseeing was a good excuse. I was just happy to follow her and 'experience' California and all its Seventies vibe.

As we sit high above the beach, basking in the sunshine, my skin still prickling with goosebumps from the chill, we see in the distance what looked like a group of little children walking on the sand towards us. Some are holding hands; some carrying buckets perhaps to catch crabs or collect seashells. I watch them, only vaguely interested, the sun making me a little drowsy.

As they come closer, the sight comes into focus: these are not children at all. They are young people, high schoolers like Leslie and I. Typical California kids, blonde, tanned, with the long limbs of teenagers used to athletic outdoor activities. And with a gasp, I realize that they are all, boys and girls, completely naked.

Until that moment, I had not seen a naked body since my brothers were toddlers. In conservative Malaysia, bodies are kept discreet, behind closed doors. Clothes are changed in bathrooms, or under curtains of sarongs. Naked bodies are viewed on a need-to-see basis: by your mother, by your doctor, by your spouse. Even on beaches or by rivers, you might see a naked male torso or, at most, the bare shoulders of a woman as she bathed or washed clothes, her sarong tied across her chest, never a fully bared body.

Yet here they are, these golden boys and girls, naked, as the Americans say, as jaybirds. I do not know whether to stare or look away. To stare seemed rude but then these people did not seem interested in modesty. Still, it is hard to look away. Embarrassed as I am, my eyes are still drawn to those slim figures on the beach.

I am fascinated by the naked boys. To me, they looked vaguely silly, with their bits dangling as they walked along. Don't they feel vulnerable? And most of all, don't they feel cold?

Temperature must surely be relative. There I was shivering in what must have been the low twenties celsius. Back home in equatorial Malaysia, I was used to the high twenties or the low thirties, coupled with high humidity. Yet here were these tanned creatures, buck naked, strolling along that windy beach as if they were in the tropical heat. I clutch my arms around me, now feeling even colder, and turn to Leslie to ask if we could go.

* * *

My stay in California lasted three months and as part of my American cultural immersion, I attended Miraleste High School with Leslie, the third of the five Hesse girls. Although the Hesses lived in a wealthy community, with large houses scattered all over the hills facing the blue Pacific Ocean, to my astonishment, they had no driver to send them to school like I always did back home. Instead, at 8 a.m. every weekday, the four younger Hesse children walked up to the bus stop on the crest above their house on Portuguese Bend Road and took the orange school bus to Miraleste, returning the same way at about two in the afternoon. On most of those California mornings I would leave with Leslie and return with her in the afternoon, in time to eat Betty's famous chocolate chip cookies. But on some days, she had extra-curricular activities, so I had to return on my own.

The first time this happened, I panicked at the sight of all the buses lined up at the school driveway. I could not remember the number of my bus and it must have left before I could locate it. Not knowing any other way to get home, I phoned Betty up to come and get me.

She was not impressed. 1974 was the year of the energy crisis, caused by the oil embargo imposed by the Organization of Petroleum Exporting Countries (OPEC) against countries that had supported Israel during the Yom Kippur War, including the United States. The whole country was put on notice to conserve fuel. You could only fill up your car with petrol on alternate days, depending on your licence plate. Odd numbers on odd-numbered days of the month, even numbers on even-numbered days. Everyone was careful not to waste petrol on unnecessary drives, which must have been difficult for car-mad Los Angelenos.

I had only a vague awareness of the state of things during those fuel-rationing days. America to me then was the land of plenty and I would wander, googly-eyed, along supermarket aisles whenever I accompanied Betty grocery-shopping. I had never seen so much abundance in one place. Nor had I ever seen anyone shop for two weeks' worth of groceries at once before; bags and bags of vegetables, boxes of cereal, cartons of milk, jars of peanut butter and 'jelly', bundles of meat and chicken and ingredients to make cakes and cookies, as well as toilet paper, detergent, toothpaste and shampoo. All of these had to be loaded into the back of Betty's station wagon and when we got home, unloaded and taken into the kitchen and then put away into the refrigerator, freezer or pantry.

Back home in Malaysia at the time, supermarkets were still a novelty. Going to Weld Supermarket whenever we were in KL was like going to Harrods. It was air-conditioned and filled with expensive imported food, like cheese. In Alor Setar, fresh food was bought at the 'wet market' and dry goods at the local sundry store. We would buy fresh meat for two days at most; we did not have a standalone freezer.

The very idea that there would not be enough petrol to go around in abundant America and that we had to be careful not to use it up too quickly was something that had not sunk into my Malaysian teenage brain. Until the day a grumpy Betty had to come pick me up at school. I paid more attention to bus numbers after that.

* * *

For all his horizon-broadening expectations for me in California, I doubt if my father could have imagined what Miraleste High School would be like. I was excited to go to the school and had expected that my new schoolmates would greet me like my St. Nicholas' schoolmates had greeted Lauren. I assumed they would want to know all about life in Malaysia, half a globe away from their shiny city by the ocean. But I had not counted on almost complete disinterest.

Perhaps the diversity of America made a little foreigner like me invisible. Perhaps I looked like the many Hispanic girls in the school, although I had nowhere near the same sultry swagger. Or perhaps, in my eagerness to promote my country by wearing my batik dresses, I just looked uncool. In an effort to learn something new and make some friends as well, I joined the journalism class that produced the school newspaper, Torreon. The kids there seemed a bit more eccentric; one boy walked around every day in top hat and tails. I felt I fitted in more among the oddities of the school. The friends I eventually did make did have something in common with me; they were all foreign students, huddled together in the library puzzling over the shallow friendliness of their hosts in that land of endless sunshine.

In the other classes I joined, I realized that, as less developed a country as Malaysia was compared to the United States in the Seventies, my education had been pretty good. In Geography class, the only student who knew what Number Ten Downing Street was, was me. In Mathematics, whenever there was a test, the other students asked me not to take it. They had noticed that I was very adept at solving equations and were afraid I would raise the grade curve too high. I never got to wear my baju kurung because nobody ever asked me to talk about my country.

There were some things I did appreciate about my American high school experience. I was surprised by the casual friendliness between the students and their teachers, instead of the deference that I was used to back home. The assignments that students were set did not just involve pen and paper. When they studied the history of migration to the United States, students had to go home and interview their grandparents about where they came from. Lauren and Leslie's paternal grandparents, whom they called Dadn and Nana, had come from Germany, while their maternal side hailed from Scotland. One day they had to dress up like hoboes to illustrate life during the Depression. These were all novel ways of learning to me, used to having to memorise names and dates from dry textbooks.

* * *

Years later, Dad liked to say that he made a mistake by sending me to California at sixteen. I had gone as this innocent small-town daughter of his, and returned a different person entirely, a bit more questioning and, to him, less polite. On top of that, I was substantially bigger, having consumed rather a lot of Betty's chocolate chip cookies in my time there, a fact Dad pointed out almost as soon as I stepped off the plane at Subang. I don't really know exactly what it was about me that Dad found had changed but it seemed illogical to send me off to the US at such a young age and not expect the experience to have some impact on me.

Despite that disappointment in whatever that had changed in me, six months later Dad sent me off to the UK to do my A-levels. In the interim I went to Lower Sixth Form at Sultan Abdul Hamid College (SAHC), Dad's alma mater. I had spent a brief time there before I went to TKC in the Fourth Form because all St Nicholas' students who qualified for the Science stream were obliged to move there since our girls' school did not have the capacity to teach science subjects. Girls from other schools, such as our rival Sultanah Asma School, also made up the still small female population at SAHC.

Going to a boys' school no matter how briefly was a very unnerving experience. For one thing, we were not used to teachers who shouted at students. It seemed the only way to control a school full of rowdy teenage boys but unsettling for girls who had come from a school where silence was a premium. Close-up, boys were also odd creatures, prone to a lot of gangly masculine roughness, disguised as athleticism, that, had we been more worldly, we would have recognized as mere showing off.

My first stint at SAHC in the gap before I transferred to TKC was very brief but my second was much longer. By then my old girlfriends had settled in and some were even pairing up with the boys. I took part in the choir which won the state competition and later faced my old choirmates from TKC at the national level. I worked on the school newsletter which then involved a lot of manual typing and cyclostyling and had so few writers that any bit of nonsense anyone, including me, wrote was accepted. Once I gave a bad review to a play some students had put up and faced the crude precursor of trolling when the upset actors sent me nasty notes and called me names.

Like many other students my age in the early Seventies, I had hoped to go to the UK to study for my A-levels and then university. The government was providing scholarships to many students, mostly Malays, to go abroad to become engineers, doctors and other scientific professions. At TKC, the very brightest had already been sent to Australia to do their matriculation because their school year started earlier. The rest of us had to wait until the northern autumn to depart for our studies.

A few years previously my brother Mirzan, then only thirteen, had been offered a scholarship, along with three other boys, to go to a public school, as boarding schools were known in the UK. It was an experiment by MARA, a government statutory body focussing on education for Bumiputera children, to send younger students abroad rather than wait until they were about seventeen. Mirzan was so excited about going especially since the other boys were all his classmates but Dad did not believe in accepting scholarships for his children. After many tears and pleas, my brother did go eventually, Mum sobbing away as his tiny figure walked across the tarmac onto the airplane while we watched from the viewing balcony of Subang airport.

When it came to my turn, Dad again refused to let me accept a scholarship. He reasoned that there were more deserving children than me but knowing I did not want to be left behind instead chose a boarding school in the United Kingdom for me out of a magazine advertisement. I was finally going to have my Enid Blyton adventure.

I should say that although he sent me to school in England himself, it did not mean that Dad was very wealthy. He had his private practice and earned enough from it to give us a comfortable life but we never thought of ourselves as rich. Neither were we poor, which was why Dad would not let anyone else pay for our education, especially not using taxpayers' money. As with our piano, I always knew how much things cost and so I knew that my parents had to sacrifice a lot to let me study overseas. They also didn't want me to feel I was special; I received the same allowance each month, £75, as scholarship holders.

In my excitement about going to an English boarding school, I had not paid much mind to what was happening in Dad's political life. By 1974, with Tun Razak as Prime Minister, he was back in the UMNO fold, appointed as a Senator and back to the Supreme Council in 1973. He stood again in the 4th General Elections in August 1974 in Kubang Pasu constituency in Kedah and won.

When Mirzan and I were about to leave for England in early September 1974, Mum handed each of us an envelope and told us not to open it until 5th September, two days after we arrived at our destination. Neither of us thought much about it then, but we did remember to read the letter inside the envelope when we woke up on that chilly autumn morning. There we read the most unexpected news: on that day, Malaysian time, Dad was to join the government as Minister of Education.

4

Finding Myself in the UK

Although I had already spent two years at boarding school in Malaysia, English boarding school was a new adventure for me. I started off in a small all-girls school, Hollington Park, in St. Leonard's on the south coast, a school that Dad had found in a magazine and which he relied on an officer, Encik Karim, from the Malaysian Students Department in London, to check out.

In fact, my parents outsourced all of my school preparations to Encik Karim. At the time neither they nor I thought this was unusual. Very few of the students who went abroad in the mid-Seventies were accompanied by their parents. Most parents could not afford it and would not see their children again for another two years at least. Many years later after I had graduated and returned home, Mum bemoaned that she had not been there to cook for me while I sat for exams. She had KL friends who had parked themselves wherever their children were studying and had ensured that they only needed to think about their books during their exams. I found the notion of Mum hovering around me at university somewhat alarming and restrained from doing the same to my own children. I did however shop for all their school essentials myself.

In 1974, it was Encik Karim who took me to the school outfitters in Hastings. My Hollington Park uniform was typically English; a pale-yellow shirt and brown skirt for every day, a brown corduroy pinafore for 'formal' occasions and unlike the white canvas shoes I wore to school back home, a pair of brown leather shoes that looked like the ugliest boats I had ever seen. These were packed by the outfitters and sent directly to the school in a green steamer trunk complete with my name painted on the side, except for the pinafore, one shirt, a brown sweater and the shoes, that I planned to wear when I finally travelled down to the school, a few days later.

There I was given a little room just under the roof gables with two beds, a cupboard and two small tables, high up in Castlemaine House that I shared with a Malaysian girl from Penang. She was nice enough and we were both glad to be sharing the room. I warned her that if she woke up in the early morning to see a white apparition next to my bed, it was only me performing my subuh prayers. She was also on her parents' scholarship but with a very different outlook than me. One freezing day, she showed me a stack of cash they had given her, some of which she decided to use to buy a fur coat because she could not stand the cold.

All the sixth formers lived on the same floor and shared one large unheated bathroom with a bathtub and no shower. Until I finally got a rubber shower mixer that I could fix to the hot and cold taps, I would sit in the bathtub and try to bathe by splashing water from the taps onto my soaped body, a task that never left me feeling wholly clean. I found the English habit of sharing bath water—where one soaks in the bath, and then leaves it for the next person—absolutely horrifying.

Hollington Park was not an experience that I would ever treasure. I found it hard to adjust to the many new situations I found there particularly the weather and the general indifference of the school staff towards foreign students, especially the few that, like me, had entered in the Sixth Form. I could not believe that we were expected to go outside into the cold for our physical education lessons. Surely this was cruel, especially for students who had come from just above the equator. Before we broke up for the Christmas holidays, we had to march through the nearby fields in freezing weather to go to a service at a church that seemed to have been built in the middle of nowhere. I considered this akin to child abuse until I learnt that this was normal for the British girls who simply wore their warmest coats, hats and gloves, and trudged on, upper lips suitably stiffened.

As a dutiful daughter, heeding my parents' pre-departure advice not to forget my cultural and religious identity, I tried to fast during Ramadhan. Despite explaining this to the Deputy Headmistress, a tall, large-boned blonde woman aptly-named Miss Wheelhouse, she refused to give me permission to skip meals. I had to sit in the dining room at breakfast and lunch, forced to watch my schoolmates tuck into toast and eggs and my favourite dessert, semolina pudding. Luckily in those short autumn days, dinner came quite early.

I spent that entire term with only the one pinafore and shirt because I could not find the rest of my uniforms that the outfitters had sent. Before we departed for the holidays, when everyone's luggage was brought out of the storeroom, I finally found my trunk filled with the pale-yellow shirts and brown skirts, sweaters and socks that I had needed. Not a single teacher had asked me why I wore the same uniform every day of the term.

I grew rapidly disillusioned with my boarding school experience. Although I made some friends, there were no midnight feasts or pranks on each other. I did not find my classes too difficult but when I tried to join the school choir, I was shocked to find that we were all required to sight read the notes, a skill I did not have. Still I kept my unhappiness to myself, writing only sunny letters home.

Midway through the term, Dad came on a working trip to the UK and I went to spend a weekend with him in London. By then I had decided that Hollington Park was not the fun-filled Enid Blyton school I had expected, and I planned to do something about it. Summoning up all the courage I had over dinner, I begged Dad to take me out of the school, citing how miserable I was there. His first reaction was to refuse, having paid a lot of money in non-refundable fees for the term. That made me feel guilty and I returned to school and resigned myself to suffering through the next two years while I did my A-Levels.

A few days later, Dad came down to St. Leonard's to visit me at school. As the newly-appointed Minister of Education of Malaysia, he arrived with an entourage including officials from our High Commission to the UK. They discovered that British protocol was very unlike that of our own. Only a lowly teacher greeted him at the front entrance and then, the headmistress, the poshly-named Miss Garland-Collins, kept him and the officers accompanying him waiting in a frigid reception room. This disrespect seemed pretty galling to Dad; this was exactly why he, along with many others, had advocated for independence from the British after the war. He took a dislike to the headmistress and also found the school unimpressive, the hallways dark and with an air of crumbling age about it. He might have felt a little guilty too. After all he was the one who had chosen the school from a magazine advertisement. By the Christmas holidays, I was out of there.

That solved one problem but gave rise to another. It was not easy to get into another school in the winter term. My guardian, Pak Wan Baharuddin at the Malaysian Students Department in London, a crusty old man who had lived in the UK for decades, knew every Malaysian leader since independence and oversaw all their children's education, had a trying time finding me another school. During the holidays I had made friends with some other Malaysian students who were attending United World College in Wales, a very outdoorsy school where students learnt how to conduct sea rescues. It sounded like fun but Pak Wan convinced me that given how unathletic I was, it probably would not suit me.

He finally found me a boarding Sixth Form College in Suffolk two hours out of London where he had already sent two Royal sisters. The Bransons College brochure had lovely photos of students of both sexes sitting out in the sunshine in jeans instead of uniforms and promised a lot of outdoor activities including ballooning. I was sold; nothing could be more different from Hollington Park.

Bransons College, located amidst the stark landscape of rural Suffolk, turned out to be nothing like its brochures. It had only twenty-nine students, including some from foreign countries, and was headed by a grumpy woman in her eighties, constantly vibrating with Parkinson's disease, called Mrs Dixon. An elderly couple, Mr Alan Clack and his luxuriantly white-haired wife, assisted her. There were no permanent teachers, just those who came to teach as a sideline to earn extra income. Not that they were necessarily bad teachers. Mrs Penrose, my history teacher, was excellent; to this day I still use the essay-planning method she taught us, listing all the points I need in an orderly manner. The same quality could not be said of the British students there, most of whom had been expelled from other boarding schools or were simply not accepted elsewhere. And yet they would sometimes come to me and say, 'These essays must be difficult for you, Marina, being in English and all!'

I was at Bransons from January 1975 to the summer of 1976, keeping my head down to do my A-Levels in History, Economics and British Constitution. Every two weeks or so, I would make a reverse-charged call home from the payphone in the school entry hall and occasionally I would spend a weekend in London with one of my classmates. On other weekends, my Greek roommate Mimi and I would spend our afternoons at the cinema in the nearby town of Ipswich watching Woody Allen movies.

One cold day in January 1976, I read in the English newspapers that our Prime Minister Tun Razak had passed away from cancer in London. I was so detached from political news from home that while I had vaguely known of his illness through friends, I had not connected it with Dad. Sad as it was, I did not think of it as having any particular impact on my life. Six weeks later, Mum called to tell me the truly shocking news: Hussein Onn, the new Prime Minister, had appointed Dad as his Deputy, a development that was wholly unexpected by almost everybody. I did not know how to react to this; my modest Kedah upbringing found it mildly embarrassing. I finally decided to keep the news to myself and hoped that nobody at school would find out.

One afternoon as I was hanging out with my schoolmates in the common room, Mrs Dixon approached me, her head shaking involuntarily as usual.

At Bransons, I was called Ina, to differentiate me from another Marina, although the English kids said it made them think of Ena Sharples, a character from the soap opera Coronation Street.

'Ina, I suppose you've seen the news about your father?'

'Yes, Mrs D.' I replied, a look of alarm on my face. She correctly read it as my not wanting any fuss to be made about the tiny article in *The Times*.

'Alright then,' she turned and left. I had learnt how to keep that upper lip stiff.

* * *

I managed to get enough A-levels in 1976 to enter either the London School of Economics or the University of Sussex to read International Relations, a subject I thought would be a good foundation for the journalism career I hoped to pursue. My interest in journalism had been a lifelong passion because I loved to write. When I was still at Branson's College, I applied for a summer job at Vogue UK magazine and was invited for an interview by one of the assistant editors. I travelled down to London and went to see a friend before the interview, desperate because I had no clothes suitable for a magazine that specialised in the glamorous and luxurious world of fashion. Neither did my friend, but we managed to put together an outfit that was marginally more sophisticated than my usual sweater and jeans with hems so frayed that Mum once cried when she saw them. The editor was friendly, but she quickly ascertained that I had no discernible skills to offer, although I would have done the lowliest of jobs just to be in that environment. Needless to say, I did not have my start at Vogue UK.

Again, unlike today when my children continually keep me abreast of their university application process, I chose the universities I wanted to apply to and navigated the complicated procedures, visited campuses and attended interviews on my own, updating my parents only by the letters I wrote each week. I eventually chose Sussex partly because I realized that London held too many temptations that might distract me from my studies. The university was located just outside the seaside town of Brighton, an hour away by train, far enough from the big city to let me concentrate on my books yet near enough for me to go there for weekends if I wanted to.

Soon after I arrived at the University of Sussex in 1976, a rumour circulated on campus that the daughter of Ian Smith was studying there. Smith was the Prime Minister of Rhodesia, later renamed Zimbabwe, who unilaterally declared independence from Britain in 1965 and refused to grant the right to rule to the black majority until 1980. Sussex had a leftist reputation, being the first of the 'red brick' universities set up in the 1960s to allow access to higher education to students who could not get into the traditional elite colleges like Oxford and Cambridge. The main hall was named after Nelson Mandela and one of my professors was a Czech who had escaped following the

Russian invasion of his country in 1968. I'm not sure why the rumour spread about Ian Smith's daughter except that some students seemed indignant that the progeny of a racist should be studying in such a leftist university, an early precursor of cancel culture. Whatever was the case, despite not knowing her, I felt some empathy with Smith's daughter because with my father as Deputy Prime Minister, I was beginning to feel the burden of being his child.

It turned out that Smith did not have a biological daughter at all although his lone step-daughter may have well carried his name too. But if indeed she was at Sussex, she had two distinct advantages over me. She was White and had the most common English surname. As long as she toned down her presumably Rhodesian accent, she could go about the campus undetected.

On the other hand, Obathmi Pindling, the son of the then Prime Minister of the Bahamas, and I could not be so anonymous. Obie, a friendly guy who loved soul music, lived together with six others and me in the Park Village student residences, individual three-storey houses with eight single rooms. I remember his mother coming to visit him once, elegant and resplendent in a fur-collared coat. There was no way that this could escape the attention of the rest of the students, peeking out of our room windows. My own parents once turned up looking somewhat less glamorous but still, the hired Bentley that had brought them could not have gone unnoticed. Luckily for me, Park Village was situated in a far corner of the campus next to the adjacent Falmer Park away from the central hub of the university and so my parents' arrival escaped the notice of all but a small group of students.

Sussex had a reputation for being a hyper-politically aware campus. There were protests for one thing or another every other day. Although I never took part in any of them, and especially after the Smith daughter episode, I became sensitive to any news about Malaysia.

Whenever Malaysia made the headlines for the wrong reasons, I would cringe. At the time, the Vietnam war had ended with victory for Ho Chi Minh's forces and the South China Sea was awash with South Vietnamese escaping the communist regime. Many of them inevitably landed on Malaysian beaches in such numbers that the government was hard-pressed to accommodate them, eventually designating Pulau

Bidong, an island off Terengganu state as the island where these refugees were to be processed. Our loquacious Foreign Minister at the time, Ghazali Shafie, declared that if any more refugees came, we would 'shoot' them. Understandably, this caused howls of outrage all over the world. I can't be sure that my fellow students read the newspapers any more than any of today's. But I did, and flushed red when I read what Ghazali had said. He then tried to soothe ruffled Western feathers by saying that he meant to 'shoo' them away, hardly the most plausible explanation. Nobody bought it anyway and I was left even more crimson-faced. It became even more imperative that I keep my family connections secret; I didn't want to feel I had to defend my government all the time. I didn't realize at the time that when you're abroad, you are always called on to represent your country.

Sussex at the time had a student population of 3,000 on its small verdant campus, with its stark modern buildings in the Brutalist style that was fashionable when it was built in the 1960s. By today's standards, that student body was miniscule when compared to the current body of some 17,000 students. Most of the small population of Malaysians were in the science faculties studying engineering on government scholarships. I was the only one I knew who was in the School of Social Sciences. My friends were mostly other foreign students, from Sri Lanka, India, Kenya although my best friend was an English girl I met in the very first week of the first year.

In the very early days of acclimatizing to university life, there were many social events meant to acquaint students with one another. At one of these in my first week at Sussex, I was standing to one side idly watching other students dancing and drinking. I had only just gotten to know my housemates and had gone with them to the social. Suddenly a blonde girl, clearly more than a little inebriated, rushed up and yelled in my face: 'Are you Malaysian? My boyfriend is Malaysian, and I miss him so much!'

I was not sure how to respond to this. How could she tell I was Malaysian? And what has her boyfriend anything to do with me? I feigned disinterest and asked where her boyfriend was from. 'PJ' was the reply. I lived in the Kuala Lumpur suburb of Petaling Jaya too, having moved there from Alor Setar when my father joined the government in 1974.

'What's his name?' I shouted back over the pounding music as other students crowded around us jigging about in what the British called dancing. She told me and I started in surprise. I actually knew him. Jill Greatorex, for that was her name, agreed to meet up the next day at a less noisy corner of campus and we chatted about mutual friends whom she knew through her boyfriend and their school, United World College in Wales. And that was how I found my best friend at university.

Jill lived in Lancaster House, one of the large dormitories on campus, not far from where I lived in Park Village. We visited each other almost every day but I spent more time in her communal kitchen because it was larger and had more people coming and going, a sociable place where while chopping and frying, we talked about lectures and lecturers and gossiped about other students. It was at one of those visits in Jill's kitchen that I learnt, in the most humiliating way, that I had to become my own person, with my own opinions.

I was sitting on a stool in the kitchen one cold winter day chatting with her dorm mates as usual, when in walked a tall man, looking slightly older than us, with light brown buzzcut hair, a long pale face and a serious demeanour.

I forget whose friend he was but amidst the clattering of pots and pans around us, we got talking. His name was Raziel and he was from Israel. He said he had some Malaysian friends who had told him about Malaysia's New Economic Policy and how it apparently discriminates against non-Malay minorities. I listened to him, my heart sinking. I am pretty sure he did not know who I was; all he knew was that I was Malaysian and that was enough for him to launch into his spiel, delivered in a calm authoritative manner, telling me what was wrong about my own country.

If I had been a bit more knowledgeable about Israel then, I might have challenged him about his country's own discriminatory policies against its Arab minorities. But I was a naïve young student, more interested in partying than politics and world affairs and I didn't know how to explain the NEP, a time-bound affirmative action policy, to him. Under his relentless questioning, I felt stupid and humiliated and could barely hold myself together. I was being attacked by someone who seemed to be more knowledgeable about my own country and I felt defensive and defenceless.

I'm not sure how I held myself together. Despite the busyness of the kitchen, it felt as if there was only Raziel and me there. Everyone else were either too involved in cooking or other conversations or were politely staying out of ours. Eventually I managed to extricate myself, went to Jill's room where she was trying to write an essay, and burst into tears. I hated Raziel for making me feel small in front of everyone but most of all I hated myself for being so ignorant and helpless, unable to defend my own country from these criticisms.

That kitchen incident however made me conscious about my so-called opinions about many things. Were they my own or was I just parroting what I had heard my father say? Every time I offered an opinion in class or in conversations with classmates on almost anything that involved politics or world affairs, a little voice inside me said, 'Is that really your opinion, Marina? Or did you just regurgitate what you heard Dad say?'

Not that I believed that Dad was necessarily wrong all the time. But because the opinions I spouted were not wholly mine, I had nothing to back them up with. I was simply repeating what he said, sometimes not even directly to me, without always understanding the basis for them. It was as if I had a radio scanner for a brain, picking up bits and pieces of information from other people's conversations and repeating them to make myself sound smart. This put me on shaky ground if anyone asked me follow-up questions. I risked facing even more humiliations, not just in dormitory kitchens but also in class.

To say I bucked up from that pivotal moment would be a lie. I managed to party, not parlay, my way through to the final year. Luckily for me, Sussex's system involved no exams until the third year where, in the School of Social Sciences, you're suddenly hit with three extended essays as well as sit-down exams. In that year I finally got serious and started to study, admittedly a bit late. In fact, it was only in those last nine months that I finally understood and took a deeper interest in the books I was reading for my classes. In the end I managed to scrape through with a Lower Second, which my Dean told me was exactly what I deserved. He also noted that had I taken a degree in partying I would have gotten a First, a remark I never recounted to my parents for obvious reasons. I'm not sure they truly understood the UK system of grading; what mattered was that I passed and graduated. Dad was also too busy with his new job to scrutinize my mediocre performance. He deputized Mum to come to my graduation ceremony at the end of July where to my relief, they gave out our scrolls in alphabetical order rather than by grades.

I suppose it's not unusual for students to only get serious in their third year as I did. In my undergraduate years at Sussex, I lived the full university student life, going to class, studying in the library, partying with friends. By the final year however, I had to think of what I wanted to do next. Since my teenage years I had dreamt of becoming a journalist because I felt that the only talent I had, if you could call it that, was writing. I wanted to be that hotshot reporter who investigated issues and brought them to light and made changes in the world.

My father would snort at these ambitions. He had a testy relationship with the press and my wanting to join the Fourth Estate sounded almost like a betrayal, as if I was crossing over to the opposition. Still, he never forbade me outright. In that respect, mine were unusual Asian parents. Despite both being doctors, they never forced any of their children to take up medicine, leaving the choice of careers entirely to us. Despite that liberal attitude, it has to be said that they had a penchant for dramatic sighs whenever their doctor friends talked about the children that had followed in their footsteps. As a result, they have one journalist, one businessman, one engineer/businessman, one former businessman/current politician, one homemaker, one vegetable farmer and one communications executive in the family. I think it does make for more varied, if somewhat unfocussed, dinner conversations.

In my last year at Sussex, I faced the prospect of going home, which I didn't want to do. Like many students who had experienced the freedom of being in the liberal environment of the UK, I thought going home was akin to going to prison, where I would not be free to do what I wanted. I also thought there were no prospects for me back home as a journalist, at least not in the romantic notions I had about journalism, having read *The Times* and *The Guardian* for several years by then. Again, these were decisions I made entirely in my own head, without reference to anyone. I told my parents I did not want to go home yet as diplomatically as possible, and I think they understood that life as a top politician's daughter in Malaysia might be tricky. When I eventually did return home and was taking driving lessons, Mum felt the need to warn me that my instructor might ask me for favours because of who my father was. They were sensitive to the hazards that I might face with the public and didn't resist too much when I said I wanted to stay back in the UK a little longer. To me it had seemed the right decision then but as I saw Mum off at Heathrow airport after attending my graduation, I felt an unexpected sense of loneliness. I was out in the world far away from home on my own.

Before I finished my course at Sussex, and to finally study a course relevant to my ambitions, I applied to several universities in the UK to take a master's degree in Journalism. It didn't turn out to be a smooth process. Application forms were long on detail and short on places for foreign students, unlike today when they need our money. Most of all they required applicants to be knowledgeable about current affairs and have their own opinions.

I managed to secure one interview at the University of Wales and travelled all the way to its Cardiff campus for my appointment. I had written a long rambling essay, filled with glib generalities, to accompany my application. Having gotten tired of filling in so many such forms with very little guidance from anyone, not even friends, I had become far too casual about this important task. In one case, in answer to the question about what I thought was my greatest achievement, I had written 'filling in this form'. No career counsellor had told me that university admissions officers rarely had a sense of humour.

In Cardiff, I faced a panel of four sour-faced men who proceeded to go through my essay line by line asking me to explain what I meant. I had not bothered to keep a copy of it which meant that I had forgotten most of what I had written. And boy, were they picky! In typical radio-scanner fashion, I had repeated a line my cousin had said to me about America being full of fake people. Naturally my interviewers asked me for evidence I didn't have. I was rightly made to feel like a foolish little girl, verbose only on paper, unable to defend a single opinion that, in any case, was not at all original.

On the train back to London, instead of feeling ashamed of myself, I seethed at the so-called injustice of being 'bullied' at the interview. I saw another passenger looking through what looked like job application forms and glared at him, likening him to the tough questioners I had just faced. Back on campus, Jill listened sympathetically as I recounted what happened, making it sound as if I was badly treated, even though I deserved everything I got for being so unprepared.

Once I calmed down, I had to seriously think of what else I could do to stay on in the UK. I had to look for a job, any job that would give me a work permit so I could stay on legally.

* * *

As any jobseeker knows, looking for and applying for jobs is a soul-destroying effort. In the summer of 1979, I had very little idea how to go about looking for jobs beyond looking at advertisements in the newspapers. I only knew I wanted to stay in London and if possible, I wanted something related to writing or journalism. But everything seemed to be against me. Firstly, I was a foreigner and that set me up against all the stereotypes that magazine or newspaper people, most of whom were British and White, had against us, just like my Bransons schoolmates who thought my English must be worse than theirs. Secondly, I had no portfolio of writing samples to speak of. I had written some short essays when I applied to universities for my Masters but since they all rejected me, I assumed none of them were any good.

As Autumn neared, I began to be desperate. Dad happened to be in London on another work trip around then and he had been interviewed by *World Times*, a newsmagazine in the fashion of *Time* or *Newsweek* that aimed to present the Asian perspective on world issues. Spectacularly over-ambitious in its name, the magazine was owned by a London-based Bangladeshi businessman. During his interview Dad must have mentioned that I was looking for a job in journalism and before I knew it, the man offered to take me on as a reporter. By that point I did not have the luxury of saying no, especially when they said they would sponsor my work permit, so I accepted. My weekly pay was nothing to shout about but I was thrilled to be earning my own money at last.

The *World Times* office was several rooms in an old corner building on Fleet Street. That address alone impressed me because it meant it neighboured all the newspapers I admired, such as *The Times* many years before Rupert Murdoch bought it. Just by being on the street I could breathe in newsprint and hopefully bump into some of the famous journalists I admired at the time.

At *World Times*, although I was happy enough to have a job, it didn't escape my notice that despite its mission to present the 'Asian perspective' on global issues, very few of its staff were actually Asian. The editor was Robert Govender, a gruff South African Indian, tall with a round bald head circled by a band of grey hair, who had fled the apartheid regime after being targeted for his activism. He was the first person to call for a boycott of the then all-White South African sports teams whenever they travelled overseas. With that storied reputation, it was no wonder that the office was sometimes visited by people like Donald Woods, the author of the biography of Steve Biko, the anti-apartheid activist who had been killed in police custody in 1977. Woods himself had to leave South Africa for his book and friendship with Biko. The book eventually became the basis for the movie *Cry Freedom* in 1987.

The rest of the staff were an odd collection of people. The Managing Editor was a blowsy White woman called Chloe whose background remained a mystery to me. She would literally float into the office on what seemed like random days in floral dresses looking like she was off to a garden party. The Marketing Manager was a ramrod-straight very affable older White man with an impressive handlebar moustache called Dennis who had once been in the British Army. Whatever his soldierly past, Dennis at least had a great sense of humour and a smile for me every day. Then there were two young reporters, a White man and a White American woman. The man, Peter, and I became friends, and we would sometimes grab lunch together. The woman though once yelled at me when, in all innocence, I asked her for some leads for interviews that I could do for a story I had been assigned. I was mystified as to why she was so angry until I realized that it had originally been her assignment but for some reason it had been given to me, a new and very junior reporter.

The only Asians besides me were two Bangladeshi staff, an accounts clerk and a very young photographer. The owner would be in the office occasionally but did not give much direction editorially. Everything was left to Robert Govender and although he turned up for work every day, I was never sure what he did. He also did not give me much guidance, probably viewing me as an ingenue that the boss had foisted on him. I worked on whatever assignments I was given as best as I could and taking my own initiative to contact people I needed information from. Robert gave me some book reviews to do which I was very excited about because it meant I could also interview the authors. At one time I was going to interview Jonathan Dimbleby, the journalist and broadcaster, on his book *The Palestinians*. When the copy of the book arrived at the office, I managed to read a few chapters before Robert took it away for the weekend, leaving me with only a truncated impression of the book to go on. I still went to meet Dimbleby at his home and he very sweetly indulged me, recognizing that I was a young reporter trying to do my best not to be overwhelmed by someone far more experienced in interviewing people.

I did not stay long at *World Times*, but I am grateful for the opportunities it provided me, haphazard as they were. I met some famous people at movie screenings or product launches. Once, I saw the stage actress Carol Channing in all her blonde false-eyelashed glory at a book launch, looking perfect for her role as Dolly Levi in the musical *Hello Dolly*. My proudest moment was writing an article on British Black music where I got to interview Eddy Grant, lead singer of *The Equals*, a British reggae pop band.

But I had grown uneasy over the lack of direction at the magazine and wondered where, apart from the newsstands nearest the office, it was actually being sold. I got my answer one day when Dennis took me down to the basement and showed me a sight that sent chills down my spine. There, in that musty room, sat piles and piles of unsold copies of *World Times*, doomed to be either shredded or sold off as recycled paper.

I knew then that my future did not lie there, and again without telling anyone, I quit, despite not having any other prospects. That meant that, for several weeks, I had no job and not much income apart from some savings. Afraid they would insist I return home, I did not dare tell my parents. The days had become much shorter and gloomier as winter neared and I was alone in the flat, not sure what to do about my situation except that I did not want to go home yet. Once I caught a cold; there are few things more miserable than suffering a cold in the damp English winter and having no one to talk to.

Not that I was completely friendless in London. I had some friends, both English and Malaysian, as well as my brother Mirzan who was studying at Brighton Technical College, now Brighton University. Most of them were still studying or working but they would come around occasionally just to hang out, cook dinner and watch TV. It was on one of those evenings, as we laughed and joked, that I got a call from Mirzan who had not joined us that night.

My parents had decided that rather than informing me directly, they would make my brother the bearer of bad news. They really should not have placed such a burden on him because he was not equipped to know how to put things gently. This was what he said over the phone to me: 'Kak Ma, Abang Jit. Accident. All dead.' He might as well have sent a telegram.

I let out a howl that must have frightened all the other tenants throughout the entire apartment building. My friends, until then happily sitting on the floor chatting, turned to me in shock. I could not stop crying and was barely intelligible, the shock and grief so sudden and massive that I was inconsolable.

Kak Ma was Asmah and Abang Jit was her husband. She was my Chik's younger sister and had lived with us briefly in Jitra where I became very close to her, confiding in her all manner of childhood worries. She had married her cousin Aziz who often came to our house to play the violin and accompany Mum on the piano. They had three young sons. On that fateful day they had been in KL and were driving home to Alor Setar in a packed car, with one of their sons, my father's two older sisters, my cousin Aziah and her stepmother Mariam. Before they left, they had stopped by our house at Bukit Tunku to say goodbye. Our staff, seeing that overstuffed vehicle, persuaded my two aunts, Mak Teh (Rafeah) and Mak Ngah

(Habsah), to stay behind. They were not to know then how that decision would save their lives.

That night, probably due to the long exhausting journey in the days before the North-South Highway was built, Abang Jit had fallen asleep at the wheel somewhere near Sungai Petani, about an hour before Alor Setar. All of them were killed instantly.

Distraught and despondent, I did not protest much when in late December of 1979, my mother asked me to come home. And so, my student life in the UK, after five years, ended rather abruptly.

When I look back at my student days, I realized how independent I was forced to become, learning things by myself along the way. For instance, it had not occurred to me that I needed to bring cooking utensils with me to university. I navigated everything, good and bad, on my own and even though I always had my parents as backup, I often chose not to turn to them for advice or even tell them when I had problems. In some perverse way I thought I needed to protect them from worry about me, because I was sure that my student experience was very different from theirs. Sussex University may have been an enclave of liberalism but Brighton itself was the headquarters of the right-wing National Front and skinheads roamed its streets. I once had to wipe spit off my coat as I walked through a London Underground tunnel. As I left Britain in 1979, Margaret Thatcher had just come to power, ushering an era of demonstrations against her 'full-cost' policies for overseas students, miners' strikes and IRA bombings. Reluctant as I was, I knew that staying on in the UK at that point was no longer viable for me.

Part 2

The Middle (1980-2003)

5

Home Again

When my mother called me in London to ask me to return home, she had prepared a bait. She suspected that I was miserable and lonely in Britain and the news of the fatal accident had only made me more depressed. Her lure was a job as a cadet reporter at *Her World* magazine that she had somehow come across. I never knew the true story of the job offer but she rang me up one morning to tell me about it.

My reaction was probably not what she expected. I burst into angry tears. I thought she was conning me just to get me home and accused her of 'spoiling' things for me. What exactly I meant by that I couldn't say because I had nothing that would really keep me in London anymore. When I finally calmed down, I laid out the choices I had and grudgingly admitted that I had none. I retrieved my passport from the Home Office in Croydon telling the smiling clerk I didn't need a work permit anymore and left the English cold to fly back to KL's tropical heat.

I started work at *Her World* magazine on 2 January, 1980. On the given day I turned up at the Berita Publishing offices, on the fourth floor of the *New Straits Times* Building, dressed in my best midi-length blue and red skirt and cream silk blouse to meet Ayoub Ismail, the General Manager.

I know that I was not expected at *Her World* because the long-time editor of that venerable women's magazine, Ayesha Harben's eyebrows shot up when she was called in to Ayoub's office to meet me.

If you've never met Ayesha before, you'd always be a bit taken aback when you do. I had known her name from reading the magazine off and on over my youth and had assumed that she must be ethnic Indian. She is definitely of subcontinental origin but with the height, fair skin, brown hair and green eyes that betray some Caucasian blood. It turned out that her father was Anglo-Indian and both he and her mother had migrated to Malaysia where their eldest Ayesha and their three other daughters were born. A true Malaysian story.

I can't say that Ayesha greeted me very warmly at first, but she introduced me to the other staff, gave me a desk and typewriter and let me get on with it. Even though *Her World* was not my romantic notion of journalism, I dove into it, grateful that I had a job at all. I was happy to accept any assignment she threw my way and eager to learn how a magazine was produced. Despite having worked at *World Times*, I had no idea about production which was done elsewhere at some unknown location. Until the head of the art department, a smiley man named Tony Chong, showed me, I had no idea how the pages came to be. How people did pagination and layout were mysteries to me. Those were the days before computers were used by anyone but scientists working in laboratories; everything was done by hand. If an article took too much or too little space, you literally cut and pasted words as necessary.

It did not take long for Ayesha to realize that not only could I write, I also did not balk at work. As a cadet, I would be sent out to cover events such as fashion shows and product launches and interview people for various articles. There used to be regular column called 'Bachelor of the Month' and I had to interview the candidates for the feature, mostly young executives who didn't mind having themselves touted as God's gifts to women. Today perhaps no magazine would have such a column nor send very junior female reporters to handle the assignment. But I viewed it as part of the job and despite being single myself, never found any of my interviewees of interest at all.

I did love fashion however and eagerly assisted the photographers who shot the covers and fashion spreads for the magazines and got to know the models, makeup artists, hairdressers and designers who came along to the Balai Berita studio. After a while, I would volunteer to produce many of the covers and fashion spreads myself and occasionally went to Singapore to do the shoots for the *Her World Annual*, a yearly special edition. There I worked with the photographer Willy Tang, shooting models dressed in designer clothes from various high-end boutiques.

Seeing how enthusiastically I would initiate assignments, Ayesha allowed me to explore every opportunity that came my way. One year I scored a free ticket from Malaysia Airlines to go to Paris and cover the pret-a-porter shows there, in return for an article in *Wings of Gold* in-flight magazine and acknowledgement in all the articles I wrote about the trip. It was a thrill, seeing all those famous designers like Marc Bohan of Christian Dior and models including my favourite Ines de la Fressange, in the big tents set up in the Bois de Boulogne. Being on my own, unlike the big crews that magazines like Vogue sent, I had to take photographs of the fashions myself. I had a camera I barely knew how to operate but it allowed me access to the spots right below the catwalk with the other photographers. Despite winding up with sore knees, I couldn't have been closer to the glamour of Paris.

In the early days of my job at *Her World*, then housed in the same building as the *News Straits Times* newspaper, many of my colleagues understandably viewed me with some hesitation. Was I this princess who had gotten a glamorous job because the boss wanted to please my parents? It didn't help that before I obtained my driver's licence, I would be driven to work by Mum's chauffeur and bodyguard, a rather embarrassing situation for a lowly junior reporter earning all of RM800 a month. Aware of the ignominy of being chauffeured every day, Mum insisted I take driving lessons and earn my licence and soon enough I was able to drive her spare car, a light blue Mitsubishi Galant, to work. My employers at the *New Straits Times Press* however decided that, despite my low stature in the company rungs, for security reasons, I had to be given a parking place within the company grounds like other senior executives while other employees had to park outside on the street. Perhaps their decision was hastened by the time when I attempted to park my car on the curb outside the building's gates and, forgetting to lower my gear, promptly drove it into the drain. Maybe I was actually a security threat to other people.

Unlike the United States, the children of senior Malaysian politicians are not entitled to government-mandated security like the Secret Service. I drove myself to and from work in my Mitsubishi like anyone else, which led to some interesting situations.

One rainy morning I was rushing to work from my parents' home in Bukit Tunku cutting through the Lake Gardens area to get to my office in Bangsar. At a T-junction amidst the lush greenery of the park, I was a little impatient and stepped on the accelerator to turn right without waiting for a car to fully cross in front of me. The unmistakable sound of metal against metal grated in my ears. In front of me, in the fine drizzle, I saw some black objects fly up into the air. The other driver and I both stopped and went to inspect our cars. To our astonishment, there didn't seem to be a single scratch on either of our vehicles. With nothing to argue about, we decided to get on our way.

I drove off and soon came to a set of traffic lights by the National Museum where I stopped at the head of the line of cars bound for work. As I waited for the lights to change, a policeman, big and bulky in his white shirt and black uniform trousers tucked into leather boots, strode towards me, a grin on his face. With his right hand, he made a circular swinging gesture, as if he were twirling a pearl necklace. I was puzzled, until he reached my window and twirled his hands again, indicating that he wanted me to wind down my window. Those were the days when you had to turn a handle to crank your car window open.

'Tell me, young lady,' he said, a smile on his face that I could not decipher as either friendly or menacing, 'What is the number on the Agong's licence plate?'

The question mystified me. Was this a special day when the correct answer would win me a prize from this traffic policeman? I thought hard and tried to picture the Agong's Rolls-Royce, its gleaming royal yellow paint vivid in my mind. But I could not see what numerals were on His Majesty's licence plate.

The policeman asked me again, 'What is the King's number plate?'

I looked at him blankly. Meantime the lights had changed to green and the cars behind me, getting impatient and realizing that the policeman was not about to let me go soon, started moving past me and taking off as fast as they could. Best to let that young woman handle her own problems this drizzly Friday morning.

Finally, after scouring my brain as best as I could, I came up with an answer. Or rather, a non-answer. 'I don't know,' I said, 'Agong 1?'

The policeman's round previously genial face scrunched into a scowl. At twenty-two, I had not yet learnt that one should never be a smartass with an officer of the law.

'The King's car has no number plate. YOU don't have a number plate. Are you the King's daughter or something?'

In that split second, I realized what it was that I saw when I had my little accident not ten minutes ago. My collision with the other car may have been slight, but it had been enough to break my licence plate, sending it flying into the air. Pieces of it were probably still lying on the ground at that fateful junction.

'I can explain, Tuan!' I said excitedly. At least I knew what I should address any policeman, regardless of rank. But he was not having anything of it. It was a wet Friday morning, and his job was to stand in the rain directing traffic. Spoilt young girls driving their own cars without licence plates was not his idea of a good day.

'Show me your driving licence!' came the stern order.

I sighed. I knew that we were headed to a potentially awkward situation, one that was going to be embarrassing for both of us. But refusing to show my licence was also an offence. Slowly I took my crisp new licence, only a month old, out of my wallet and held it out the window to the man.

The policeman took it, his mouth turned down in disdain and studied my license. I watched, heart in mouth, as slowly his expression changed from sternness into one of incredulity. If there was a thought bubble coming out of his head, it would read 'Oh shit . . .' After a long pause while he turned my licence over and over, probably wishing it belonged to someone else, he turned to me.

'Which Mahathir is this?'

By any definition, Mahathir is not a common name. It is not the equivalent of Smith or Jones, not even Johnson or Blair. It is more akin to Thatcher or Corbyn, which would cause you to immediately make the most obvious associations. Furthermore, most Malaysians with that name would spell it Mahadzir. But my grandfather Mohamad, who taught English in school, was insistent that his son pronounce the 'th' sound in English correctly. Hence, he spelt my father's name the unusual Mahathir. For the policeman, there was no mistaking which Mahathir progeny he had the misfortune to encounter that morning.

'That one,' I whispered, cringing.

His bulbous brown face turned white. It took a full minute before he recovered enough to ask me to explain what happened. In quick gulps, I rushed out my story and persuaded him to follow me on his motorcycle back to the accident spot. There, just as I thought they would be, lay pieces of black metal on the road, some bearing clear white markings of my car number.

'OK, this is what you do, Miss,' said Mister Traffic Cop, now back to his original tan. 'You go to your office, get a piece of cardboard, write your car number on it and tie it to the front of your car. Then you get the real replacement done.'

I nodded in relief and gratefully got back into my car to drive to my office, about five minutes away. To avoid the risk of being stopped by another diligent traffic policeman, and the entire episode being repeated, my new uniformed friend escorted me on his motorcycle all the way to the *New Straits Times* building.

I dined out for several weeks on that story. I wonder if he did too.

* * *

Until my second child was born in 1999, I drove myself everywhere. Sans bodyguards of any sort. Like I said, Malaysia is just not that sort of country, where the children of politicians are automatically assigned a security detail.

My solo drives around KL would sometimes get me into awkward situations. In the mid-Nineties when I worked as a public relations executive, I was once stopped by a policeman for allegedly talking on my phone. In my defence I was actually waiting for a traffic light to change, rushing home after work. I had not realized that you can't hold a phone to your ear even when you're stationary.

After making me park at the side of the road, the young policeman marched up and demanded my driving licence. I gave it to him and waited for the inevitable shock. He read my name and looked at me in surprise, taking in my nondescript small car, the successor to my Galant, the fact that I was driving myself and my lack of muscular companion.

'Ah,' he said, as if weighing what to do about this situation.

'Yes,' I said, bowing my head in apology. 'I'm sorry, please write out my fine notice.'

He looked at me and smiled almost shyly.

'Well actually it's OK. This is just a warning.'

Relieved, I was about to thank him when he added, 'But I would like to ask you something.'

'OK, how can I help you?' I waited to see if he would confirm the many stories I had heard about encounters with policemen.

'Do you think you could get an EON dealership for my brother-in-law?'

I was so surprised that my jaw literally dropped. I couldn't believe what I'd heard. EON was the marketing arm of PROTON, the national car project which my father had initiated and promoted. People bought it because it was a good car at a reasonable price. Obviously, an EON dealership was a lucrative one. I had in fact been part of the public relations team that had organized the launch of the first Proton car in July 1985. Although I did know the bosses at Proton and EON since they were my clients, it was ludicrous to think that I would ask them for a dealership for anyone.

'Um . . . no,' I said when I finally regained my voice, 'I don't know anything about that.'

I searched in my bag for something to give him to compensate for his disappointment. Why are women always eager to please men, even when they might be corrupt? Eventually I found a red ribbon pin made by the organization I headed, the Malaysian AIDS Council, and handed it to him.

'Here, have this! And thank you!'

With that, I sped off, leaving a bemused policeman with a red ribbon pin in his hand. I don't suppose he told that story to his brother-in-law.

* * *

My experience abroad however was quite different. In the 1990s, I travelled to Manila, the capital of the Philippines, for the opening of a photographic exhibition, Eyes on ASEAN, that I had organized. Mrs Ming Ramos, the wife of the then President Fidel Ramos, was invited to open it. Naturally this meant that Malacañang Palace knew that I was going to be in their capital.

I arrived at Ninoy Aquino International Airport with my friend Wong Mei Wan to be greeted by a whole phalanx of policemen and women dressed in the presidential security uniform of barong Tagalog, the translucent white shirt made of pineapple fibre, and black trousers. 'Ma'am,' they said, they would be my escorts and security detail for the entire time I was there.

I found this highly amusing, unused as I was to being surrounded constantly by very hefty men and women wearing communication earpieces. One of them told me in all seriousness that she was my food taster, presumably to ensure that, rather than be delighted by Filipino cuisine, I was not poisoned. Undoubtedly Manila had a far more dangerous reputation at the time compared to Kuala Lumpur, but my six bodyguards seemed a bit over the top. Still, I was grateful for the ease at which they transported me to places I needed to go to in that traffic-choked city.

I had the same security the next time I went to Manila to organize a major photographic shoot for a book on the Philippines that I was working on with the French publisher, Editions Didier Millet. They again accompanied me everywhere including to some corporate offices where I went to meet potential sponsors. I noticed that Filipino office staff were generally unsurprised at their presence. Presidential children must go in and out of people's offices often, or bodyguard entourages were commonplace in that city. Eventually I began to feel guilty at the use of Filipino taxpayers' money to accommodate me besides some embarrassment at having them hover in the reception while I tried to persuade company CEOs to part with their money for the book. After that occasion, I stopped informing Malacañang I was coming to Manila and visited several more times on the same project quietly and generally anonymously. Not that the city, even with eight million people, was big enough to hide in. In one of Manila's smaller shopping malls, I was recognized by the President's son-in-law's bodyguards who were shocked that I was wandering around unguarded. I just winked and moved on.

* * *

In 1981, slightly more than a year after I returned home from the UK, Dad was appointed Prime Minister after Hussein Onn retired due to ill-health. At that time, none of us imagined that Dad would remain in office for twenty-two years. It was already a bit surreal that he was Prime Minister at all and that our lives had changed so substantially from the simpler days of my Alor Setar childhood. When he became PM, I was just twenty-four, Mirzan was still at university in the UK and Mokhzani and Mukhriz were in school at Mara Junior Science College in Kota Bharu, Kelantan. My sister Melinda was the only other child at home and was studying at a college in KL.

After first moving to a rented house in Petaling Jaya when he first joined the government in 1974, the family was offered the official residence of the Deputy Prime Minister at Number 3, Jalan Tunku when Dad was made DPM in 1976. Number 3 was an old colonial-style house nestled up the monkey-filled hills of Bukit Tunku. Down the road from us, at Number 1, was, ironically, Tunku Abdul Rahman, after whom the area was named. I loved that house because although it looked big and grand, inside Mum had made it cosy. While downstairs were formal public areas with a large sitting room and dining room, upstairs was a comfortable family home. My three brothers still had to share one bedroom but since they were mostly away in school and university, it didn't matter very much. My sister Melinda and I had each our own small bedrooms, private nooks where we could relax undisturbed.

Our evenings were spent in the upstairs family room with its flowered wallpaper and sofas that always made you want to curl up and lie down on them. Dad would return from work and wind down by watching our favourite TV programmes like *Eight is Enough* or *Fame* in that room together. It was also where I found a scowling Dad once when I ran up the stairs after a very late night out.

Number 3 was also quite a social house. Apart from the usual Hari Raya open houses, my parents would often host musical evenings where they would invite musicians and singers to entertain a small set of friends. One evening they had the Prime Minister Tun Hussein Onn and his wife Tun Suhailah over to listen to Tun Hussein's favourite gambus player, Fadzil Ahmad. I remember Tun Hussein laughing happily when the song *Dia Datang* was performed.

Inevitably when Dad became PM, we had to move again, this time to a house over at Federal Hill, across from Parliament House. Known originally as Sri Timah, it had belonged to Malaysian Mining Corporation before it was bought by the New Straits Times Group. Then it was sold to the government when it was looking for a suitable residence for the Prime Minister that would be named Sri Perdana.

That first Sri Perdana was a large house situated on top of a hill along the stretch of Jalan Damansara that led to Bangsar and further on to Petaling Jaya. It had an expansive multi-level garden with some big conical trees. I doubt if I went down to the garden much: once you're down there, climbing back up to the house was a chore for even the strongest legs. When I got married the first time, most of my guests watched the ceremony via close-circuit TV that had been set up in the tents at the lowest flattest level of the garden, because we simply could not accommodate everyone in the house.

To enter the compound, you drive past a tall iron gate and a guard house up a steep paved road that branched at the top to the right to the porch and the main doors and to the left to the side entrance. That's only if you are a VIP. The rest of us, family, friends and workers, entered through a side gate, next to a car park and housing for staff, and drove up to the entrance to our living quarters by the side of the building. The policemen at the guardhouse may give you a cursory look if they are familiar with you. If not, they may call up to the house to check that the guest is expected.

As with the Jalan Tunku house, we lived above the shop. On the ground floor were the formal public areas, with a carpeted living room, a low-ceilinged inner reception room and, down a few steps, the formal dining room used to entertain guests like Margaret Thatcher, the Sultan of Brunei and various other foreign VIPs. At the back of the house connected to the dining room by a long corridor was the kitchen, equipped to handle formal dinners usually catered by hotels. When we first moved in, we were all fascinated by the gigantic icemaking machine, as big as a freezer with a glass top, that seemed to spew so many cubes of ice you could get hypothermia just by sticking your head in.

Upstairs was our living quarters which resembled a large apartment. This time we each had our own bedrooms along a long wide corridor that opened up to a living and dining room and best of all, a kitchen. Although most of the serious cooking still came from the downstairs kitchen, brought up by the specially installed dumb waiter, at least we now had the facilities to make our own drinks and snacks whenever we wanted.

My parents' taste in décor tends towards comfy sofas, cushions and rugs and so our living quarters tended to be long on comfort and short on style. By the standards of many of today's mansions, the Sri Perdana we lived in was very simple, almost plebeian. I had to beg Mum to please take off the plastic sheet overlaying the tablecloth from our dining table and to stop using those cheap red paper napkins that looked as if someone had stolen them from a seafood restaurant and get some better-quality ones instead. If you wiped your mouth with one of those napkins, the grease simply moved from one side of your face to the other.

Living on a bigger hill may have seemed more secure than the previous house but this was an illusion. It may not have been too easy to get past the main gates and the guard house but once you're within the compound, there is not much to stop you from going to areas that you shouldn't be going to. A particular weak point was the Hari Raya Open House.

On the first day of Hari Raya each year, the gates would be thrown open and the public would stream in to greet Mum and Dad. It used to, and still does, amaze me how many Malaysians, and foreigners, were willing to get dressed, pack their kids up and queue outside in the heat for several hours just to shake hands with Mum and Dad and grab some satay and *kuih*. But they did, every year without fail. My parents, then much younger and stronger than today, would stand in the formal living room and shake hands with every single person who came up from the front porch. A bodyguard standing next to them would then give children duit Raya, money packets usually containing crisp small notes, that Mum had prepared herself the day before, and then the visitors would pass on to the inner reception room on their way to the dining room where tables of food would be laid out. My brothers and I would usually be standing in the inner room also to shake hands with everyone and hopefully also catch some of our friends who might show up.

The Malaysian open house is truly a phenomenon like no other. Where else in the world would the head of government open his doors to literally any man, woman or child to walk in and actually take their hands in greeting, without a security officer tackling them or at least, knocking their hands out of the way? There is no frisking of anyone, nor are there metal detectors set up, in case someone decides to bring a little blade or some other sharp object at this opportunity to meet their leader up close. Police presence was very light and almost invisible. We just trusted the people, and it didn't occur to us that we had any reason not to.

Those were the years before mobile phones so very few people would linger to take photographs with Mum and Dad and hold the line up. At most they would hand over a letter or gift or ask for an autograph. But still, almost 8,000 people would pass through the Sri Perdana doors by the end of the day, and my parents would stand there, smile and take the hand of every individual, young and old, whoever they were, from the time doors opened until they closed around 6 p.m. Only at lunchtime would they, and we, retire upstairs for a quick lunch. Then Dad might catch a short nap before refreshing himself and going downstairs again for the rest of the open house hours.

I always enjoyed these open houses, because after a few years you began to recognize the regulars and it felt like a yearly reunion. Besides the politicians from both sides of the aisle and the diplomats, there would be all sorts of interesting characters. There used to be a woman we called Queen because she always walked in regally in a long gown and a tiara. Some annual visitors would corner us to show us the photo they took the year before, in case we forgot them. One year, Hari Raya and Chinese New Year coincided and many of our visitors, especially the women and children, turned up in hybrid costumes, baju kurung with mandarin collars, or cheongsams with long skirts underneath. Our Chinese visitors greeted us with Selamat Hari Raya, and we replied with Gong Xi Fa Cai. And then both of us would beam with the novelty and pleasure of it.

In those days, security was so light as to be almost negligible. There were two ways to reach the private living quarters upstairs. One was by the stairs adjacent to the side entrance, the one we normally used. Another was via the back stairs going up from the kitchen. At the top of those stairs were our bedrooms, beginning with mine on the left and Mokhzani's on the right. During open house, nobody is upstairs as everyone is occupied downstairs in the public areas.

A few days after one such open house, Mum received a call on the house phone from a stranger. He said he was calling to alert her about the very poor security at Sri Perdana. How did he know this? He had come for open house on his own and while looking around the public area had noticed the back stairs. Unchallenged by anyone, he took the stairs up and found himself in our living quarters where he proceeded to open unlocked doors and peered inside our rooms. Nobody had stopped him as he wandered all over our apartment until he finally returned downstairs to the dining room where the crowds were. He took nothing nor left with anything except for the impression that we were rather careless. We were lucky that he had enough civic consciousness to provide this feedback. However, the lesson was learned, and from then on, there was always someone stationed at the bottom of those stairs lest anyone else be tempted to satiate their curiosity as well.

Apart from that incident, and some cases of finding uneaten satay behind our curtains, the open houses were the highlight of our year, even though we often ended the day fatigued to the bone. I think the public enjoyed it too, despite the long waits in the heat and gardens that were not truly convenient for big public functions like these. When they built the new Sri Perdana in Putrajaya, I fervently hoped that they would design a large flat area specifically to cater to open house. But no, when my parents moved there several years later, the public still had to wind themselves up and down steps, mostly outside, to shake Mum and

Dad's hands. I thought they should get medals for such good-natured patience.

* * *

I was at Berita Publishing for four years, rising to become Acting Editor and then switching over to the management side when the post of Promotions Manager became vacant. Writing articles, I found, was too easy for me so I learnt as much as I could about magazine publishing including producing photographic shoots, dealing with sponsors and organizing big charity events such as the annual 'Her World Charity Fashion Gala'.

The Eighties was the beginning of the big charity dinners when a fashion show would be the highlight of the evening. Women, dressed in their best designer clothes, came to look at the latest fashions hot off the Paris runways. Men came to look at the models. They paid big money for the privilege, either by buying tables at exorbitant prices or by buying 'lucky draw' tickets which could win them exclusive luxurious prizes or by putting their hands up to bid for even more expensive items in the auctions. Proximity to VIPs or celebrities was also a draw. The nearer they wanted to be to the VIP Guest-of-Honour, usually the PM, the more they had to pay for their table. If you could get the VIP to do something special, like sing a song for instance, there was more money to be made for the charity.

All the money we collected went to various charities, less some expenses that we kept as low as possible, usually under 30 per cent. Donors, the people who bought tables, received tax exemption certificates from the charities. It was a good way of raising funds for those in need, with all the effort on our side. In the three years that we had the Her World Gala, our team at the magazine raised hundreds of thousands of ringgit for the charities we selected, usually those that helped women, children or the disabled.

Lest anyone think this was easy to do, let me lift the curtain on what goes on in the background to bring such a beautiful glamorous event to the KL elite. In the 1980s, there were no high-fashion designer boutiques in the city, so we had to bring the show from Singapore.

This meant negotiating with the boutiques, getting customs clearance for the clothes that needed to be re-exported, obtaining Immigration permission for any foreign models that we might hire, getting contractors to build the catwalk and provide lighting and sound systems for the show. I would spend a lot of time filling in the customs declaration forms and sitting at the then Subang airport sometimes until late at night with Immigration officers while I waited to clear all the cargo containing clothes and visas for the models.

Meanwhile, we had to sell the tables. I wrote hundreds of appeal letters to be sent to companies asking them to buy tables at the dinner at various prices in return for a good time and a tax exemption certificate. Many said no but enough said yes that the event was worth holding.

Arguably the most difficult part of the event, and many such charity events, is collecting the money from the companies who donated and bought tables. The major corporations were fine. But it was the individuals and smaller companies who would sometimes be difficult to get hold of after the event. Chasing after them became a long-drawn-out process which in turn meant that we could not close our books and give the money to the charities. Some of the charities, so dependent on donations, became quite frustrated with us for our slowness in handing over the money raised.

As for me, I learnt so much not just about how to organize big charity events like these but also about patience and perseverance in dealing with people, companies and bureaucracy. I had to learn the diplomatic arts as well as that of persuasion. Malaysians are generous but they usually want a lot of bang for their buck so we had to devise a programme for the evening that was creative and different from what they would get anywhere else.

I was also often caught between the show creators and the contractors. One year we had a show featuring the designs of the renowned designer Yves St Laurent that came directly from Paris. The French team were very particular, to the point of being mistrustful of the skills of our local contractors, whom I had worked with several times and trusted. There was that time when I had to be the middle person between the French team and our local person as we set up the stage and runway in the hotel ballroom. The French stage manager would shout instructions at me in a mixture of French and English, and I would translate for our contractor. He in turn would shout his reply which I would then translate for the stage manager, minus the insults and vulgarities. In the end, the show was beautiful and war between France and Malaysia was averted.

My experience in these events did not go unnoticed. One day I got a call from an Australian woman called Jeanette Robertson-Lomax who wanted to talk to me about a job in her public relations firm, Daniel J Edelman, an American firm that was in partnership with the Melewar Group in KL. I was flattered to be noticed and I knew that by then I had enough of a track record to be hunted for my own talents. It didn't dispel all my doubts about myself but I was ready to move on. After four years at Berita Publishing, I left to join DJE as an Accounts Manager, handling the public relations for a number of clients, whether corporate or government.

My first assignment was to launch Durian Shake for MacDonald's. It was a product so novel that it hardly needed any PR, appearing on the front page of the newspapers on the day it was launched. Over the three years that I was employed at DJE, I worked for clients such as Singer Sewing Machine, the launch of the Proton Saga, the launch of the Putra World Trade Center (PWTC) and the first event that was held there which was the 1986 Pacific Area Travel Association (PATA) conference. The last two involved having Dad as the guest-of-honour which provided some awkward moments for me.

When major buildings are built in KL, there are two events that are commemorated before they are opened: the ground-breaking and the 'topping-up'. Both are treated as major opportunities for publicity and very often politicians are the main VIPs that are invited to officiate these ceremonies. I was not around for the ground-breaking ceremony of the Putra World Trade Center but the topping-up in 1985 was on my watch. And Dad was to do the honours.

The PWTC was the first dedicated convention and exhibition center in Kuala Lumpur, with a big hall that can seat 3,000 people and a large space that can hold every kind of exposition including car exhibitions. The complex includes the 40-floor Menara Dato Onn, the headquarters of UMNO. Topping up the center meant holding the ceremony on the roof of the tower 175 metres above the ground. To get there, we had to transport all the guests, including the guest-of-honour, Dad, in rickety metal lifts that climbed up the side of the towers. It was not the sort of thing that people with acrophobia would enjoy. Indeed, one of my colleagues, standing at the reception table at the foot of the tower watching the lifts make their slow ascent, fainted before we even began proceedings.

Once we got everyone to the top, which was bare except for some tents, tables and chairs that someone had managed to hoist up there, the ceremony began. It was the usual formal event beginning with a doa selamat, a blessing, followed by various speeches, Dad's being the last. Finally, the host, the developer of the building, had to hand over a gift to Dad. In this case, we had decided to give him a bonsai tree in a large rectangular ceramic pot. Looking back, I realize the irony of giving a dwarf plant to commemorate a tall building.

I handed the bonsai to the client to hold while the MC announced what was to happen. Unfortunately, the MC's introductions went on for a bit which meant that the client was left holding a plant that felt heavier and heavier by the second. He turned to look at me, but I did not dare take it from him in case the MC stopped talking and it was time to present the gift. Eventually, he handed it over to Dad who barely touched it before his aide-de-camp (ADC) leaped forward to take it from his hands.

That was not the worst thing that happened that day. As the ceremony wound down and he was leaving, Dad suddenly spotted me. As staff of the PR company, I was usually backstage or trying to blend in with the crowd. To my horror, not only did Dad see me, he began to walk in my direction. My eyes widened as I slowly shook my head trying to signal him not to come any nearer. Eventually he got the message, smiled wanly, turned and left.

At dinner at home that night I scolded Dad for approaching me that day. 'It reminds them that I'm your daughter, not just the person servicing their PR account!' I wailed. I badly wanted to be judged for myself and my own quality of work. If people were made to be aware of who I was, it would be difficult for me to know if they truly thought my work was good or were giving me far too much slack. My parents were highly amused at my discomfort, but they understood. From then on, if Dad officiated any of my clients' functions, he would pretend not to see me and no one but my bosses would know that the woman running around arranging chairs, organizing the bouquets, shepherding the performers and handing out press releases was his daughter.

Me, the firstborn, 9 June 1957

My first birthday party at 929, Jalan Maxwell, Alor Setar, June 1958

Family portrait at the studio, Alor Setar. I was about 3 and Mirzan, 2.

Mirzan, aged 3 and me aged 4

Mum dressed us all in red and white with our initials 'Ma', 'Mi', 'Mo' and 'Mu' embroidered on our shirts, Alor Setar, circa 1966. L-R: Mokhzani, Mirzan, me and in front, Mukhriz

Standard 1A, St. Nicholas' Convent, Alor Setar, 1964. With Miss Ong Eng Eng. I am in the same row as Miss Ong, third to her left.

Family portrait, Pondok Maharizan, Titi Gajah, circa 1969. Back row L-R: Me, Mum, Dad, Melinda; Front row L-R: Mirzan, Mokhzani, Mukhriz

Mum came for my graduation from the University of Sussex, Brighton in 1979

Dad cradling his first grandchild, Ineza, aged two months, Kobe, Japan

L-R: Mokhzani, Melinda, Mirzan, me, Mukhriz, Sri Perdana Bukit Damansara, circa 1974

Tara's and my wedding at Sri Perdana, June 1998. Our guests-of-honour were the then
Deputy Prime Minister Anwar Ibrahim and his wife Dr Wan Azizah Wan Ismail.
On Anwar's left is my late mother-in-law Susi Sumaryo.

Election night, 1999. The BN won but not as well as before.

Hari Raya 2015, during Dad's retirement we could have most of our family together for the festival, and we liked to take funny group photos. Front row L-R: Mokhzani, Mastisa, Tara, me, Dad, Elena, Mum, Mia, Mirzan, Jane, Norzieta, Mukhriz; Back row L-R: Khadijah, Ineza, Shasha, Mazhar, Yasmin, Hakeem, Marisa, Ally, Othman, Mohamad, Serena, Omar, Lara, Mahathir, Maizura

Me speaking at a campaign rally for the 14th General Elections, the Esplanade, Georgetown, Penang, 28 April 2018

Me with Mum and Dad, Election Night, 14th General Elections, 10 May 2018

Then Deputy Prime Minister Dr Wan Azizah with Anwar Ibrahim and
Tara and I at my niece's wedding reception, Shangri-La Hotel,
Kuala Lumpur, 22 February 2020

Dad and I at the reception hosted
by my niece's in-laws, at Shangri-La
Hotel, 28 February 2020. An hour
or so after this, Dad was no longer
Prime Minister.

6

Be Fast or Be Last

In Dad's first tour of office, I rarely accompanied him on his official visits to foreign countries. In part, that was because I could not take time off from work. But often it was because I was never invited, since I had no official function and taxpayers' money could not be spent on me. Besides I knew what those trips were like. Dad's favourite excursions were to factories, destinations that were far from appealing to a young woman like me. Even holiday trips abroad would sometimes include a visit to a car or airplane factory because Dad always wanted to know how they were made.

But I did request to join his entourage for a special one. In 1985, Dad made his first official trip to China. It was to last eight days beginning in Beijing and taking in Xian, Shanghai, Hangchow and Guangdong, the first official visit by a Malaysian Prime Minister since Tun Razak's in 1974. To my delight, Dad gave me permission and I took leave from work for the journey of a lifetime.

China at the time was only just emerging from its long isolation as a Communist country under Mao Tse Tung. The Paramount Leader of the People's Republic of China was Deng Xiao Ping, and the Premier was Zhao Ziyang. The country had not quite woken up to the economic greatness that it is now. We knew very little about it then and were not sure how to prepare ourselves for the trip, thinking we were going to a very poor country that might not have all the amenities we were used to.

I remember buying liquid body wash to bring along, in case they didn't have soap. One of the accompanying businessmen had been pressed by his wife to bring his own sheets, because they were not sure what sort of hotel they would be housed in.

Among the entourage, travelling in a chartered Malaysia Airlines jet, were members of the Cabinet, the Opposition, various top-level civil servants and many businessmen. Mum was of course accompanying Dad along with her personal assistant and me. Arriving in Beijing, we were taken to the government's guest house where we were to stay. It looked like something out of a Zhang Zhimao movie, with dark wooden furniture in a style reminiscent of the 1930s and plenty of satin— curtains, cushions and bedsheets. In fact, that was my impression of China in 1985, that it was very much stuck in another era, like one giant movie set. Outside in the streets, everyone we saw wore blue Mao suits and sometimes it was difficult to tell men and women apart as they rode by on their bicycles.

One of our first stops was the Great Hall of the People where Dad was to meet his counterpart Zhao Ziyang. The hall was indeed great, with very high ceilings, floor-to-ceiling columns, the same old-fashioned furniture and a distinct smell that I later realized must have come from the copious amounts of tea that they drank. Dad sat in an armchair next to Zhao while the rest of us were arranged in matching chairs in a rectangle facing them, so many of us that I'm sure those at the furthest end barely heard what they said. In any case, this meeting was largely ceremonial so there was nothing beyond the usual platitudes and niceties.

The Great Hall of the People was located at Tiananmen Square, which like many historic places in China, was built on a scale that emphasised power, immense and impressive. We were there some four years before the 4 June 1989 massacre when the military fired on and killed protestors in the square, so we didn't have to stop ourselves from making any awkward remarks. On its North end was the Forbidden City, a humongous palace complex built in the 15th century to be the imperial palace and winter residence of the Emperor of China. Naturally we were given a tour of it and again it looked like a film set of every historical Chinese movie you've ever seen. Full of buildings filled with ornate carvings, statues, porcelain and lavish furnishings. There were giant courtyards where the Emperor would view his army and his people, sitting way above them in an ornate gold throne. In China, size truly matters.

My memory of China is primarily of this show of power through bigness. But there were moments that stood out. The Great Wall turned out to be much steeper than I imagined, blown constantly by the freezing winds from the northern steppes. The first time we saw the terracotta warriors in Xian, it was impossible not to gasp at the sight of hundreds of life-size statues that looked like they might just come to life at the wave of a magic wand. We met old Chinese Muslim men with long white beards looking like Confucius at the pagoda-like Great Mosque of Xian, built in 742 A.D slightly more than a century after the Prophet Muhamad was born and about four hundred years before Islam was brought to Malaya by Indian Muslim traders.

In Shanghai one night, Dad wanted to go to the Peace Hotel to listen to a group of old men play jazz music. Again, it felt like a trip back in time; the décor was still the art deco style that the original owner, the businessman Sir Victor Sassoon, built in 1929. It smelt somewhat musty and a trip to the toilet was apparently not for the fainthearted.

Perhaps my greatest memory of that China trip was through my tastebuds. I counted that we had 21 meals in all, elaborate many-course meals, including a variety of appetizers. There was no let-up; every lunch or dinner, and sometimes meals in between, was a heavy display of Chinese cuisine. In Xian, we had to applaud the wait staff for serving us, a quaint custom we thought must surely be attributed to Communism's egalitarianism. By the time we reached Guangdong at the end of the trip, we were ready for pizza. I returned from China swearing not to eat Chinese food again for a long while.

I have been back to China several times since and the changes it has gone through have been remarkable. Where once they only wore plain blue jackets and trousers, young Chinese now wear Chanel to go to breakfast, dressing their dogs in matching jackets. All sorts of designer architect high-rise buildings have risen; Shanghai is the most vertical city I have ever seen, with a pulsating energy that matches New York. China has become the biggest market for luxury goods in the world;

you can hardly buy anything without a logo emblazoned all over it. Of course, all this fantastic development has come at a price including horrible pollution and not a lot of freedoms for individuals and whole groups of people.

The last time I was in Beijing in 2013, I thought it was rather ironic that the only people who now actually wanted to live in unheated traditional Chinese houses in the hutongs, or old neighbourhoods, were Western expats.

* * *

It may seem that if you're a member of a top politician's family, you're constantly walking on a red carpet with minions bowing and scraping at your side. The truth is a lot less glamorous, at least when Dad was in office. If you ever travel with Dad, whether on official trips or private holidays, the thing that you most need is speed. Once you get a signal, usually the sound of car engines warming up and swarms of people moving towards an exit, you have to make a mad dash to keep up. Because nobody will wait for you, the insignificant unimportant person, even if you're a daughter.

I have learnt this through experience. If you're following him, first make sure you do have a designated car in the convoy that tails Dad's car in front. If you bump a bodyguard out of his designated seat, you may find yourself lifted by the arms and unceremoniously dumped out of the vehicle. The security details' focus is only on one person and if you get in the way, then you're just collateral damage.

Over the years, I learnt to spot my assigned car and not linger when it's time to depart. This requires you to be supremely well-organized. If you forget anything, then there is no waiting or turning back to get it. If it's something truly important like a passport or wallet, too bad.

On several occasions, rank amateurs have found themselves left behind because they made the mistake of losing focus. Travelling with Dad means training your beam laser-like on what you have to do, which is, to get into your car. It is not your job to think about your next destination; that will happen by itself provided you have a competent driver. But he will leave with an empty car once the entourage starts moving if you don't manage to heave your body into the back seat before then.

VIP entourages are like locust swarms. They move in a buzzing group, powered by nature and oblivious to any slow outliers. Once it moves, it moves. Whether it is a convoy of cars or a pack of humans, the only person it will slow down for is Mum. Because Dad will always wait, sometimes impatiently, for her.

When I was younger and more fleetfooted, I was rarely left behind. But the older slower me learnt the hard way just two years ago in London when I wanted to spend time shopping with Dad. I arrived at his hotel slightly late only to find that he had left for his favourite store, Marks and Spencer. Mum had not felt like sprinting with him so had stayed behind. I took a taxi and found him easily enough in the men's department of the large main branch on Oxford Street. After getting what he wanted, mostly shirts and handkerchiefs, he proceeded next door to Selfridges department store where he headed for the basement level where they sold gadgets of all kinds. If there's one thing Dad loves looking at, it's new gadgets.

This was where I made my mistake. Something caught my eye, a computer keyboard that looked like a typewriter and I stopped to take a closer look. And when I turned round to look for Dad, he and his swarm had disappeared. Selfridges may not be as big as Harrod's, the largest store in the world, but it is still immense. Searching for anyone even if they're surrounded by a phalanx of bodyguards is like searching for that N in a sea of M's. Or in this case, the M in an ocean of Ns. Worse still, there was no phone signal down there.

I became frantic, not because I had lost him, like a mother who loses a child and fears it might be in danger, since I knew he would be at no risk at all. I panicked because my plan to spend time with Dad had been torpedoed by my own inattention.

I spent a good twenty minutes searching for him around that basement floor and on the ground floor, an unlikely hunting ground since it housed the cosmetic and women's handbags sections. Finally, I got outside where mercifully I found a signal and could call Dad's ADC to find out where they were. It turned out they had left for another store in another part of the city.

I finally found him again at Whole Foods concentrating on different types of cheese. 'You left me!' I accused him, my arms crossed over my body, my voice slightly amplified. He looked up at me surprised. 'I did?' Had he not noticed I wasn't there?

After almost a quarter century at the top of the heap, surrounded always by staff and security who move him from place to place with efficient speed, Dad often forgets that the rest of us are just flotsam and jetsam in the rushing stream that is his entourage. Except if Mum is with him, he rarely looks around to ensure that we are keeping up. I did think that his security would at least have warned me that he was already on the move, the Sinatra equivalent of Bill Clinton's Elvis. But no, their eyes are on one person and one person alone, the only one whose security is their responsibility: Dad.

7

Mum

No story about Dad can exclude Mum. They are a team. While Dad was the law, ultimately in our family when we were children, Mum was the enforcer—which of course did not make her popular. Every day she would have something to nag us about, so I at least thought of her as a tyrant. Dad was a bit more hands-off though if he ever did explode, the earth would literally shake and we would cower in fear of the 'hurry-cane', otherwise known as the rotan. Although it was deployed very sparingly, the cane was an ever-present sword of Damocles, ready to fall if we ever transgressed. Our possible transgressions were in fact few: lying, stealing and rudeness to anyone. Failing at school tests might get us a pinch on the thigh and a humiliating scolding. They were always enough.

As a teenager in the Seventies, I was not an easy child. Not that I was particularly rebellious. When you grow up in a small provincial town like Alor Setar, and attend a Convent school, rebellion was just not in your vocabulary. I heard about girls who smoked, had boyfriends and even got pregnant but they were so rare that they were a novelty. If teenagehood was a time for us to find our identities, I spent a lot of mine being a scowling grump, constantly finding fault with Mum, shrugging off her attempts to have women-to-women moments. I suppose daughters rarely think of their mothers as cool, and as teenagers instinctively push away from them because they don't want to be like them. When we are young, we only see the characteristics of our mothers we don't like. It is only later, perhaps when we become mothers ourselves, that we finally appreciate our mothers' virtues, those we hope we inherit. When I get annoyed with my own daughters, I will mutter under my breath, 'Wait until you have daughters!' and then catch myself wondering if Mum ever thought the same thing too when I was young.

Still, it took a long time for our relationship to get on an even keel. Mum came to Brighton to attend my graduation from the University of Sussex in the summer of 1979. Dad could not come because he was busy with work. She came and stayed in my tiny flat on the beachfront and proudly helped me put on my cap and gown for the ceremony where I received my scroll from Sir David Attenborough, the natural historian and broadcaster. Afterwards we went for lunch at a restaurant in the town where we ran into many other families whose children were also graduating. We had a nice time, just the two of us, but at one point, I forget who said what, and a steel curtain of tension came clanking down on us. That was always typical of our relationship; short periods of closeness followed by longer periods of tension, usually because I thought Mum was old-fashioned and could not understand what was important to me.

In 1986 I got married to my then husband Didier Roussille, a Frenchman I had met at a resort on the East Coast. In my usual way, I kept him a secret from my parents until he converted to Islam and proposed to me and then presented them with almost a *fait accompli*. We had a huge reception at the PWTC because as President of UMNO, my father felt he needed to invite representatives of the entire membership from all over the country, I said farewell to my job at DJE and we moved to Japan where Didier had been transferred first to Tokyo, and after five months, to Osaka. I became pregnant fairly soon and on a short trip home, announced that the only people I wanted with me when I gave birth were my husband and my mother. This had surprised but pleased her enormously, especially as this was to be Dad's and her first grandchild. She took the responsibility very seriously and looked forward to joining me in Kobe, where we had moved from Tokyo.

In facing the birth of my first child so far away from home, I had not realized what a sacrifice Mum had made to be with me in the spring of 1987. At the time Dad was facing a big crisis at home, faced with rebellion within his own party and all sorts of agitations outside that threatened to spill over into a possible repeat of 13 May 1969, later to be known as *Ops Lalang*. I was not particularly aware of what was going on politically back home in those days before social media. Japanese TV didn't cover much domestic politics in small Southeast Asian countries. Besides my facility with the language then would not have held up enough to understand the news. Whatever English-language news there were was skimpy; Japan was more interested in what happened across the Pacific Ocean in the United States than down south in our part of the world.

Mum arrived about three weeks before I was due, with a helper, Fauziah, several bags of rice and a half-finished sweater for the baby that my Aunty Leha was trying to knit. I had asked her to bring the rice from home because I found Japanese rice too sticky to go with Malaysian curries. At the time Japan did not allow imports of foreign rice into the country arguing that it didn't suit their palate. It was yet another 'non-tariff barrier' to protect Japanese farmers who were, and still are, a very strong lobby. I will confess now that Mum was a rice smuggler. Hopefully the statute of limitations on such 'crimes' has expired.

At the time I lived in Sky Mansion II, a block of flats in Kitano-cho, the hillside old part of Kobe with its many European-style houses built by English and Dutch traders. Kobe was, after Yokohama, the second Japanese port to open up to the world and therefore was more cosmopolitan and welcoming to foreigners. There was already a large expatriate community comprising largely of Proctor & Gamble executives and their families whose children all attended the international school Canadian Academy. When I first arrived already three months pregnant and needed to find doctors, I was referred to CHIC or Community House International Center, a place for expatriate residents to meet, take Japanese language lessons and classes on Japanese culture. Within a few hours, my first friend in Kobe, the also pregnant Sarah Williams from Scotland, turned up at my door with all the information I needed.

My time in Japan was truly my initiation into full adulthood, having to decide on things like where to live and how to make it a home. We had settled on Sky Mansion because it was built for expats. Unlike the small and dark apartment we first rented in Tokyo that was once visited by a burglar and had water leaking from the upstairs flat, our Kobe flat was large and bright with three bedrooms, two bathrooms complete with full-sized Western bathtubs and best of all, a large kitchen fully-equipped with non-Japanese-sized American appliances. It was shaped like a large pentagon with the windows on one side from one of the bedrooms and the kitchen facing an alley and the large floor to ceiling glass windows in the living room and the other two bedrooms facing the greenery of the Kobe Club next door. Its size was so unusual for Japan that when I found a large L-shaped sofa for my living room, I got my first taste of the diligence that the Japanese are famous for. The salesman insisted on visiting us first to ensure that it would fit in our home, given the normal minuscule size of most Japanese apartments. Almost as soon as he popped his head in our door to see the vast expanse of our empty living room, he nodded and retreated, convinced at last that we were not trying to fit an elephant into a mousehole. Most of our furniture however was bought on a trip to Singapore from IKEA and Habitat and shipped back to Kobe. With the limited budget Didier's company gave us, it was actually cheaper to do that than to try and furnish it from stores in Japan.

Japan, with its orderly clean streets, its impossibly polite people, its very strange TV programmes is an experience I recommend to everyone. I spent my first months in Tokyo and then Kobe exploring every corner near where I lived, peering into shop windows and trying to figure out the street signs. I was happy to be there with my husband and excited about the coming baby. I was beginning to realize that running a home, especially with a newborn, was a management job, managing budgets, time and people every day. I did not miss Malaysia much; in the days before emails and mobile phones, writing letters and the occasional phone call sufficed. The Kobe Club next door, a Western-style recreation club set in several acres of grounds with a swimming pool, restaurant and a large ballroom, served as a place to socialize.

It was there that I met the group of friends who became key to my survival in Japan.

Before the baby came, I had full days alone while Didier went to Osaka to work. I filled them by enrolling in Japanese language classes at CHIC. One day I attended a cake-making class at the Kobe Club and met a whole group of women from various parts of the world. There was Khatijah from Singapore, Claire and Ton from the Philippines, Karen from the US, Carol from the UK and Sunita from Hong Kong. And of course, my first friend Sarah. Those women, most of them the same age as me and with small children as well, became my tightly-knit group of mates. From then on, we met very often usually at each other's homes and shared information on how to navigate this strange country that we found ourselves in.

* * *

In Kobe I introduced Mum to my friends, and they warmed to her immediately. We would organize lunches and teas for her either at their home, or mine or at a restaurant. She enjoyed having a normal life, like mine, with this casual socializing, instead of the more formal and restricted life of a Prime Minister's wife. At the same time, she kept a secret from me, that she was very worried about what Dad was going through at home. She said very little about what was going on, focussing instead on my wellbeing as I approached my baby's arrival. She would accompany me to see my doctor at Kobe Kaisei Catholic Hospital, carrying Aunty Leha's knitting in a paper bag to finish while she waited for me.

Focussed on my imminent delivery, I was not sensitive enough to Mum's worries. There was the day when I entered her bedroom, the bright sunny one that faced the greenery of the Kitano-cho hills behind the Kobe Club, and found her at her dressing table, eyes red from weeping. She had not spent so much time away from Dad since the late 1960s when she went for a course at the University of Michigan at Ann Arbor. This time, she was in tears out of worry for Dad or because she was homesick, I didn't know. Ever the recalcitrant daughter, I was not in the mood to indulge Mum and to my shame, I didn't ask her.

I was due to give birth in the prettiest of the Japanese seasons, in springtime, just as the cherry trees were about to blossom. As it happened, they were a little late that year so that the thousands of pink flowers erupted just when I was stuck in hospital after delivering Ineza, a delivery that was not without its drama.

My daughter was due on 10 April, but I had been warned that it could be two weeks on either side of the due date. This uncertainty made calculating how long Mum could be with me a particularly difficult one. The later my baby waited to arrive, the more the likelihood that Mum couldn't be there with me.

The date came and went uneventfully. By then I was large and heavy and decidedly tired of being pregnant. I wanted to get it over with. There was still no sign of any movement the next few days until on the afternoon of 13 April I found some discharge, a brown, gel-like substance. Wrapping it up in toilet paper I waited for Mum to return from her trip to the stores to show her. Neither of us were sure what it meant. It had been twenty-three years since Mum had her last baby.

By evening however, I started to feel some pain. Not very intense but enough of it at regular intervals that we began to think that it might be time to head for the hospital. Kaisei Hospital was about a twenty-minute ride away up in the hills of Rokko, an affluent suburb between Kobe and Osaka. We did not have a car, but we did have wonderfully generous friends. Before she left for holidays in Scotland, Sarah Williams, who lived two minutes away, had made her husband Alan promise to stand by and drive us. Regardless of what time I needed to go to the hospital.

When we finally decided it was time to go, it was about 10 p.m. I dressed in the mint-green fleece track suit that I had taken to wearing during the last months of my pregnancy, grabbed the bag filled with clothes and toiletries I had readied for hospital and Mum, Didier and I got into Alan's car and headed to the hospital.

At Kaisei, we were quickly ushered into the labour room. No other expectant mother was there that night. I lay on one of the beds while Mum and Didier settled down in chairs to wait with me. The contractions had become more intense by then and I tried to remember the Lamaze breathing techniques from the classes that Didier and I attended.

At one point a nurse came in to shave me in preparation for delivery. Unlike most Japanese who can be polite and gentle to distraction, this nurse was brusque and efficient. As I lay on the cold hard table, in a room adjoining the labour ward, my nether regions exposed, I had another contraction and tried to stay her hand as I cried out in pain '*itai, itai!*'. She grumpily told me that it was nothing compared to what I would go through when actually delivering my baby. I understood enough Japanese to know what she said and complained weepily to Mum who tried to soothe me, stroking my hair.

Eventually I fell asleep and so did Mum. Didier sprawled across another bed, snoring loudly. The contractions had not increased in intensity. In the morning, I was given a light breakfast. It seemed like we were in for a long wait. I began to wonder if we should have come in so early.

A young nurse, smiling gently, came in to check on me. Her equipment was rudimentary; she simply placed an instrument that looked like double egg cups held bottoms together on my bulbous stomach and listened. Studying her face for clues on what she was hearing, I saw her frown—a puzzled look on her face. Quickly she went to fetch the doctor on call, who happened to be my obstetrician Dr Nakajima. He listened to my stomach with his stethoscope, nodded his head and said to me, 'We need Caesarean.'

At the time, Mum and Didier were standing behind the doctor and the nurse facing me. Mum must have seen the shock on my face and moved quickly to my side to ask me what's wrong. I could barely whisper the word 'operation'.

Mum turned quickly to Dr Nakajima, a look of alarm on her face. The nurse had told him that she had heard the baby's heart slow down whenever I had a contraction. His stethoscope had confirmed the same. It meant that the baby was in distress and had to be taken out by Caesarean section immediately.

This was not something I had prepared for, to have to undergo a Caesarean rather than give birth naturally. All those Lamaze classes, techniques to manage labour pains through breathing exercises, were for nothing.

The nurses prepped me quickly and after quick hugs with Mum and Didier, anxious looks on their faces, I was wheeled into the operation theatre where Dr Nakajima was waiting.

I had opted for a spinal anaesthetic so that I would stay awake throughout the operation. To administer it, they had to roll me on my side so that my spine would be exposed, and the anaesthetist could inject me easily. Kaisei, being a Catholic Hospital, had many nuns working as nurses including in the OT. One stood left of the operating table and in my fear and anxiety, I flung my arms around her body, hugging her tight as the needle went into the base of my spine. Then they quickly rolled me onto my back again and began.

Every second of that operation remains in my memory from the moment Dr Nakajima traced what felt like a pen on my stomach to the pushing and pulling to get the baby out, to when they were stitching me up again. But the weirdest memory I have is that although every person in the theatre was Japanese except me, and they only spoke to each other in their own language, I understood every single word. I had been in Japan only a year by then, but I suppose that's what is meant by total immersion: consciously and unconsciously you absorb the language, and even in the most traumatic of situations, it does not sound alien to you.

My baby daughter was born on the morning of 14 April 1987, in a flood of brown amniotic fluid, a sign of foetal distress. Her head had gotten stuck between the placenta cord and the wall of the uterus in such a way that whenever I had a contraction, she couldn't breathe. That was what caused her heartbeat to slow down. I would never have known had it not been for the nurse and her double eggcup.

I don't remember the baby crying. I only knew it was the girl I wanted and then they rushed her off to be cleaned while I was being sewn up. I lay back on the table, the overhead lights in my eyes, unable to see what was happening because of the cloth barrier they had put up just below my breasts. Relieved that my baby was delivered but unsure as to how she was, I sobbed away as the doctors worked on me. At one point, I heard someone ask in Japanese 'Who's crying?' A head poked over the barrier and then turned back to his colleagues. 'It's the patient.' As if it could have been anyone else.

Meanwhile Mum and Didier had been coping with their anxiety in different ways. Didier never smoked in front of my parents but that morning, overwhelmed by the rapid turn of the situation, he asked Mum for permission and had a cigarette. I assume he had it outside but at that time in Japan, they were not very strict about such things.

Mum as always looked for spiritual succour. Wandering around the hospital corridors she found the hospital chapel, with its pews and altar with all its Catholic symbols. Sitting in a far corner, away from the giant cross in the front of the room, she prayed for the safe delivery of her first grandchild. I suppose God always listens and doesn't mind where you're asking from.

I was kept in the hospital for a week to recover from the operation. After my delivery they wheeled me into a single room, just awake enough to hear Mum calling Dad on the telephone by my bed to tell him the news. He was in Sarawak and at that moment was shaking hands with hundreds of people at a gathering when his aide handed him what must have been a satellite phone, this being long before the mobile phone was invented. I heard Mum tell him he was now grandfather to a baby girl, a real 'dato' at last. And then I heard her mispronounce her name: Ineza Mélanie Mahathir Roussille.

How did I get this name? As many women do during pregnancy, I had spent many hours thinking up names for my baby. Since I didn't know what sex it would be, I should have been thinking of both boy's and girl's names. But I spent almost all my time dreaming of girls' names and don't recall even a single boys' name that crossed my mind.

Didier was French so I wanted to honour both sides of my baby's heritage by picking names that were acceptable to both, and, most importantly, could not be mispronounced by either side. We toyed with many names—at one point Didier suggested Eglantine, an unwieldy name that reminded me of an acquaintance in France who had a penchant for wearing Carmen Miranda hats. Having grown up in a family with alliterative names, I wanted certain initials. 'I' to go with Didier's Muslim name Ikhlas that reflected his sincere nature, and 'M' to match mine. I had also wanted to include my father's name

Mahathir; in fact, I had suggested we invent a new surname, Mahathir-Roussille, a name I used after marriage. But Didier enquired at the French Consulate and was told, to my great puzzlement, that to use that surname would denote that our child was illegitimate. So finally, we settled on Mahathir as her third name.

I had long been an admirer of the model Inés de la Fressange, a tall, lanky, dark-haired and dark-eyed woman who loped on the catwalk in a casual boyish style I found appealing. Inés is another form of Agnes, which sounds hard in English but much softer in French. I wanted to Malayanise it further by adding an A at the end and so it became Ineza. I was quite pleased to find out that the closest equivalent to this name of my invention was Inessa Ardan, a Russian revolutionary.

Her second name, which was to begin with M, was more difficult to come by. I loved the name Melody because of its musicality but Didier, unbeknownst to me, had consulted with his family in France for names as well. This resulted in my being presented with a list of saints' names by my mother-in-law Esther Bètouliers that I promptly set aside. Melody, Didier told me, was not a good name, it would become a joke and she would be teased for it. There must have been some French cultural reference I was not aware of, or perhaps it sounded too much like 'malady' but whatever the reason, we could not name her that.

The night before I had to go to hospital, we had watched *Gone with the Wind* on TV. One of the characters, the object of disdain by Scarlett O'Hara, was called Melanie, played by Olivia de Havilland. I liked that name well enough and so it became her second name, Mélanie.

Mum stayed with me for a few days after Ineza's birth and then hurried home to be with Dad. We were both sad that those few weeks of closeness at such a special moment in my life had to come to an end, but I understood. She had fulfilled her promise to be with me when her first grandchild arrived and as things happened in such dramatic fashion, I was glad that she was there to share those moments with me. It had been an emotional time for her. In Kobe she had found its only mosque, a short walk from Sky Mansion and had gone there to pray for both my and Dad's wellbeing. She left Fauziah to help me for the next few months but I still leaned on Mum for emotional support. One day she received a call from me bawling away because it had hit me only then that I had a little human being who was totally dependent on me to care for. She cooed soothingly but I'm sure in her head, she thought, 'Welcome to motherhood.'

A few weeks later, after I had settled back at Sky Mansion and was more confident with the baby, she returned to Kobe with Dad to show him his first grandchild. I still have a photo of him sitting on my large sofa, cradling Ineza in his arms, just as he had done with me thirty years before.

* * *

My appreciation of Mum evolved a great deal after her stay with me in Japan. Even when I returned to Malaysia in 1988, it was often her that I turned to when I had problems. My marriage was cracking but as always, I kept it to myself until Mum heard the whispers and confronted me. She understood my agony even though she was fond of my husband. Dad, on the other hand, would hear nothing of it. To him, married people should stay with one another for the children's sake. Again, I had exhibited my mediocrity by not keeping the marriage together.

My parents' devotion to one another is legendary. After sixty-five years of marriage, they have settled into a cosy calm intimacy that is an example for all of us, within and outside the family. It was their model of marriage that I aspired to, one where there is mutual respect, plenty of understanding of each other's foibles, on a bedrock of deep love. It was also a standard that I felt unable to live up to and as much as I tried, in the end I decided that I did not deserve such unhappiness. Fortunately for me, while I needed Dad's permission to marry, I did not need it to separate. One morning in 1994, the Federal Territory Syariah Court granted Didier and I our divorce. Dad never brought the subject up again until 1997 when I told my parents I wanted to get married again. He still thought, unrealistically, that I should reunite with my former husband for the sake of our daughter.

Dad's attitude towards me sometimes seemed at odds with his towards Mum. From the outset, he has never insisted that she stop work, understanding that the effort she had put in to obtain her degree was not to be wasted. As a result, she made a career for herself, from practicing in the Alor Setar General Hospital to leading the public health programmes in Kedah to heading the rural health training school in Jitra. Even when he became the Prime Minister, and she found herself having to perform new duties, mostly formal and charitable, she kept going to her office, bodyguards in tow, at the Public Health Institute in Bangsar where she was the head. Mum was always a civil servant but one whose contract had to be renewed every few years until she took early retirement in the mid-eighties. Yet she never complained, did her work and plunged into her role as spouse of the PM with the same commitment and gusto as she did everything.

Not that she isn't without her special quirks. Everyone now knows that she took up the violin in her eighties and performs occasionally at special charity events. But in the same way that she diligently worked at her medical degree, she takes to other hobbies with a laser focus. When my youngest siblings Mazhar and Maizura were babies, she read up on all the latest books on baby-rearing, settling on the recommendations of Dr Glenn Doman who believed that infants can be taught to read at a very young age. There was Mum flashing cards in front of the gurgling Maz and Mai; words, the national flags of different countries and domino cards so they would learn numbers. The theory was sound, but it depended on mothers who had the time to devote themselves to teaching their children. Eventually Mum sent the two to a kindergarten that practised the same methods, when her official work kept her too busy. But she believed in it enough that I too received Dr Doman's book and card sets when Ineza was born, although I was never as good at card-flashing as I should have been.

When I was about to marry Didier, Mum discovered that Esther, her soon-to-be *besan*, did not speak English. Esther and Mum were the same age at the time, about sixty, not an age where anyone normally takes on a new language. But Mum decided to study French so as to be able to communicate with my in-laws. As usual she dived into her lessons with all seriousness, finally taking and passing an exam at the Alliance Francaise. Unfortunately, Didier and I separated so she didn't get to use her new skill very much. Instead, she would text me in French and I would be forced to use my poor written facility in the language to reply.

Mum's main focus though was, and is, always Dad. She always advises other wives to accompany their husbands on travels as much as they can, and she has always done the same. With him, she has been to an astonishing number of countries from Africa, to riding the Andean mountains in Argentina, to enduring the seasickness crossing the Drake Passage to Antarctica. On a trip to Bosnia, during the war with Serbia, she tried to hide her fear on a helicopter ride with Dad to view the conflict areas. When they returned, Dad remarked to me, 'I think Mum was scared.' I rolled my eyes. She took up horse-riding because he did but after one fall, she had to admit that it had shaken her too much and gave it up.

For all her role as enforcer to Dad's lawmaker in our childhood, in our adulthood, Mum has evolved into a mediator. Where sometimes Dad and I have had loud differences of opinion, usually over issues of policy, it is Mum who will step in to calm the waters. She strives always to be neutral, to not take the side of either father or daughter. I usually already know what Dad thinks about any particular issue but find it hard to convey to him without getting worked up, especially on those aspects that he considers 'liberal'; human rights and sexuality, for example. Mum would call me to listen and understand my side of things—sometimes even agreeing with me—and then convey it back to Dad in as gentle a way as possible. In many ways she has become the safe conduit for messages that may be contentious, because we always know that she will view them with a very human lens and will translate them from that perspective. If Mum was in government, she would be an excellent facilitator for rapprochement between warring countries.

8

A Second Chance at Life

After two years in Japan, Didier decided he wanted to strike out on his own and we came home to KL at the end of 1988. Having not been in paid employment while abroad, I had to figure out what I wanted to do next. I had not wanted to go back to working for anyone; instead, I wanted to leverage on my Japan experience by starting a small business exporting *batik* clothes to a Japanese department store. It did not do very well; despite my two years in that country, I had much to learn about doing business with the Japanese.

My former colleagues at DJE approached me to work part-time with them on some projects. On a trip with them to Singapore in January 1989, I received an early morning phone call from my husband: Dad had had a heart attack and was in hospital. I hastily packed my bags, left a note for my boss and rushed to Changi to catch my flight home. My friend who picked me up at Subang airport said she barely recognized me because I looked so haunted. I felt so guilty for being away when it happened.

Arriving at the KL General Hospital, Mum took me to see Dad. I couldn't help but give a gasp of shock at the sight that greeted me. Unused to ever seeing him weak and helpless, I was not prepared to see him lying in bed hooked up to tubes and machines, dependent on the expertise of his doctors. He was only sixty-three at the time but fairly heavy and a heart operation, where the heart needs to be stopped while it is being fixed and then restarted is always a risk. His surgeon however was the best we had in Malaysia. Mr Yahya Awang, a tall, distinguished man who also happened to be Hussein Onn's son-in-law, put together a top-notch team of Malaysian cardio-thoracic surgeons, anaesthetists and nurses. He took care to brief us all on the procedure and when I asked what was the backup plan if anything happened to him before the operation, he smiled gently and said he would be sleeping in the hospital so that he would be rested and ready bright and early before he picked up his scalpel.

Dad too knew about the risks of such a major operation, which had to be done within a week after his attack. On the day before surgery, I happened to be sitting by his bed. He had been awake and strong enough to write a letter that he handed to me. I looked at it and then back at him, puzzled.

'If anything should happen to me, give this to Anwar.'

Anwar Ibrahim was at the time Dad's Minister of Education and protégé.

'And don't open it!'

I didn't know a piece of paper in an envelope could feel quite as heavy as that letter he gave me that day in 1989. But as fate would have it, I had no reason to open it nor to pass it on to Anwar. Over the years I have kept it safely, even when I moved house, and maybe the day will come when I will get to read it.

It wasn't so surprising that Dad had a heart attack at the end of the Eighties. In the previous years he had to face many crises, chief among them the challenge to his leadership of UMNO in 1987, and the events that led to Operation Lalang. These were the events that had troubled Mum when she was with me in Kobe and which she had felt so bad about leaving Dad. Even though he did not have the heart attack until two years later, I suppose the build-up in stress was too much for the body to take. He did not have a cholesterol problem, the doctors found, so it must have all been work-related stress. Later, I realized that one of the symptoms of an impending cardiac arrest is a short temper. There was one day when, for reasons that I no longer recall but which could not have been very important, Dad got very upset with me just after we had tea at home in his sitting room. I was very shocked because it was such a sudden flare-up, the likes of which I had not seen in a long time and I went home in tears. I think he too realized after a re-evaluation of his life after the operation that it is not worth getting too uptight about anything. I have not seen him lose his temper since then. In fact, he's often the calmest person in the room whenever there's a crisis, as there were many more to come in the following years.

We were happy that the operation was successful of course, not just for his sake but also for the country. To our relief, it made Dad also re-look at the way he managed stress, understanding that his health depended on it. He began to exercise the discipline that he always tried to instill in us and all who worked for him, by eating properly and sparingly, getting enough exercise and sleep and knowing when to switch off and relax. Every year he tried to take a holiday with Mum, preferably somewhere remote enough that no 'wellwishers' could just drop in on him. If we could, we joined them because it was a joy to see him not thinking about work but instead laughing and joking with us. We ate pizza in Italy, boated in the Mediterranean and shopped at his beloved Marks and Spencer. Occasionally, I could not stop myself from making some remark that annoyed him. Once we were talking about the TV character Murphy Brown played by Candice Bergen having a baby out of wedlock. Dad had tutted disapprovingly, and I lobbed a little grenade, 'She should have had an abortion.' That earned me a glare and silence that lasted until at least the next day.

9

HIV and me

The years after I returned from Japan were eventful to say the least. Apart from going through Dad's heart operation, I had started writing my column 'Musings' in *The Star* newspaper every fortnight, expressing my views on all sorts of issues. Along with some large fundraising events for the famine in Africa and other charities, I had gained a lot of newspaper coverage and the attention of the public. My old bosses at DJE also made me director of a photographic book project, *Malaysia: Heart of Southeast Asia*, bringing in photographers from all over the world to record seven days in the life of the country. Through these experiences I gained much insights into the issues of the day as well as enhanced my skills in organizing, communicating and most of all, fundraising.

I wouldn't say any of this drove me to activism. Even though I had strong opinions about certain causes, such as women's rights, violence against women and child rights, it never occurred to me to actively champion any of them. To me then as a young woman, an activist was someone unwashed forever marching in uncomfortable circumstances for some radical cause or another. When I was at the University of Sussex, a campus known for its left-wing reputation, I had not taken part in any student politics. I didn't vote in student elections and neither did most of the so-called liberal and leftist students in my time. As a result, in one year our entire student union office-holders were members of or sympathetic to the Conservative party.

I did however have some activist blood in my veins. Dad had been one from his early years. As a medical student at the University of Malaya in Singapore he had written a newspaper column often criticising the colonial government under the name C.H.E Det, a play on his family nickname. I was not to know forty years later that column-writing would also pave my way to action.

My forays into fundraising did not go unnoticed. One day in April 1993, I received a call from a longtime women's rights activist I knew, Mrs Ramani Gurusamy. She was a member of the National Council of Women's Organisations (NCWO) that was forming the Malaysian AIDS Foundation with the primary responsibility of raising funds for its grant-making programmes. They did not have enough women on the Board, she said, would I consider joining it?

I remember being a bit startled at this invitation. I thought of myself as very junior to Mrs G as we called her and did not know how I could contribute. But I had also been thinking about the AIDS pandemic during those years, having lost some friends to what was then an incurable and untreatable disease. I had always wanted to help; here now was my chance.

I agreed to have dinner with Mrs G and her colleagues and unknowingly walked into a trap, a benign one. By the end of the evening, I was made Chair of the Board of Trustees of the Malaysian AIDS Foundation (MAF).

The foundation had been set up a few years before I joined with a small fund of only RM300,000. This was meant to support the work of the Malaysian AIDS Council (MAC), an umbrella body of, at the time, 18 non-governmental organisations that were carrying out HIV prevention programmes among groups such as drug users, sex workers, migrant workers, estate workers and also included professional medical associations. It had been set up by the Ministry of Health to facilitate their funding to the NGOs through a single channel rather than a myriad of small groups. The MAC then had decided that they needed to fundraise from other sources as well, hence the decision to set up the Foundation which was launched in 1992 by the then Raja Permaisuri Agong, the Queen.

In 1993 both the MAC and the MAF had only a small staff of two, a general clerk and an accounts clerk. Everyone else was a volunteer.

While the MAC had grants from the Ministry of Health to run some programmes, none of these were meant to pay staff salaries or any operational costs. We operated out of a small office in Jalan Maharajalela, near Stadium Merdeka, that consisted mostly of a tiny office and a room for meetings. That was where we had our Board meetings but also where we jampacked the place when we had representatives from all our affiliates for our Council annual general meetings.

I had never chaired anything before, much less had any clue about the protocols of conducting meetings, recording the minutes and passing resolutions. There were also statutory requirements that had to be adhered to. For these I relied on my fellow board members who had more experience than me in these organizational matters.

It didn't take me long to understand that the organization suffered from a lack of dynamism. Few people knew about it and even less knew what AIDS was about. As a result, we didn't have many donors and worried constantly about where money would come from and whether we could hold on to our staff.

Once I had a grasp of the weak financial position that the MAF was in, I decided to apply what I had learnt from my fundraising experience to raise money for its programmes. That was when I realized that AIDS was an entirely different thing from photography or famine.

People think that as the PM's daughter, it would be easy to open the doors of companies and get money from them. Only half of that is correct. Doors certainly opened when I called up personally to arrange appointments with the most important person in the company, the person that I had researched would be most likely to give me a straight answer without having to refer to anyone else. I suspect that many people were curious about me, at the time a thirty-six-year-old who was suddenly in the papers a lot not for attending glamorous parties but for organizing large fundraising events and penning my thoughts in the newspaper. Nobody had really known any previous daughters of the PM. They mostly stayed in the background and didn't draw attention to themselves. Was I the real thing or just a publicity hound?

This general curiosity resulted in my ease in getting appointments with corporate CEOs and Chairmen to present my proposals to them. Some of them already knew me from my book project and knew that I was serious in my work and delivered what I promised. That experience trained me in how to approach people and persuade them to part with their money for a good cause. I always knew I had succeeded when they passed me on to their corporate communications departments to follow up.

But I also knew when the fish would not bite. There was an easy test that I devised, based on a more psychologically-adept friend's suggestion, that has held true until today. If the person I've just pitched a project to sponsor or a charity to donate to walks me to my car at the end of the meeting, I knew I had failed to convince them. The reason is simple: if they were going to say no, these corporate figures, generally decent people, felt enough guilt that, as an act of subtle gentlemanly atonement, they would accompany me to my car. In those days I always drove myself so in many cases, these company chairmen and managing directors, men who were always chauffeur-driven, found themselves walking me to the far reaches of their own carparks that in all likelihood they had never seen themselves. Seeing me get behind the wheel of my little Proton rarely changed their minds. I knew that the more courteous they were, the less likely they were to spring any money for my project. Based on this observation, these days I can take bets with my colleagues as to whether our pitch succeeded or not. Most times, I win.

But AIDS was a different ballgame. In the mid-90s, Malaysia had about 6,000 cases of people who had been infected by the virus, most of whom were injecting drug users. For at least two decades prior, Malaysia had a very tough approach when it came to drug trafficking. Anyone caught with more than 200 grams of marijuana was presumed to be trafficking and faced a death sentence if convicted. Those in possession of less than that was considered a drug addict and sent to a government rehabilitation center. None of these drug laws have worked as the growing numbers of drug users testify. Then in the late 1980s, HIV arrived and found its way very quickly through the drug-using communities, principally through the sharing of dirty needles.

Drug use was already stigmatised for many years when the government launched its war against drugs. The arrival of HIV only solidified that stigma, so that even rehabilitated drug users found it difficult to get a job once they were cleared of their addictions. This often drove them back to drugs including to injecting and ensured that even more people using drugs, primarily young Malay men, became HIV-positive.

Against this background, as well as early reports from the West that HIV was found mainly among gay men, the prejudice against people with HIV was exceptionally strong. Many people could not believe that I was working in such a 'dirty' field. Incredibly, some even accused me of seeking publicity by working with what they considered the dregs of society. My response was that if I merely wanted publicity, I had every opportunity to work with much more comfortable causes such as cancer or with children. But I chose to work in what was possibly the most difficult subject.

In those days, ignorance, even among those who were supposedly educated, led people to behave in truly unconscionable ways. I remember one man, well-respected as a senior in his field, looking at an exhibition on HIV, turning to me and with dead seriousness asking, 'If they can't be cured, why don't we just shoot them?' Another man, an officer in the very Ministry that was in charge of the AIDS response, blithely assured me that even if it was his own brother who had HIV, he would throw him out of the house. The lack of compassion and empathy was astounding, and I knew I had a lot of work to do to raise awareness of the disease and epidemic.

To do that, I had to learn as much as I could on every aspect of the epidemic. In many ways, AIDS was the perfect disease for me to take on. Much like Covid-19, whose causes and impacts go way beyond medicine, AIDS involved a myriad of factors. What makes a person become infected and whether they survive or not has little to do with biology. It has everything to do with their station in life. A poor person, with little access to education and information, is far more likely to become infected than a wealthier person who is able to read about the disease and how to prevent it. Any person who has a drug-using habit or who has a tendency for unsafe sex, that is, sex without a condom, is extremely vulnerable to infection. Getting a diagnosis involves knowing where to get tested and what to do afterwards. But most importantly, even if all things are equal, keeping one's HIV status confidential to avoid the stigma and discrimination is another challenge in itself. There was also a gender and sexuality aspect to HIV: for a while it seemed like men were more vulnerable to infection. But, in many ways similar to how migrant workers are forgotten in the Covid pandemic, the female partners of HIV-positive men were neglected until much too late.

AIDS suited me as a cause because it had a multiplicity of dimensions. Not only did I have to learn about the biological and medical aspects of the disease but also the socio-political causes of it. There were legal, economic, class, gender and religious issues to be dealt with to truly understand the length and breadth of the epidemic. It was fascinating and intellectually stimulating. But it could not just be theory for me.

My education in HIV came not just from the doctors, scientists and researchers who worked on the problem but also from the people most affected by it: the drug users, sex workers, migrant workers, the LGBT community and refugees. And of course, from the many women, both those who had been infected and those who had to care for their loved ones. Long before it became fashionable, I was getting a crash course in intersectionality.

My background in journalism and public relations proved to be a boon when I worked in HIV. Communications to the general public is important in any epidemic but HIV was trickier because to speak effectively about it required talking about taboo subjects such as sex and sexuality, as well as drug use. What words did I need to use that would not provoke a negative reaction against me and the cause?

I decided that communications relied on two things: what I said and how I said it. To take the stigma out of HIV education, I had to take the nudge-nudge-wink-wink out of it. It was always important to use the proper terminology and not slang. I had to eliminate any sense of vulgarity. For example, it was okay to say 'penis' but not 'dick'. As long as I kept it sober and scientific, most people had no problem with it.

I was also extra careful in how I presented myself. Almost always I would dress in a baju kurung so that I looked like the safest person to listen to. When people saw how conventional I looked, they generally dropped their guard and therefore I could talk frankly about the dangers of HIV and know I would get through to at least some of them.

It was extraordinary what people would say when they felt safe enough. I once gave a talk to staff members of a government-linked company, mostly men, mostly Muslim and generally conservative. When it came to question time, one of them raised his hand and said that his company put him and his colleagues at risk by sending them overseas unaccompanied by their wives. In other words, they could not be blamed for seeking the company of sex workers when they were lonely. I had to hide my shock at such a blatant confession of male privilege, as well as irresponsibility. After all they could have just worn condoms. Using everything I had to restrain myself, I just smiled and said that was something they needed to take up with their company. But when I returned home, the question that most bothered me was this: why were they emboldened by the absence of their wives and yet not at all deterred by the presence of the God they prayed five times to every day?

These were among the many contradictions I heard throughout my time at the Malaysian AIDS Council and Foundation. Men of stature and achievement would tell me that they took an HIV test every year and they've always been fine, not realizing that they were also telling me that they were having unsafe sex in between the tests. I sometimes found myself educating executives about the dangers of oral sex over lunch, not the most delicate subject to have while facing food.

Yet some people in officialdom were jittery about me talking too frankly about how people get infected. My attitude was simple; if they ask me, I shall answer. Once I was in Kota Bharu, the capital city of one of the most conservative East Coast states, Kelantan, giving a talk to women about HIV when one of them put up her hand to ask a question. 'I am asking on behalf of a friend,' she said. Uh-huh. 'She wants to know if sucking is dangerous.'

On another occasion I was in a large school hall speaking to secondary students about the disease. For that audience, I was very careful how I approached the subject, keeping to the scientific facts, explaining how the virus transmitted from one person to another in the most diplomatic way possible. When it came to question time, a bespectacled boy who must have been no more than thirteen, ran up from the back of the hall to the microphone and asked, 'What is so special about condoms?' The teachers sitting in the front row flinched and paled. 'Well,' I said, 'Condoms are made of good old Malaysian rubber and the virus cannot go through them. So, if you wear them, you can't get infected.' The teachers breathed a sigh of relief, pleased that it was me, rather than they, who had to answer this question.

I am always puzzled why so many adults are reluctant to provide children with the information that could potentially save their lives. Mostly I think it is because of their discomfort with the facts that they have to give, facts that they felt could not be mentioned in polite company. But like that little kid who asked me about the condoms, children are smart and naturally curious. This curiosity, if not handled well, could be dangerous for them.

In one large hotel ballroom, an elderly man said that while he realized that the information was important, he felt that we should not move too fast to educate young people. I responded by giving an example of why this education, including sex education, was so urgent. There had been a recent letter to a local newspaper's 'agony aunty' written by a young boy who said that he was worried because he was being pressured by his peers to have sex with a sex worker. While girls are expected to protect their virginity before marriage, no such sanctions exist for boys. Parents turn a blind eye to boys experimenting with sex, without thinking of the very real dangers to their health, including sexually transmitted diseases. Of these, the most fatal, especially in the Nineties when there was still no treatment, was HIV.

To slow down on educating young people, as the old man suggested, was foolish and irresponsible. Why should we endanger our young when a little bit of education could save their lives?

Similarly, in a forum for Members of Parliament organized by UNAIDS, a man from the conservative Islamic party PAS asked me why I kept talking about countries that had HIV and not about those that did not have HIV, 'such as Saudi Arabia.' I said I'd love to talk about countries that were HIV-free but that I didn't know of any. Even Saudi Arabia, the country where Muslims aspire to visit the two Holy Cities, Mecca and Madinah, had cases of HIV. I had frequently met Saudi doctors at AIDS conferences.

Another asked why I kept talking about condoms. I gave an analogy. I said that if I asked had they slept with someone other than their spouses in the past two weeks, I could guarantee that one hundred percent of the audience would say no. But some of them might be lying. It's those liars that I'm concerned about. If the rest were telling the truth, then they could just store the information I just gave them about condoms in their heads as knowledge that hopefully they'll never need. But for those who may be lying, that information may well save their lives.

In Malaysia it's rare for a woman who looks and dresses like me to speak so frankly like that. People, especially men, find it hard to take. Often it puts them on the defensive, especially if they are caught out from lack of knowledge. But to me, fudging such important information was just not on. We endanger people by not being truthful with them.

* * *

My colleagues from the Malaysian AIDS Council gathered in my living room one rainy afternoon in about 1996. Just the day before, we had been told that we finally had a meeting with Dad to discuss the HIV/AIDS issue with him. It was a request we had put in with his office a full nine months previously. If anyone thought the President of MAC would get priority because I am his daughter, his office seemed determined to prove that this was definitely not the case. But that day they finally called me and said that since no less a personage than Nelson Mandela had cancelled his visit to Malaysia, there were now empty slots in Dad's schedule which we could take up if we wanted. As Parliament was in session then, we could have a slot at his office at the Dewan Rakyat building amidst the verdant gardens in the centre of Kuala Lumpur.

Dad is a formidable person to present anything to because he is usually so well-briefed and listens so intently that he is able to pick out any false notes that might arise. People have been known to become so overcome by nerves that they were barely able to speak, thus inviting an unforgiving stare from him. The first time I had to present formally to him, with my bosses at the time in a project to rehabilitate the Central Market, I basically spoke into my chest and refused to look at him. Even without seeing his face, I knew he was highly amused and couldn't wait to tell Mum about it.

This was the reason my colleagues and I were meeting at my house. We had to rehearse our whole presentation because we knew we had to be ready to answer any question he might throw at us. Nobody wanted to be struck dumb by an unanticipated query and have to suffer one of his signature withering looks.

We need not have worried so much. With me was Dr Christopher Lee, the infectious diseases specialist who later headed the Infectious Diseases unit in the Ministry of Health, Dr Sharifah Hapsah Shahabuddin, the head of the National Council of Women's Organizations, and my colleagues who worked among the various groups most vulnerable to HIV such as drug users and sex workers. They all knew their particular section of the epidemic more than almost anyone in the country. Although not everyone would be presenting, I wanted the group to be as inclusive and diverse as possible so that Dad could appreciate the breadth and depth of the epidemic in our country.

We also wanted to bring a secret weapon, a living breathing person with HIV. Nobody can embody the full impact of the epidemic as an individual as well as a family member, a work colleague and a general member of society as a person who had actually been infected by the virus. Our choice was very deliberate. Miss L was not a drug user nor a sex worker. She was a teacher in her thirties at a small-town public school who had unknowingly been infected by her partner. Since being diagnosed, Miss L, a tall quiet young woman with a short bob and glasses, had been giving talks to various groups about her experience of the disease in an effort to put the human reality to this much stigmatised epidemic. She bravely agreed to put her face, and humanity, to this very important presentation.

Came the day of the appointment, six of us assembled at Parliament House and made our way to the office in the tower section of the building. A small simple room, there was just enough space for us to squeeze onto a sofa and a few chairs and set up a projector and screen. We were still using transparencies and overhead projectors in those days before laptops and PowerPoints.

When Dad finally arrived, I introduced everyone and began the session by informing him that we had come specifically to talk about the economic impact of the epidemic; how, without good prevention programmes, it was stalking the very age groups we needed to develop our country. He had been a doctor, so he knew enough about the biological and medical aspects of the disease. Our goal was to provide him with new information and perspectives on the epidemic that he may not have been privy to.

Dr Christopher Lee spoke about how most cases were being handled by the public hospitals because private hospitals were refusing to treat their own HIV patients, out of fear that this would affect their business, and sending them on to the government services. Government doctors were becoming overwhelmed especially since there was, in the mid-1990s, not much treatment for people with HIV.

People were also afraid to be tested because of the stigma of AIDS and out of fear of losing their jobs. But without treatment and care, they would eventually fall ill as their immune systems deteriorated and would have to leave their work. Without insurance or any other sources of income, they would have no money to put food on the table, much less pay for the medicines they needed.

Dad listened carefully, nodding his head as we showed him the costs of the epidemic on our economy, how it could decimate our workforce. Then we unveiled our secret weapon. Without telling him who she was, I introduced our final speaker, Miss L. She was clearly nervous as she got up to speak, beginning with a bow and formal greetings as if she was making a big speech. Then she said, 'I am a teacher, and I am HIV-positive.'

I looked at Dad's face and saw his eyebrows shoot up. Before him stood a young Chinese woman in her prime who, once she got over her initial nervousness, spoke fluently and articulately about her experience of the disease. She talked about keeping her diagnosis a secret which was difficult when she occasionally fell ill or when she had to take days off to travel to KL to see her doctor, Dr Lee. The risk of being seen if she went to her local clinic was too great so she would travel three hours or so every few months from her small town to be checked on by Christopher Lee.

Miss L was the first HIV-positive person to speak directly to the head of the government about the impact of the disease on a real human being. I had tried not to use my personal access to him to lobby for HIV/AIDS because I thought it would not be fair to other organizations that did not have such advantage so I could not gauge how much he understood about the pandemic. But I think Miss L educated Dad more than I could have that day. She helped dislodge any preconceptions Dad may have had about the disease and I hope he gained a better understanding of who the epidemic truly affected. It was happening to ordinary people, many of them women who were partners of drug users or clients of sex workers and who had no idea of their partners' status until it was too late. Some women had been abandoned by their own families and blamed for their diagnosis despite having been unaware of their risks from their own partners. Yet at the time the national response was almost solely focussed on men, especially drug users without considering that they had wives and partners they could infect through sex.

Our meeting ended with just a few questions from Dad. We could not really judge how much he had absorbed from our presentation. But we were pleased to have had the opportunity anyway, especially after waiting almost an entire year for it. We only knew of our impact some two weeks later when Dad was Guest-of-Honour at the Red Ribbon Gala, a fundraising dinner we held to raise funds for the MAF. In his speech, he expressed his disappointment as a doctor himself at learning that there were private doctors who shoved their HIV cases onto their public hospital colleagues instead of treating them themselves. After his speech, I walked over to Christopher Lee's table. He had tears in his eyes.

My own reward had come earlier. Mum told me she had asked Dad how the briefing went, and he had replied that it was excellent.

10

The Staid with the Colourful

During my twelve years working in HIV/AIDS, frustrated sometimes with the slow pace of change, I developed a penchant for—there is only one word for it—ambushing people. After listening to a speech by a religious official that was completely devoid of compassion, I asked several HIV-positive people in the audience, very hurt by his words, to go shake his hand, not to agree with him but to forgive him for his ignorance. To his dying day, he never knew how we proved that HIV could not be transmitted through touch.

Another time I introduced an HIV-positive woman to the Minister of Health at an event. She was a former sex worker, gaunt with skin darkened by the medicines she was taking. He shook her hand and asked her what she did. When she replied, 'I'm too ill to work right now,' I saw him blanch and hastily turn away.

Even Dad was not spared.

In 1999 Malaysia hosted the 5th International Conference on AIDS in Asia and the Pacific (ICAAP). This is a biannual conference that brings together scientists, doctors, researchers and activists from all over the region to discuss the AIDS response from the South Pacific all the way to Turkey. It lasts for about five days and includes seminars, panels, meetings, lectures as well as cultural events. It is the only conference I know of where the staid and straight mingle with the curious and colourful. In 1999 it was even more colourful because it was organized by a non-governmental organization, the Malaysian AIDS Council which I headed.

When people ask me what AIDS conferences are like, I like to remind them of the scene in the first *Star Wars* movie where Luke Skywalker walks into a bar and encounters all sorts of weird and wonderful creatures from different parts of the galaxy. At AIDS conferences it can feel the same especially if you're a novice. You walk into any room and you'll meet all sorts of exotic creatures, the full span of the diversity of the AIDS world. There are the usual bespectacled doctors and academic researchers, mostly older men and a smattering of women, many of whom come from countries with robust intellectual environments like Australia and the UK. Then there is 'the community', the motley assortment of the groups most vulnerable to the virus due to their marginalized social status: the drug users, sex workers, LGBT, migrant workers, refugees and not least, women. AIDS conferences, at the regional and international levels, are probably one of the few serious conferences where such communities are seen and, most importantly, heard.

In 1997 at the 4th ICAAP in Manila, I had pledged, as host of the next conference in Kuala Lumpur, that the 5th would be open to everyone and every community. To bid for the conference, I needed Cabinet-level approval because there were all sorts of red tape that had to be navigated. Chief among them was a law, the Prevention and Control of Infectious Diseases Act 1988, that prohibited any foreigner with an infectious disease from coming into the country.

The law was devised in the old days of cholera, the plague and other highly infectious diseases and is probably, like many of Malaysia's laws, a holdover from British colonial days. In 1988, it was amended to include the Human Immunodeficiency Virus (HIV). It is likely that in those early days of the AIDS epidemic, too little was known about how it is acquired and spread. A person who carries the virus may be asymptomatic for many years before it is detected through a blood test. It can also only spread through very specific ways where body fluids are exchanged through sex or the sharing of needles. This was unlike tuberculosis that can be spread by coughing, or Covid-19 where people can become infected just by being near an infected person in the right circumstances. The wording of the Act essentially said that anyone who knows they carry the virus can be prosecuted for spreading it.

People with HIV are central to any conference on HIV/AIDS because only they can talk about what it is like to live with the virus, including the many discriminations they have to face due to their status. There was no way that we could prohibit anyone with HIV from coming to the ICAAP; that would defeat the purpose of the conference itself. But the 1988 Act was an instrument that the government could use to do exactly that.

This is where I was lucky to have a doctor father for a Prime Minister. He understood, having once been exposed to a person with HIV in the form of Miss L, that it was not a disease that you can catch like the flu. Unless a person living with HIV was planning to deliberately spread the virus through sex or the sharing of hypodermic needles, it was highly unlikely that casual encounters with an HIV-positive person, as in a large conference, was a danger to anyone. We got an agreement from the government that the Act would not apply to the delegates at least for the duration of the conference. It meant that we could go ahead with the ICAAP.

Inevitably, once the news got out that the ICAAP was coming to KL, some of the conservative factions of society geared up to object. PAS, ever willing to ignore the science, raised the 'spectre' of the disease spreading among the Malaysian populace. They suggested that I was getting preferential treatment by getting approval for such a 'dangerous' conference. I countered that would happen only if PAS members were planning to have sex with the delegates. In which case I would supply them with condoms.

The 5th ICAAP opening ceremony was held at the only conference centre in KL at the time, the UMNO-owned PWTC so they earned quite a bit of money from the rental of the space. All the hotels nearby and further afield, whatever star rating they had, were also filled with delegates who, when they were not listening to conference speakers or attending workshops, were out eating at restaurants and shopping. Like any big conference, the ICAAP, with more than 4,000 delegates, brought a lot of business to the city.

* * *

AIDS conferences are opportunities to jumpstart the education of many people about HIV/AIDS. The front-liners at the conference, the hotel receptionists, restaurant servers and housekeeping staff, the technicians and the cleaners at the conference centre, were aware that many of the people who were participating in this big meeting were likely to be HIV+. With the low level of knowledge about the disease at the time, we needed to educate the vast swathes of people who would, in one way or another, come into contact with the delegates so as to prevent any fears and discriminatory incidents.

In the months before the opening of the conference, we set up programmes to educate the people who worked in the hotels, at the conference centre, and most importantly at the Kuala Lumpur International Airport, the gateway for the majority of the international delegates. If Immigration officers freaked out in any encounters with a conference delegate as they checked their passports, even though they could not ask the arrivals about their HIV status, we would be in trouble. It might lead to the shut-down of the immigration services for our delegates and we would have to spend all our time running between the city and the airport 75 kilometres away trying to solve these issues. Luckily for us, airport officials welcomed these educational talks for their staff. Obviously, they were aware that their officers were often the first point of contact with foreign arrivals and therefore were exposed to every infection possible. Our volunteer teams spent weeks giving talks on HIV to airport staff, sometimes at midnight when the night shifts got off duty.

Naturally, Dad officiated at the opening ceremony where some 4,300 delegates, the largest ever for the ICAAP then, had gathered. Also present were Mum, the Minister of Health, Dato Chua Jui Meng and the Executive Director of the Joint United Nations Programme on HIV/AIDS (UNAIDS), Dr Peter Piot, as well as the heads of the five co-sponsoring Asia-Pacific civil society networks. We also had some VIP foreign guests including the Queen of Bhutan who was an ambassador for the UN Development Programme.

The ceremony opened in total darkness. After a few seconds, on the giant screen in front of us, a movie began with a door opening and a man stepping out of a bus. Directed by Din Said, director of several feature films in Malaysia, the short film told the true story of Jack Singh, the first Malaysian person with HIV to publicly talk about his status. Jack, a former policeman, lived with his mother and sisters on the outskirts of KL. The film showed their life at home, eating and talking just like any other Malaysian family. It highlighted the fact that Jack was very much accepted by his family and that he was no danger to them. When the movie ended, the room darkened briefly before a spotlight appeared on stage where Jack and his mother stood, hand in hand, bravely facing the world together. The entire audience, including Dad, stood up and applauded. It was no small feat for that family to come out in front of so many people especially members of the Malaysian government.

My organizing committee's brief was to put together an opening ceremony programme that showcased as many members of the vulnerable communities as we could fit in. We saw it as one of the many advocacy opportunities presented by ICAAP, to make a difference to the AIDS response in Malaysia. What better avenue than when the leader of the country was present. A young gay man from Fiji, handsome in his cream linen suit, represented the pre-conference Community Village and spoke of their expectations of the conference, to be treated just like any other human being and to come up with solutions to the many problems that such marginalised people faced. Other HIV+ people also gave speeches, bringing the reality of the pandemic to the world.

After I made my welcome address and various officials had spoken, including the Minister of Health and Dr Piot, it was time for Dad's keynote speech. The emcees began by introducing the next presenter. Out came Kartini Slamah, a transwoman born in Sarawak, dressed in a tight *sarong kebaya*, her hair teased up and pinned with a large red flower. Kartini had long worked with sex workers, educating them on how to protect themselves from infection in the back streets of Chow Kit in KL, an area she knew well having once also plied her trade there. In her low-voiced perfect English, Kartini had the honour of introducing the Prime Minister of Malaysia and inviting him to give his keynote address.

If Dad or Mum realized who he was being introduced by, they never said a word to me. Neither did any of the other VIPs sitting in the best seats in front of the very same stage where UMNO bigwigs sit when they have their General Assembly every few years. The only people who had noted it were my activist friends from around the region who had long worked with Kartini. They slapped me on the back afterwards and said, 'You're very naughty, Marina!' But in all honesty, I had not thought of it as an ambush. I viewed the entire conference as an opportunity for advocacy against stigma and discrimination and was determined to ensure that the communities most suffering from it were visible.

Some weeks before the conference, Dad's office had asked me for points to include in his speech. I was a bit surprised since they could have consulted the Ministry of Health for those. But I decided it was a good idea to provide him with some policy suggestions.

The draft went to his office and I did not hear from them again. At the opening, Dad began with a long-winded description of his government's efforts to combat HIV. It had obviously been written by the Ministry of Health, was dull and did not tell us anything new.

As I massaged my fingers with nervousness, the speech got more interesting. Dad began talking about the exorbitant price of the HIV drugs, a point I had included. The first anti-retroviral drugs available had been developed by the major international pharmaceutical companies. They helped to lower the amount of the virus in people's bodies, allowing their immune systems to remain healthy for a long time. These drugs were a major breakthrough after the early days of the pandemic when deaths were inevitable. But the problem was how expensive they were. In Malaysia then, they would have cost a patient some RM2,000 per month, a sum that was beyond the means of all but the richest.

There was however a way around it. Although these drugs were protected by patents, the World Trade Organization (WTO) Trade-Related Intellectual Property (TRIPS) agreement signed by many countries including Malaysia included a clause that allowed for compulsory licensing. It meant that governments could break patents and produce cheaper versions of the drugs if they were meant to save lives. HIV drugs obviously fit the bill; reducing the virus in the body meant that people were less susceptible to the debilitating opportunistic infections that took advantage of a weak immune system.

When Dad mentioned compulsory licensing, I had to smile. I could feel a thrill run through the audience like an electric shock. Most of the doctors, researchers and activists knew exactly what it meant. One person who did not was the Minister of Health. He turned to me and asked, 'What is compulsory licensing?' and in about ten seconds I had to explain to a cabinet minister what it was and what it would mean to Malaysians with HIV.

Dad also induced a frisson of excitement by suggesting convening an AIDS Summit among the heads of the ASEAN governments. The Prime Ministers and Presidents of the ten ASEAN member countries had never talked about a pandemic before. Again, this was a suggestion I had included in my talking points for Dad. I reasoned that if the ten ASEAN countries negotiated together to bring the price of the HIV drugs down, they would likely succeed. Together, ASEAN's population in 1999 was 500 million people, a market Big Pharma was unlikely to ignore. A guaranteed sale to the ASEAN Ministries of Health, similar to the Covax programme for the coronavirus vaccines, would force the pharmaceutical companies to agree to the demands for lower prices. Otherwise, they faced having their patents forcibly broken and generic versions of their drugs produced. That idea became the front-page story in the newspapers the next day, along with a photo of Dad and Kartini onstage.

Later Dad said to me, 'You made me promise many things!' I just smiled. It's not my fault that his staff had cut and pasted my points into his speech without really researching the implications. But I also knew the idea of threatening compulsory licensing, for that was all it was, would appeal to Dad. He was well aware of the injustice caused by expensive drugs to the developing world. Drug companies justified the high prices by the cost of years of research and development they spent in order to come up with the drugs. Still the human cost of these prices, where millions of people had no access to these drugs, was morally unjustifiable. Politically, it was also a fight worth taking on.

My 'ambush' bore fruit five years later. In 2002 Malaysians living with HIV were able to obtain free first-line antiretroviral drugs, AZT, from government hospitals. Instead of paying an unaffordable RM2000 a month, they only paid RM200 for the consultations and service.

Previous to this, only pregnant women who were HIV-positive could get free treatment in order to prevent them from transferring the virus to the babies they were carrying. But after the hard work that we did, persuading the Ministry of Health as well as the Ministry of Trade and Industry to invoke the TRIPS clause that would have allowed compulsory licensing, the pharmaceutical companies voluntarily dropped their prices. This was the only way they could continue to sell their medicines without having to face competition from the import of generics.

Two years later another miracle happened. For years, my colleagues and I at MAC had been advocating for measures to reduce the harm of drug use. Malaysia's HIV epidemic had been largely fuelled by drugs, specifically by the users who injected themselves and then shared the same needles. This was the most efficient way for the virus to transfer from one human body to another, the needles and syringes effectively being the transport vehicle for infected blood. Breaking this chain of transmission would stop the virus from spreading among the drug-using community and further afield to their spouses and partners. I had attended many conferences and meetings and listened to delegates from countries like Australia and Portugal proclaim their successes with needle-exchange programmes. Drug users who injected were encouraged to bring in their used needles to specific collection centres in exchange for clean new needles. In this way, dirty needles possibly containing the virus could be taken out of the environment and safely disposed of, lessening the danger of anyone making use of them, or worse still, accidentally pricking people who stepped on one.

To me, this made a lot of sense. But I knew it would not be easy to convince anyone back home that it was a good idea. Our drug laws are severe; anyone with a hypodermic needle is assumed to be a drug user. The police implemented this law very strictly and would be difficult to persuade. Luckily, we had an ally, a former top policeman Zaman Khan who had become an advocate for HIV after two of his nephews died of AIDS-related illnesses. He got us appointments with the Royal Malaysian Police top brass which paved the way for a programme to bring police officers from Australia to talk to them about their successes.

Also opposing us were a group of former drug-users. Their focus was a return to dignity through abstention with a lot of religious support. For the most part, the programme worked, and the group became the darlings and poster boys of the government drug rehabilitation system. They were part of MAC by virtue of the fact that they could reach out to their peers and educate them about prevention of HIV. Some were also HIV-positive.

But they vehemently opposed our needle-exchange and methadone maintenance therapy proposals because these programmes did not require users to become drug-free first. I had always likened the problem of HIV among drug users to a house on fire. Do we put out the fire in that single house before it spreads to the neighbouring homes or, do we fire-proof the other houses first? To us at the MAC, dealing with the spread of HIV was equivalent to putting out the original fire first, in our case by supplying clean needles or getting people onto methadone maintenance programmes. Methadone was a synthetic opioid that gives you the same high as heroin but without the side-effects, is ingested and allows you to hold down a job. It's the fact that those on methadone maintenance treatment were still high that the former drug users, now given to wearing neat shirts and ties, objected to.

These harm-reduction programmes were also opportunities for giving people information on HIV as well as getting people off drugs. They allowed social workers and doctors to come into contact with people who would normally be in hiding. When drug users came in to exchange their dirty needles or to take their daily dose of methadone, counsellors could speak to them about how to further prevent HIV infection and also to extol the benefits of getting off drug use altogether.

Once they got over their initial squeamishness, the Ministry of Health was supportive too, partly I think because the fact that Dad was also interested helped. During the 5th ICAAP in 1999, Dr Peter Piot of UNAIDS had a meeting with Dad in his office in Putrajaya. Sitting in his spacious sitting area with its carved wooden armchairs facing windows overlooking the Putrajaya lake, Dad asked Peter to explain what this needle exchange programme he had heard so much was about.

Peter is an eminent virologist, having been one of the researchers who had discovered the Ebola virus. He is also one of the few scientists

I know who has real empathy with the people who are most vulnerable to disease, the ones who do not work in offices and labs but who most need his knowledge. More importantly he's a good communicator, someone who can explain things in plain language. He was the perfect person to speak to another plain-spoken person like Dad.

With Dad, Peter's strategy was to talk about his fears for his children. He said that he was terrified should any of his children become infected with HIV because at that time, there was little treatment for AIDS-related complications. Any programme that halts the spread of the virus should be welcomed, needle and syringe exchange programmes among them. I know Dad listened without saying much, because that's his style but he must have absorbed something.

Some five years later, I was in my car on my way home from work when my mobile phone rang. The call was from Dr Chua Soi Lek who had succeeded the earlier Chua, Jui Meng, to become Minister of Health in the Abdullah Badawi Cabinet. I picked it up with trepidation, as I often do when I get calls from anyone in government. But he had good news for me. He called to say that the Cabinet had given the go-ahead to needle exchange programmes and he was going to announce it in a press conference.

I remember feeling relieved and happy that we had finally broken through the wall of official resistance to something so radically different from the usual approach to drug use in Malaysia. But I also worried about how the public would take to this announcement when we had done so little to educate them first. The very idea of giving drug users syringes and needles so that they could continue using drugs albeit more safely, would be anathema to any lay person. In 2005, just before I stepped down as President of MAC, I gave a farewell interview to a vernacular newspaper where I said that there was no real need to make a public announcement of the harm reduction programme just then. It was wiser, in my opinion, to establish the programme quietly, monitor and evaluate it and if successful in its prime objective, to reduce the numbers of drug users with HIV, then announce it to the public. Even if anyone objected, we would have evidence that it worked. The Minister was not very pleased when my interview came out because he thought I was being critical of his announcement and being ungrateful. Almost two decades later, with an upscaling of Malaysia's needle and syringe exchange programme as well as its methadone maintenance therapy, the numbers of drug users who are infected with HIV has reduced drastically from a high of 66 per cent in 2005 to 11 per cent in 2016.

Our HIV problem has now transferred to the one that we most hated to deal with, sex, one that is somehow more controversial and difficult to manage than even drugs and needles.

Before I knew it, I had been at the helm of the Malaysian AIDS Council for ten years. Not only was I known as 'the AIDS lady' in Malaysia, but I was also getting known overseas. I represented the Asia-Pacific region NGOs on the Programme Coordinating Board of UNAIDS, had spoken at the UN General Assembly, at several of the World AIDS Conferences and at the World Economic Forum in Davos. I had met a lot of people around the world, not just the top scientists, doctors and researchers working in HIV/AIDS and many of the NGO leaders but also celebrities who had taken up HIV as a cause like the actor Richard Gere. By 2002, I was getting tired of all the talking and travelling and wanted to step down.

It would be another three years before I could because Dad threw a spanner in the works.

* * *

In the same year that I had begun to mull leaving MAC to pursue other interests, Dad shocked the entire country by announcing that he was resigning as President of UMNO and therefore also as Prime Minister. I will go into the aftermath of that announcement in the next chapter but for now, beyond the personal effect it had on me, it also caused me to look at my future differently.

I had planned to step down as MAC President after my term finished in 2003. By then I would have served five two-year terms, far longer than I ever imagined when I first took up the post. Although I had loved the work and the friends and colleagues I made, I was beginning to resent having so much MAC work that I was unable to pursue other creative possibilities. In the year 2000, I had developed with Lina Tan, a friend and experienced film and TV producer, a TV series for young women called 3R-Respect, Relax, Respond. With three fresh young women as hosts, 3R broke new ground by providing information about women's rights, by challenging stereotypical roles that young girls were expected to play and by talking about issues surrounding relationships, work, violence and health, all in a breezy MTV-style way. It became a hit, because it was unique and gave its young female audience the space to talk about issues that truly mattered to them, rather than what was merely expected of them.

3R was an exciting new challenge for me and I wanted to explore it as well as other ideas and projects I had in mind. To do all that, I had to leave MAC and the MAF which I concurrently chaired. By 2003 I was exhausted with the endless work of advocating for evidence-based programmes, looking for funding and the constant travelling. In 2001 for example, I travelled three times to New York to attend the preparatory meetings for the United Nations General Assembly Special Session on HIV/AIDS as well as the Special Session itself. The physical and emotional toll of having to repeat the same things over and over again and seeing the number of deaths rise as people kept talking and obfuscating and generally doing very little to help became too much. Worse still, in September 2001, two jet planes flew into the Twin Towers in Lower Manhattan, just three days before I was due to attend another UNAIDS-sponsored meeting in New York. Over three thousand people died, and the entire world became a more depressing and angrier place.

But it occurred to me that if I resigned in the same year as Dad, it would look as if my position depended on his being in office. I knew my colleagues would be worried that our programmes and fundraising efforts would be affected though I thought our successes would surely speak for themselves. Not wanting to shake up the organization too much at that point, I grit my teeth and allowed myself to be re-elected for another term, vowing it would be my last.

* * *

When I finally left MAC and MAF in December 2005, I had been there for twelve years. In that time, I may have achieved some wins for the cause, such as getting free anti-retroviral treatment for People Living with HIV and made HIV/AIDS a mainstream topic for discussion among the Malaysian public. I also left a very solid organization with enough funds in its coffers to sustain itself and a system of delivery of its goals that I hoped would work efficiently.

I have much to be grateful for in my years in HIV. In those dozen years, I grew as a person in so many ways that I don't think would have been possible had I not had the good fortune and privilege to have led the MAC and MAF. In the most tangible ways, I unearthed within myself leadership qualities I never knew I had, managing a disparate group of NGOs who sometimes had little in common besides an interest in HIV. I built up enough confidence to speak in public on many subjects related to HIV not just in English but also in Bahasa Malaysia. I made friends with all sorts of people, locally and internationally, and learnt to feel at ease with all of them. And funnily enough, in a field derided by so many as being shameful and taboo, I got to know my faith better.

This might seem strange to many people except those who actually work in the field in HIV/AIDS. Seeing the suffering of so many people, often through no fault of their own, you start thinking a lot about life, disease and death. Knowing how some people are vulnerable to disease because they were unlucky enough to have been born where they were or as they were, with very little chance to get the education they needed to bring themselves up in life, you start thinking about justice. Are some people meant to suffer injustice and discrimination all their lives? Are those of us who were luckier meant to turn our eyes away from their fate?

I had been brought up with a solid religious foundation. My parents had ensured that I knew all the basics about my religion: our core beliefs and the pillars of faith that identified us as Muslims. I did well to *khatam* the Quran at age fourteen-finished reading the entire Holy Book even though I might not have understood every word of it. I knew how to pray and how to recite some basic verses. My parents also taught us some universal values; not lying, not cheating, being kind and always just and fair to others.

I found it difficult then to understand other Muslims who were so quick to dismiss and discriminate those who were infected with HIV, especially fellow Muslims. When methods to save lives depended on evidence, we had religious edicts thrown back at our faces, as if the call to save lives and to assist those in need were not in themselves religious injunctions. I became particularly frustrated at the barriers to protecting women from infection, when there was evidence from all around the world that women were increasingly vulnerable to HIV. Not only was their biology against them, their low status in many societies almost ensured that they had no chance at all. How could we protect women from becoming infected by their own husbands when there were religious officials and even family members who insisted that no matter what, women had to cater to their spouses' sexual needs? Condoms were a taboo subject; women who brought the subject up faced the prospect of violence from their already volatile husbands. It was better to shut up, lie down and pray that the risk was low.

Reality often belied the stereotypes. During my time at MAC I learnt of the unique and terrible predicaments of the transgender community, a community that is discriminated against at every turn. One year, the community organized a convention at a resort up in the hills not far from KL. They were there to discuss many of the issues they faced, from legal ones to health to religious ones. When they concluded with a list of resolutions, I was surprised to find that their top priority was to find a way to resolve how and where to pray. The physical expression of prayer—how they are dressed, for instance—is different for Muslim men and women. Without formal legal recognition, transgendered Muslims had a dilemma when they wanted to perform their prayers. Do they pray as men or as women? If they go to the mosques, are they to go to the men's section or the women's? At the moment they are welcomed in neither. But the crucial point is they wanted to be able to express their devotion to God just like anyone else. I thought, shouldn't their piety be encouraged, rather than condemned?

The response from the Muslim authorities to the plight of the transgender community, the most visible sector of the LGBT community, has mostly been of condemnation and harassment. Some transgendered people have high educational qualifications but prejudices against how they look ensure that many of the jobs that they are qualified for are closed to them. Out of desperation, many are forced to turn to sex work, for which they are further condemned. Transwomen sex workers are often arrested and sent to prison where they are incarcerated with male prisoners, subjecting them to abuse and violence. This treatment solved nothing; few trans people ever changed their gender identities or found work that helped them to enter mainstream society. The snake of desperation simply ate its own tail over and over again.

But I had grown up believing in a just and compassionate religion. I thought of the Prophet Mohamad (peace be upon him) as a kind man who would have extended his hand to help anyone who was suffering. I did not—and could not—believe that the approach of the religious authorities that I knew truly reflected what I had been brought up to believe. I also saw that other faiths, especially Christians and Buddhists, had a different approach, one that sought to provide solace and support, rather than criticism and condemnation. Surely my religion was no less sympathetic to the marginalized.

I believed strongly that religion, especially my own, Islam, had a positive role to play in the AIDS response, particularly in encouraging compassion and care and discouraging prejudice and discrimination. Looking around for religious scholars who could help me, I found Professor Fathi Osman, an Egyptian Islamic scholar, who was teaching at the International Islamic University (IIU) in Kuala Lumpur at the time. To my surprise, he emphasized justice and equality as key principles in the Quran, instead of the hellfire and brimstone I had been so used to hearing. It was a much more positive take on Islam, rather than the negative one we heard over the radio and TV that defined devoutness as a long list of things that we could not do, rather than what we can and should do.

Professor Hashim Kamali was another Islamic scholar originally from Afghanistan at IIU, who I asked whether condoms were really forbidden in our religion. Unlike Catholicism, Islam did not have a problem with contraception so why should there be such vehement opposition to condoms? Indeed, it was said that during the Prophet's time, men used sheep's intestines as a crude form of prophylactic. Our modern-day version was simply a more refined one.

Prof Hashim, a soft-spoken man with a gentle face, glasses atop a large, curved nose, studied the issue and came up with the concept of *darar*, or emergency. Briefly, in situations of emergency, it is permissible to do one sinful thing if it prevented a larger sin. For example, if trapped in a jungle with no food, it is permissible to slaughter a wild pig and eat it to survive, even though pigs are generally haram for Muslims. Similarly, even if condoms could possibly lead to sex outside of marriage, a sin, it would also prevent the transmission of disease and therefore save lives.

This was a major breakthrough for us at MAC and eventually spurred us to work with more religious scholars and officials to pursue a more compassionate approach to HIV. We held workshops alongside religious scholars around the country for grassroot Muslim leaders such as mosque imams, village heads and religious teachers, an effort that revealed a need for HIV education that far surpassed expectations. It turned out that many Muslims in rural areas were already seeing how HIV was devastating their communities.

Talking to local communities, I was amazed at how the women could see very clearly how drugs and AIDS were decimating their men. They could often describe their situations better than any social researcher could do because they lived it every day. What I could not understand was why so little was done to help them. Often when I talked about these problems to the authorities, I was met with a disinterested shrug, rather than a sense of urgency. In my years at MAC, there was no greater frustration than finding this uncaring attitude amongst those I termed 'desk jockeys', people who tried never to stray far from their desks. I often wished I could drag them to the communities that were suffering so that they could see for themselves what was happening. Then, as now with Covid, they were only interested in numbers and not the people behind them.

We did have one opportunity to get some people to see the real effect of AIDS. In 2001, MAC was invited by Dr Magid Kagimu, the founder of the Islamic Medical Association of Uganda, to send representatives to the first International Muslim Leaders Conference on AIDS in Kampala. This was an opportunity to bring the reality of HIV to some Malaysian religious leaders through peer education and we quickly found some funding for a small delegation. Led by Nik Fahmee, then Executive Director of MAC, we assembled a group that included a state mufti, the imam of the National Mosque, some Islamic

Development Department (JAKIM) officers and Muslim activists including, unbeknownst to the rest, an HIV-positive man.

They returned with eyes wide open, having seen for themselves what could happen to their communities if they chose to ignore the issue. They were also given the mandate to organize the second conference in KL.

The second International Muslim Leaders Conference in Kuala Lumpur was not without controversy. With me as Chair and under the theme 'When Theology Meets Reality', we were determined to bring the lived experiences of the most vulnerable members of the Muslim community to speak before religious leaders. We assembled women, drug users and a transwoman as speakers as well as an ustaz from Indonesia who ministered to a village of sex workers.

Participants came from all over the Muslim world, particularly Africa and the Middle East, as well as many grassroots leaders from Malaysia, and United Nations officials. To cut the story short, the ones who stirred the most controversy, the ones who had the harshest words for the vulnerable communities were those in suits, not robes. They shouted down a speaker, Dr Amina Wadud, for talking about the gender biases that leads to women's vulnerability, they objected to transgender speakers and delegates and they wrote statements to the media on all their grievances. For five days, I had to manage a situation that was watched carefully by people outside the conference. Every night I retreated to my room in the hotel to seek counsel from Mum. She told me to keep calm and said she was keeping Dad abreast of it all. It helped me a lot to hear her voice and gave me the courage to face every day when emotions ran high.

Despite that I still think of that conference as a success. Nobody walked out of it, not the delegates who had travelled from overseas, nor any of the Malaysians. The programme ran like clockwork. After the closing ceremony, one delegate, the Minister of Health of Baluchistan, the largest province of Pakistan, approached me. He wore the traditional tunic and trousers, a turban and a long white beard. The Minister wanted to thank us for organizing the conference and said he had learnt a lot. A year later, a Pakistani colleague told me that the Minister's first action when he returned home was to invite NGOs to organize a training programme on HIV for religious leaders.

Domestically the religious sector continued to be an important one for us. MAC worked with JAKIM on workshops around the country and developed an Islam and AIDS manual to be used for reference by any Muslim working in HIV. It was the result of long and hard negotiations, particularly over the inclusion of condoms as a prevention method, but many years later I was heartened to attend a JAKIM workshop for the transgender community where they proudly showed me the published manual.

* * *

When people presume that AIDS takes people away from religion, they have very little experience of what the reality of AIDS is. To my mind, AIDS brings people closer to their faith whatever it may be, because it makes you think about mortality so much more when you know it can be foreshortened at any time. What a cough is to an uninfected person can become tuberculosis to a HIV-positive person. A rash to someone else can become Kaposi's Sarcoma, a form of skin cancer, to someone whose immune system has been suppressed. People are afraid of those with HIV when in fact people with HIV are always in danger from others, physically and mentally.

But this consciousness of mortality and how you cannot take it for granted also brings with it grace. I have seen men and women, who have the virus in their veins, wake up each day to talk to others, especially young people, about what moments of foolishness can do to their lives. Judge Edwin Cameron from South Africa, a brilliant jurist, spoke up many times in that articulate judge way, about being HIV-positive. My colleagues on the UNAIDS Programme Coordinating Board, who represented other regions of the world, were kind and supportive and greeted me with warm hugs when we were all in Geneva or New York for those gruelling rounds of meetings. Another judge, Michael Kirby of the Australian High Court, became a dear friend after we met at various conferences and I served on several task forces on HIV with him. It was a world that was so diverse and representative of the entire globe, all speaking the same language, moved by a passion to do something about this pandemic, that it gave me faith in humanity. The ones who sat with their arms crossed, scowls on their foreheads, were a minority. Most people genuinely wanted to do something about HIV.

In that time, I learnt more about my religion than I would have in any other situation. It did not make me want to don a hijab, but it did make me see the way in which God tests us and how we pass or fail that test. I believe that HIV was sent to us as a test of our humanity, especially our capacity for compassion which I think is what differentiates humans from other living beings. It is a test of empathy as well, the ability to put ourselves in the shoes of others, especially those who are very different from us. I had everything going for me when I joined the HIV world; I could have chosen any other cause. But I still feel to this day that HIV/AIDS chose me, that there was a specific reason why the challenge was placed in front of me to take up. It was a gift given to me to show what I was truly made of. I may not have fully succeeded but I think it helped me become a more whole person, with more faith in whatever talents and skills that had been given me, as long as I put them to good use. That faith is what has helped me withstand whatever detractors have thrown at me in the following years.

* * *

I did make one terrible mistake, however. I already had a successor as President of the Malaysian AIDS Council, Professor Dr Adeeba Kamarulzaman, a specialist in infectious diseases who had a good grasp of the non-medical issues that needed to be addressed to truly deal with the pandemic and who had a vast international network of colleagues she could tap. But my colleagues at the Malaysian AIDS Foundation were worried that without me, it would be so much more difficult to raise funds for the programmes that would not be covered by the grants from the Ministry of Health.

We thought we needed a high-profile patron who would help us raise funds. I will admit that it was my idea to suggest Rosmah Mansor, at the time the wife of the Deputy Prime Minister Najib Razak, as a patron. It turned out to be an expensive mistake in so many ways and we were relieved when in 2018 her husband was defeated in the 14th General Elections and her term as patron expired.

In the years since, the MAC has grown much larger with a staff almost double that when I left. Their programmes are funded by the Global Fund for HIV/AIDS and TB, facilitated by the Ministry of Health. The Malaysian AIDS Foundation is still going strong with many innovative fundraising programmes as well as a whole bank of celebrities who donate their time and popularity to help promote the HIV message. I am happy that the two organizations are still working hard for the cause, with professional staff running them smoothly.

In 2018 the Malaysian AIDS Foundation asked me to return, this time as Patron, a largely ceremonial position.

11

Reformasi

I was a new bride for the second time in 1998 when one Saturday afternoon, my phone rang; Mum was on the line.

'Don't come to the house, Ina, ya!'

I was puzzled. This was the first time that she was telling me NOT to come to her house. Although I lived only ten minutes away from her, I did not visit quite as much as I should and was not planning to that day. It was understandably surprising to hear her tell me to stay away.

It took a while before I realized what Mum, speaking in the calm tone she uses when she doesn't want us to worry, was talking about. My parents were living at the time at the first Sri Perdana in Jalan Damansara, the official residence of the Prime Minister. Right across the road was the official residence of the Deputy Prime Minister who until a few days before was Anwar Ibrahim. I won't go into the reasons why Anwar was fired as DPM since there is so much that has been said about it already. But that September day in 1998, a crowd had gathered at his house to lend support amidst rumours that he would be arrested. If I were to go to see Mum, I would have to drive past them and I suppose she worried that I might get a fright.

In those days before mobile phones and social media, it was not a big surprise that I had not known what was happening until Mum called me in the afternoon. Undoubtedly, I was aware of the current crisis from reading the newspapers but unlike today when you can get news in real time, it was possible to not know what was happening across town or even in the next neighbourhood unless someone makes the effort to inform you. I was not worried about my parents as I knew they would be safe in their house. But I took heed of Mum's advice and stayed home and waited for more news.

* * *

Staying home gave me time to reflect on that year so far. 1998 was an eventful one, to say the least. In May, the Reformasi movement in Indonesia had brought down President Suharto, pressing for democracy but also unleashing violence across the country especially against the minority Chinese community. Chinese women particularly suffered from the violence, including rapes, in cities like Surabaya.

As it happened, 1998 was also the year that my husband Tara, a professional photographer from Indonesia, and I, after years of courtship, were planning to get married. We had met on one of those book projects I was working on and finally planned to have our wedding in June 1998. It was something that we had long looked forward to, being often separated in our respective countries and tiring of commuting between Kuala Lumpur and Jakarta to see each other. I had been busy with the initial preparations for the 5th ICAAP slated to take place in October 1999 but was planning to take leave at the end of May to concentrate on my wedding.

The Indonesian Reformasi nearly ruined it. In early May in Jakarta, some university students protesting against Suharto were shot dead by the military right in the middle of the city. Riots and looting occurred across many Indonesian cities including more violence against ethnic minorities especially the Chinese. There were rumours that the full might of the military would be unleashed on the people as Suharto, a former general, tried to keep hold of power. Eventually Suharto resigned on 21 May after his own colleagues refused to support him and handed the presidency to his Vice-President BJ Habibie.

With my fiancé and his family in Jakarta and friends due to come for the wedding from places like Solo where there had been a lot of violence, I was frantic with worry for their safety as well as whether they would be allowed to leave the country. I could not believe that after waiting so long, an actual revolution would torpedo my wedding. It sounds selfish now since so many people had lost their lives and Indonesia underwent so much upheaval. But I had so many conflicting emotions; worry for Tara and his family, happy that Suharto was gone but also unsure of what came next.

To my relief, things in Indonesia stabilised very quickly and the country did not descend into chaos. My fiancé, in-laws and friends flew to KL in early June for our big day. We had a full traditional *akad nikah* at my parents' home, in Sri Perdana. The Indonesian contingent, with my mother-in-law Susi Sumaryo, my fiancé and my brother-in-law and sister-in-law as well as other relatives and friends, dressed in full Javanese traditional dress, arrived bearing specially carved wooden trays of gifts as their *hantaran*. As their group walked up the driveway led by the batik designer Obin holding a large blanket made of jasmine flowers on that sunny Sunday morning, I waited in a separate room with my closest friends and my daughter Ineza, having just signed the *surat nikah* presented by the *kadhi*.

Our wedding took most of that Sunday. In the morning, as is traditional, both families delegated representatives to speak on their behalf. Tara was represented by the writer Goenawan Mohamed who told my uncle Ahmad Razali, one of my mother's younger brothers, his intention to ask for my hand. When my uncle, on behalf of my parents accepted, my mother-in-law, a tiny, elegant woman who had spent many years living abroad as the wife of a diplomat, came up to my room to slip a ring on my finger to signify my formal engagement to Tara. It was the shortest engagement ever because right after that, after a short break, we had the actual marriage solemnization ceremony.

My husband, dressed in his unaccustomed tight brown batik sarong, a short cream-coloured jacket and a *blangkon*, the traditional Javanese batik cap, sat with some difficulty on a cushion on the floor facing the kadhi. The young kadhi was dressed equally formally in a long coat over shirt and trousers and a black *songkok*, his official papers and a microphone in front of him. He read out first the obligations and rights of husband and wife in a marriage. Then, taking Tara's right hand in his, he asked if he, Tara Agus Sosrowardoyo, took me, Marina

Mahathir, as his wife with a *mas kahwin*, or *mahr*, a payment from the groom to the bride that is legally required, meant to ensure her financial independence from him. Tara had to repeat the entire long sentence in one breath and to everyone's relief and applause, he passed. Sitting just off the room in a nearby corridor with my best friend and matron-of-honour Vivienne, listening to him, I too gave a sigh of relief. We were married at last.

The morning ceremony was just for family members and my friends who had come from overseas. In the evening, as was traditional, we had a reception for more friends, mostly those of my parents. If we lived in a kampung, Malay custom called for inviting all neighbours to such an important family celebration. In the Bukit Persekutuan 'kampung' that we lived in, our closest neighbour was Anwar Ibrahim. As he was also the Deputy Prime Minister, he and his wife naturally became our guests-of-honour.

* * *

Anwar had met my husband before. In 1997, Time magazine had commissioned Tara to photograph Anwar for its cover. A young almost fresh-faced Anwar was shot in black and white, his tennis-muscled arms crossed, and his gaze directed at the camera as if challenging anyone to stand in his way. Anwar had enjoyed spending several hours with Tara for the shoot, posing in different ways and bantering with him. He also loved the resulting photo, and it has since appeared in many other publications and even book covers, without attribution to Tara.

For Hari Raya in 1997, Tara and I went to Anwar's for his Open House. It was the first time that we were out together publicly in KL so there were a lot of curious looks when we showed up. With this relationship, and the fact that they were neighbours and government colleagues of my parents, it was natural to invite them to our wedding.

Anwar also knew me. We had been working together on the Encyclopaedia of Malaysia project, he as Chair of the Advisory Board and me as the project director on behalf of Archipelago Press, the publishers. The Advisory Board comprising various academics and luminaries such as Prof Asmah Omar and the late Puan Sharifah Azah

Aziz would meet every few months in Anwar's office at the Ministry of Finance to review the progress of the project. It was my job to work with his staff to set up the meetings, fitting it into his extremely busy schedule, prepare the agenda and relevant papers. I suspect that he always enjoyed these interludes from politics and governing, hobnobbing with intellectuals to discuss cultural and historical matters. The meetings were friendly, enjoyable and productive, with many suggestions and recommendations for the editors and writers for each volume. Eventually the Encyclopaedia was published after Anwar had left office and was already in Sungei Buloh prison. After some discussion with the members, I insisted that his name remain as Chair of the Advisory Board and a full set be sent to him in prison.

With our personal relationship with Anwar, inviting him to our wedding was a no-brainer. At the main table, he and his wife, Datin Seri Dr Wan Azizah flanked Tara and I while my mother-in-law sat on the other side of Anwar, and my eldest uncle, Tun Ismail Ali was next to Dr Wan Azizah. Customarily as hosts, my parents do not sit down but instead mingled with our guests. It was a relatively casual affair. Just before dinner we had had a brief *bersanding* where Tara and I sat on a decorated sofa as the King and Queen for the day, to receive blessings from our parents and older relatives as well as the requisite photo-taking. At dinner, my brothers had regaled us with some hilarious speeches, teasing us both on our romance. I laughed so much I started tearing, made worse by the glitter eyeshadow that bothered my contact lenses. At one point as I was dabbing at my eyes, I turned to Anwar and saw him looking quite alarmed at me. I think he really thought I was crying.

This is why my entire album of photos from my wedding reception has Anwar Ibrahim and his wife in it. We were not to know how much his circumstances would change just three months later.

* * *

When the protests against the government for arresting Anwar began, I was in a dilemma. I watched appalled the TV reports on the accusations of sodomy against him. 'Is this really necessary?' I asked Dad, as we sat in the living room listening to words we had never heard on prime-time news before. He shrugged; this was what the police had charged Anwar with, a crime under Section 377 of the Penal Code.

The protests grew and the government responded in the worst way, with water cannons and teargas, a precursor to the later protests against the Bersih rallies. People were injured and arrested. The Reformasi movement in Malaysia was born and soon enough a new political party, Parti Keadilan Rakyat was established.

Those were the early days of the internet. Although mobile phones were not as sophisticated as they are today, email as a way of passing on news was burgeoning. All sorts of reports about the protests were coming into inboxes of the growing numbers of people with internet connections. Eventually this led to the growth of online news portals like Malaysiakini. Social media like Facebook, Twitter and WhatsApp had not yet been invented.

I won't pretend that those were easy days for me. Having been working in the NGO field for a number of years by then, especially on human rights, everything that was happening then made me uneasy. I didn't have any particular preference for Anwar and didn't know what the political issues involved truly were but the fact that he was accused of 'sex against the order of nature', a legal relic from British colonial days, made me extremely uncomfortable. It was a law that was rarely used since independence, and even then, only when a minor was involved. Consensual same-sex relations between adults had until then remained a private matter.

While I tried to remain above the politics and concentrated on my work at the AIDS Council, it was difficult to escape media attention. Most of the domestic media stayed away from me but the international media thought I was worthy of some comments. I knew this wasn't just because of whose daughter I was, but also because I worked in HIV with one of the vulnerable groups—men who had sex with men. The foreign media was aware, as was I, that a focus on Section 377 endangered all men who had relations with other men, regardless of whether they were VIPs or not.

Some of the international media came up with totally bizarre ideas. One Australian TV station wanted to do a story on me and Nurul Izzah Anwar, the eldest daughter of Anwar Ibrahim. At the time she was eighteen; I was already forty-one. I did not think it was wise nor fair to do a story on both of us just because we were political progeny. Another international station did interview me, but I stuck to talking about HIV/AIDS, pointing out that whatever the government did, whatever protestors marched against, the AIDS epidemic was still with us. I held everyone, regardless of their political affiliation, accountable for their responses towards the epidemic as well as their attitudes towards people most vulnerable to the virus. Prejudice, I knew, had no political preference.

Nothing allows you to know who your friends truly are as in times of crisis. I had a lot of friends working in NGOs and most of them sided with the Reformasi movement. I sympathised with them, but I knew that publicly at least I had to remain neutral. My work in HIV involved working with the government and with the ICAAP taking place in Kuala Lumpur only a year later in October 1999, I could not jeopardize it. My people, including the drug users, sex workers, LGBT, migrant workers and others who most needed help to prevent infection, were counting on the conference to showcase the issues of stigma and discrimination that they faced. There was no way that I could hold it without government support.

I did lose some friends who faulted me for not speaking openly on what I felt about the whole Anwar crisis. But my real friends stood by me, even when they did not agree with what the government did. They knew me well enough to know how difficult it was for me to have to read all the nastiness on all sides every day in the press. For months we had to bear the sheer awfulness of the trials with all its sordid details. It was embarrassing that we had to descend to such levels.

I also had to deal with the recriminations from my international colleagues. Some Western LGBT organisations suggested that the 5th ICAAP should be cancelled as a show of protest against the prosecution of Anwar. I was forced to point out that nothing could make things worse for Anwar than international LGBT organisations coming out in support of him. While he had denied the charges against him, he had said nothing about the need to repeal Section 377. To assume he was an LGBT ally was a mistake.

Luckily cooler heads prevailed and the ICAAP preparations continued. But the whole Anwar crisis in 1998 left a deep wound that has never quite healed in the psyche of many Malaysians, on both sides of the fence. And I do believe it led to the growth of much of the homophobia in Malaysian society that prevails until today.

Within the family, we rallied around Dad in our usual circle-the-wagons style. But we also knew how hard this was on him as well. For months before then, we had heard all sorts of rumours circulating about Anwar, both about his personal life as well as his political manoeuvres. I had been repulsed by some of the sensational stories people were telling me about him. I dislike gossip especially of the more salacious kind and some of the stories people were telling me seemed fit for trashy rags like the *News of the World*. The political moves, that Anwar was trying to find ways to unseat Dad in UMNO, seemed more probable and my brothers and I had tried to warn Dad about them. But if Dad has one major fault, it is that he prizes loyalty, both to him and his own to others, sometimes blindly. Anwar had been his blue-eyed boy from the time he brought him into UMNO, had given him a lot of responsibility and had already anointed him as his successor. He was not about to change his mind about him without real proof of wrongdoing. As was normal when it came from within the family, our warnings went unheeded.

When he was finally convinced, by others, that Anwar was not fit for office, he took decisive action. And we all know what happened next. I do think it did cause Dad some pain, as it does when anyone feels betrayed. A few months after Anwar was sacked, I invited Dad to officiate at a pre-ICAAP event with my Malaysian AIDS Council colleagues. As he was making his speech, a speech that should have been a routine one with all the usual praises for a job well done, he suddenly choked up and stopped speaking. I quickly brought him some water, assuming that something had caught in his throat. Mum sat in the front row looking at him with concern, just as all the faces in the audience were. After a while he recovered and continued but for the rest of the time he was with us, he seemed subdued as if he was thinking of something else.

Later that day I called Mum and asked her what she thought had happened when Dad was speaking. I was afraid that he might have been taken ill. 'No,' she said, 'I think he was thinking of someone, someone he lost.'

12

Stepping Down

Dad survived the crisis around Anwar's sacking and the 1999 General Elections where, although the Barisan Nasional retained its majority, it saw its popular vote drop to 56 per cent. The successful holding of the Commonwealth Games in 1998 may have helped his win but it was clear the winds of change were swirling and gathering force.

In June 2002, Tara and I joined my parents in Italy where they were taking a short holiday before they were to pay an official visit to the Vatican and meet the Pope. I noticed that Dad was busy writing in his customary longhand on notepaper almost every day, but I assumed that since the UMNO General Assembly was coming up soon after our return, he was probably penning his thoughts in preparation. We had a relaxed time, celebrating both my birthday and wedding anniversary and I didn't think too much about what Dad was writing, nor bother him about politics.

When we got home, we all fell into our normal routines, going to work every day oblivious to anything brewing in the air.

Then Dad shocked everyone by announcing that he was stepping down. In a true made-for-TV moment, he finished his closing speech at the UMNO General Assembly by saying that he was leaving as UMNO President and therefore also as Prime Minister. As most people would remember, pandemonium broke out, with Supreme Council members and Ministers standing up, shouting and screaming at him to rescind what he just announced. Rafidah Aziz, then Minister of International Trade and Industry, was pictured on television pleading with him to take it back. But he stood there, with tears in his eyes, saying 'No, no, no, I've made my decision.'

I was not there to witness this hurricane of emotion that coursed through the PWTC's Dewan Merdeka and out over the airwaves to the rest of the country. Thinking that the General Assembly would be its usual routine self, I had gone to Bangkok for a meeting. That afternoon, Saturday, was my first free day before I was due to leave and I had planned to go shopping with a friend. I was getting ready in my hotel room when my mobile phone rang.

'Marina!' I heard the voice of my friend Prof Sharifah Hapsah, sounding uncharacteristically urgent. 'Are you watching TV?'

'No . . .' I frowned. It seemed like an odd question. But then the last time Prof Sharifah had called me out of the blue, Princess Diana had died.

'Your Dad's resigned!'

My knees became wobbly, as if my bones had suddenly turned to mush. I felt my heart pounding so hard I thought it would jump out of my chest. My brain began asking the worst questions: 'Is he ill? Why didn't he tell us?'

Prof Sharifah's was only the first of the phone calls I was to get in rapid succession that afternoon. Everyone had the same questions. All I could say was 'I'm in Bangkok! I don't know anything!' which was the truth. Each call told me nothing more about why Dad had resigned and I grew increasingly worried. None of my own family, not even my mother, had reached out to me.

Forcing myself to think, I decided I had to get home as quickly as possible. Frantically I asked my shopping companion Gigi to help me find a flight home. Instead of going to a shopping mall, I had to get to the airport. Luckily on a Saturday afternoon, Bangkok's notorious traffic wasn't as lock-jammed as it normally was.

On the way to the airport, I phoned my brothers to find out what was happening. Mokhzani had been at the scene and had gotten Dad off-stage once it became clear that nobody was going to calm down. Mum had been watching from the balcony where the VIP wives sat, undoubtedly also stricken with shock. As always, when he was about to make such a big announcement, Dad had not given her the slightest hint. Despite their closeness, she was as caught by surprise as anyone.

Nobody had much news for me since things were still chaotic. The UMNO top brass had retreated into a VIP room with Dad, all still trying to persuade him to change his mind. But Dad can be resolute about these decisions. He had wanted to resign earlier but he had gone through an economic crisis, followed by the Anwar Ibrahim political crisis and so had to postpone leaving. By 2002 he felt things were on an even keel again, he had a successor in Abdullah Ahmad Badawi, and he could safely hand over the reins. But knowing there would be objections from some quarters, he decided to keep his decision secret and sprung it on the entire UMNO membership—and his family—at their biggest gathering.

Arriving back in KL that night I went straight to my parents' home at Sri Perdana in Putrajaya, the new administrative capital they had moved to in 1999. It was already late, but I felt I had to see Dad immediately to find out the real story, especially if he was ill in any way. He had had heart surgery in 1989 and I worried that perhaps it was giving him trouble again.

I found him in his study, calm, collected and, oddly, cheerful, as if a burden had been lifted from his shoulders. 'What have you done now, Daddy?' I asked, anxiety all over my face. He smiled. 'I am stepping down. But next year after the Non-Aligned Meeting and the OIC meeting.'

'Hmmm . . .,' I frowned, 'Sounds like you're finding excuses not to step down now.'

'No, I am leaving. But I want to finish these two events first.'

I was relieved that he had not been hiding any serious illness. But I was not unhappy that he was stepping down. Our family had never thought of him remaining in office as desirable. We wanted to have our father back, especially as the third generation, his grandchildren, was growing. For twenty-one years we had had to share him with the entire country, had to suffer through the many downs although admittedly we also shared in the triumphs. We missed birthdays and graduations, endured complicated manoeuvres to be able to holiday together, long periods when we just never saw him and quick snatches of conversation when we did. It was not a family life and we were tired of it. And we knew that Mum was too.

The next morning the entire UMNO Supreme Council trooped into Sri Perdana to map out Dad's retirement plan. I had gone home the night before but had returned bright and early to see what was happening with Dad. Mainly I was worried that the Supreme Council would persuade Dad to stay even beyond 2003. When Hishammuddin Hussein, the Minister of Youth and Sports, finally came out of the meeting and told me that they had agreed for Dad to stay on for another year, he noted that my mouth turned down in disappointment. I had hoped he would step down sooner, international conferences or no international conferences, but obviously they had no alternative to Dad's plan.

* * *

The following year passed by in what seemed like a nanosecond in my recollection. Dad hosted his two conferences and also did some final official visits including to Timor Leste, the newest member of ASEAN. In September, he attended his last United Nations General Assembly in New York. Since there was a session on HIV/AIDS at the same time at the UN, I went along as part of the NGO delegation and therefore could also watch Dad speak in the General Assembly hall, with the United Nations logo behind him as he stood at the podium. Afterwards as was customary, he received congratulations from other delegations and then retired to a room for a press conference. I remember clearly that moderating the press conference was the UN Under-Secretary for Communications and Public Information Shashi Tharoor, later to return to his homeland India to stand for elections and who is currently a Member of the Lok Sabha, the Indian Parliament.

At home, Dad as always kept his plans close to his heart. All we knew was that he wanted to go on holiday as often as possible with as many of us as possible. Dad's respite from work and political worries was to be surrounded by his grandchildren, at the time numbering 15. He wanted to revel in their hugs, talk to them about their hobbies and ambitions, like any doting grandfather. Both he and Mum's 80th birthdays were coming up in 2005 and 2006 and we finally had the luxury of planning something special for them.

Dad officially stepped down in October 2003, twenty-two years after he became Prime Minister. On that day, after two decades of being largely forgotten, my siblings and I and our spouses were finally invited to Istana Negara to watch Dad's official retirement, as well as the swearing-in of Abdullah Ahmad Badawi as the fifth Prime Minister of Malaysia. Also attending was the entire Cabinet as well as the heads of the Opposition parties.

The ceremony was brief and sombre. Dressed in formal black, Dad stood before the Agong, at the time the Raja of Perlis, who accepted the resignation of his Prime Minister. Immediately after, His Majesty awarded Dad with the Grand Order of the Defender of the Realm (SMN), the highest award in the country which carries the title 'Tun'. The wife of a Tun is a Toh Puan and for about two minutes, Mum was a Toh Puan until she too was given the Grand Commander of the Order of Loyalty to the Crown of Malaysia (SSM) which also carries the title 'Tun'. At that moment they became the first living couple in Malaysia with the same title.

Only after the awards ceremony did the swearing-in of Abdullah Badawi, a quiet, gentle man who had served in Dad's Cabinet as Foreign Minister and finally Deputy Prime Minister, take place. Again, this was a simple formal ceremony, but it was the first time that we had actually witnessed it.

My siblings, spouses and I, dressed formally, sat in a row just behind our parents as we watched the culmination of twenty-two years of being the 'first family'. It seemed incredible that two decades had gone by almost in the blink of an eye. But in that time so much had happened. We had watched our father go through many crises and come out of them on top, had almost lost him when he had a heart attack, had gotten married and given him many grandchildren. It seemed the right time for him to step down, and although we felt some sadness that this chapter in his life was closing, we were also looking forward to the next one where we would hopefully see more of him and Mum.

I for one looked forward to a normal life. Our lives for the past twenty-two years had almost entirely been coloured by our relationship with Dad. We were judged against his achievements and failures, and the weight of expectations sometimes fell heavily on us. I often felt that there was nothing I could get right. Someone would always find something wrong with me, no matter what I did. Either I was too smart, or too stupid, depending on your point of view. For years even though I was not a politician, much less an election candidate, I felt that the slightest mistake I made might cost Dad a vote. I tried to say yes to every request whether it was to officiate an event, give a speech or take photos, because I did not want to disappoint anyone. Sometimes it felt like too much, like the time a stranger claiming to be from Dad's constituency called me at home to demand I pay his daughter's university fees.

But in the grand scheme of things, I could not complain. Dad's tenure as PM had been a privilege, one that hung on voters supporting him time and again. It was not something to be taken for granted. We had to move on, to live relatively ordinary lives again.

If only it was that easy.

Part 3

The Sabbatical (2003-2018)

13

Fifteen Years of Normal

Life, after Dad stepped down, was not so dramatic a change for all of my siblings and me. By then, except for Mazhar and Maizura, who were still teenagers, we were all grown up and busy with our own families. My parents moved out of Sri Perdana and into their own home at the Mines Country Resort in Sri Kembangan which was nearer KL and therefore easier for us to visit.

Hari Raya 2004 after Dad left office was the first in a long time that we could celebrate together just as a family. For twenty-two years *Hari Raya* was always a workday for Dad and Mum because of the big Sri Perdana Open House. We would have about an hour with them in the morning for our family get-together before they had to present themselves before the public ready to shake hands with the thousands of people who had come to greet them.

That first post-retirement *Hari Raya*, wanting to have time to ourselves, the entire clan, grandchildren and all, took ourselves off to Phuket, Thailand for a few days. We knew that if we stayed in Malaysia, there would be friends and extended family who would stop by to greet Mum and Dad and it would not be a restful time for them. They would still also be obliged to visit the King and Queen at the palace for their usual festive greetings. We wanted a relaxed protocol-free time together. The only solution was to leave the country for the holidays.

Without the new clothes or traditional foods but with almost all of our immediate family together; seven children, five in-laws and almost all of the fifteen grandchildren at the time, we had one of the best holidays in a long time. Every day we wore shorts and t-shirts and spent the days lazying around chatting, watching TV or reading while the kids swam or played games. In the evenings we would go out for Thai dinners. It was the most relaxed *Hari Raya* we had had in a long time.

I wish we could have kept this plan up for subsequent *Hari Rayas*. I suspect that once he was free of the obligation to have an open house, Dad began to miss it. People kept dropping by Mum and Dad's on the first day of the festival regardless of whether he invited them or not. Soon it became necessary to make better arrangements to accommodate them. A large white tent, festooned with ketupat decorations and fairy lights, was set up on the lawn in front of the house facing the golf greens that had once hosted Tiger Woods. Caterers were brought in to set up stalls featuring traditional *Hari Raya* food like *nasi himpit* and *rendang* and stall food like *satay* and fried *kuey tiaw*, tables and chairs were set out and a PA system rigged up.

Our rituals are the same every year. On the first day of *Hari Raya* after Mum and Dad return from prayers at Masjid Negara and greeting the King and Queen, we gather in their living room to greet them and ask for forgiveness for any misdeeds in the past year. This follows a strict protocol. Sofas and chairs are arranged around their living room with my parents seating themselves on the first sofa. The entire Mahathir clan queues up beginning with the eldest, followed by the next in age all the way to the youngest. My husband Tara, being the oldest, is always first, kneeling before my parents, taking their hands in his and asking for forgiveness. Then a kiss and hug before he sits next to Mum. I go next, getting on my knees before Dad, Mum and Tara and repeating the ritual before taking my place next to my husband. Then my brothers and their spouses, followed by Ineza as the oldest grandchild down to the youngest. The routine was only slightly broken in the years when my mother-in-law was still alive and Tara and I and our children would spend alternate *Hari Rayas* in Jakarta.

Over the years the line has grown longer and longer. The younger you are the more time you spend on your knees, shuffling from one person to another. The adults however have to prepare a whole stack of *duit Raya* packets not only for the younger generation but also for all the helpers from each household, who also perform the same ritual after the family is done. After some quick family photographs usually taken by my husband, we're off to greet the already long lines of visitors queuing outside the tent.

Despite the sheer fatigue of greeting the mass of people who come to the open house at Mum and Dad's every year, they have never complained. It's not easy to get to their house which is inside a gated community with no public transport. But the fact that people still made the effort, even sometimes coming from out of town, stand in line for ages for a quick handshake and sometimes a photograph, made them appreciate the public even more. My brothers and I would also be there because it was also a chance for us to meet our friends all at once after a month of not socializing. People would turn up sweaty and tired after battling the traffic and looking for parking, but they inevitably turned cheerful once they'd greeted my parents and had a plate of noodles and a drink.

I loved our open houses even after Dad's retirement because it is such a quintessentially Malaysian custom. Our houses, or at least the public areas of it, are literally open to anybody to attend, a fact that is advertised in newspaper articles a few days beforehand. Although there are plainclothes police mingling in the crowd, to protect Mum and Dad, their physical security is not the only thing that we need to think about. One year there was a bird flu epidemic, or perhaps it was SARS, and all the guests in line to greet them had to wipe their hands with sanitisers before shaking their hands. Yet everyone cheerfully complied, understanding the need to shield not just my aged parents but themselves from any contagious disease.

For more than a decade, we enjoyed having Mum and Dad back as our parents and our children's grandparents whom they call *Tok Det* for grandpa and *Tok* for grandma. It meant that they could attend all the family occasions like birthdays, anniversaries and other special days. Or even, for no reason at all, I could have them to my house for lunch or dinner. During Ramadan, it became routine for each of us to host one another at our homes to break the fast and perform the *tarawih* prayers. As they lived half an hour away at the Mines, every trip Mum made to KL to run errands or see her doctor was an excuse to drop in on us as well.

A few more grandchildren were born during that time, including two who were born on the same day in 2001, and in 2015, they welcomed their first great-grandchild, a baby girl born to my sister Melinda's elder daughter Anisha. My parents had married late, had children in their thirties and had to wait until they were past sixty to get their first grandchild. They were so excited that in the year that Dad turned ninety they could actually meet the first of the fourth generation. Almost five years later, in February 2020, their second great-grandchild, also a girl, was born, one month before the first Covid pandemic lockdown.

With my parents in their old age, every birthday of theirs became significant and important. Their eightieth birthdays, Dad's in 2005 and Mum's in 2006, became excuses for parties and holidays. My brothers and I organized a big party for Dad at a hotel where we subjected our guests to performances by the grandchildren. The real celebrations however occurred overseas where we could just be family and let our hair down without worrying about what anyone else thought. We never did much during those trips except visit a tourist site or two and go out to eat. On one holiday, I booked a hot balloon ride for Dad and some of the grandchildren. Dad is always game for these adventures but as I watched him rise up in the reed basket under the giant bright orang balloon, I suddenly felt my heart clutch. What was I thinking! What if something terrible happened and he fell out of the sky like a stone? To my great relief, he returned to earth safely after an hour, thrilled not just with the ride but with the fact that he understood the French that his guide spoke.

For my parents, while they love visiting new places, having their children and grandchildren around is what makes them happiest. They are indulgent grandparents, happy to let their *cucu* take advantage of their affection and generosity. Their reward is absolute adoration from their grandchildren, with a lot of hugs freely given and returned.

My siblings and I have brought up our children as strictly as my parents when it concerned education but in one area, how we showed love, we differed. Dad frequently mentions how his father barely talked to him, 'because parents in those days didn't.' With his own children, he strove to be different: Mum and he hugged and kissed us more than what I observed my friends' parents did. Their grandchildren however are exposed to more verbal expressions of love. As a young child, I could never have imagined telling my parents I loved them or they reciprocating with the same. In the Asian way, you showed love by what you did, not what you said. If I wanted to show love for my parents, then I had to please them by doing well at school and generally behaving like a good daughter.

With our kids, we have been more 'westernized' if you like. Saying 'I love you' is normal, randomly kissing and hugging each other is not unusual nor regarded as embarrassing. As a consequence, my parents have benefitted from our children's more demonstrative upbringing. 'Love you, Tok!' is a routine expression at the end of a phone call. My nieces will walk hand in hand with Dad in public places. Dad of course loves it, smiling proudly and nodding at staring passers-by. My five nephews, almost all uniformly tall, adore their grandmother and keep in touch with her as much as possible. Indeed, all the grandchildren are attached to their grandparents.

There was one holiday abroad when my parents were scheduled to leave a day before the rest of us. As they said their goodbyes before heading to the airport, I suddenly heard a loud wail. Looking up I saw my Shasha, then aged about five, clinging to Mum's legs, tears streaking down her chubby cheeks. She had just realized that the *Toks* were about to depart for home.

'I don't want you to go!' she cried, as Mum tried to soothe her. Sobbing and hiccupping from her tears, we finally convinced her that we too would be leaving the next day and would see them at home very soon. Dad later told me that Mum had been despondent all the way to the airport, Shasha's cries ringing in her ears. Two days later when we arrived back at KLIA, who would be waiting for us but Mum and Dad, fulfilling the promise they had made to their twelfth grandchild.

The fifteen years of retirement were for the most part the nearest we came to normalcy in our lives. Things that other people might take for granted—being able to see their parents whenever they wanted, for example—became possible for us. Of course, Dad still loomed large in the Malaysian imagination. That was to be expected after twenty-two years. But those years were beginning to fade, in my head at least, so much so that they almost seemed like a dream, as if they did not really happen. Our lives had changed over the two decades but at the same time we had managed to go about our lives without much disruption, going to school, university, getting married and having children.

We did not realize then that things were going to change yet again.

14

The Man Whose Heart Stopped Twice

Dad's life was no less busy in his retirement. He went to his office at the Perdana Leadership Foundation every day and twice a week he could be found at the Petronas Twin Towers where, as advisor to the national petroleum company, he had an office on the 86th floor. He gave talks and speeches, opened a bakery and restaurant called The Loaf with a Japanese friend and travelled both around the country, especially to Langkawi island, and overseas. Every year he went to Japan to attend the Nikkei business conference, was interviewed often and wrote articles for various publications. He also kept up his hobby of horse-riding; on Sunday mornings he had a regular ride at hilly areas around Kuala Lumpur and Putrajaya with a group of friends, and sometimes a grandchild or two.

My life was just as hectic. Although I had left the MAC in 2005, I continued doing some international work including serving on the organizing committees of the 8th ICAAP in Sri Lanka and the 9th in Bali, Indonesia. In 2007, I was going to Colombo monthly to help organize the conference, not made easy by the fact that there was a low-grade civil war still ongoing at the time. Luckily for me, the conference was in August because in September I could not have travelled anywhere.

* * *

Dad lay in his bed at the National Heart Institute on that late September afternoon in 2007, and almost gave up on life. He had endured major surgery twice within a space of just two weeks. The first had been to repair the blocked valves that had caused him to suffer ever-frequent bouts of chest pains and breathlessness, bouts that had seen us rush to the hospital late at night, hair tousled from sleep, to be by his side. Once, on his beloved Langkawi island, he had struggled so much to breathe on his way to hospital that Mum, cradling him in her lap, was sure she was going to lose the love of her life.

Our family had not taken the decision to operate on Dad lightly. Sixteen years previously, he had his first operation to open five blockages; it was past time for another. For a year, his doctors had treated him with medication. At the age of 82, they felt his body would not be able to withstand the rigours of coronary artery bypass surgery, a procedure that required his heart to be stopped momentarily and then re-started. We knew that an intense operation like that, known as a 're-do', is always more difficult, more so at his advanced age.

But ageism, both on the part of families and doctors, also sometimes plays a part in medical decisions for elderly patients. The assumption is that not only won't their bodies withstand the rigours of surgery, but since they won't have many more years anyway, it was not worthwhile to do such an intricate, expensive and risky operation.

Researching the risks of heart bypasses for elderly patients, I came across a paper by the United States National Institutes of Health published in March 2007 that argued that while many older patients came to surgery with many risk factors, long-term survival and a good quality of life was possible. Dad has never smoked, ate fairly healthily and after his first bypass in 1989, exercised moderately several times a week. His diabetes was well under control. Under these circumstances, his surgeon Mr Yahya Awang, the same one who operated on him previously, was confident that it was worth the risk and that Dad would recover well. Without much fanfare, Dad checked into the National Heart Institute on a Sunday afternoon.

Dad underwent the first operation in the first week of September. Mum, my brothers and I, waited in a room that had been reserved for us. Unfortunately, it was easily accessed by some unwanted visitors, including a politician who had actively worked to make Dad lose in the Kubang Pasu elections for delegates to the General Assembly. He walked in and I walked out while Mum and my brothers ignored him and eventually, he felt the freeze and left.

After some four hours, word came to us that Dad's operation was successful. His three blocked arteries were repaired with veins taken from his right leg and blood flowed easily through them again. We all breathed a sigh of relief; although we knew he was in very competent hands, the thought of Dad under anaesthetic with his heart momentarily stopped still sent shivers through us.

While heart surgery in itself may be arduous on patients and their families, what is truly challenging is the recovery. Heart patients, especially those past their eighties, do not cheerfully bounce back and become as they were. Recovery is painful and slow, trying the patience of both the patient and those around them. Every day they are made to clutch a pillow to their chests while a physiotherapist pounds on their backs to make them cough out any phlegm in their lungs. In short order after surgery, they are yanked out of bed to walk so that their muscles do not atrophy from lack of use.

They are also at high risk of infection, even while in the very sanitized environment of the Intensive Care Unit. Every time we went in to see Dad, a few at a time, we had to first rub our hands with sanitizer. At one point I came down with a cold and was banned from the hospital for a week. Any germ that got to Dad would be disastrous for his weakened immune system. When the patient is moved out of the ICU into a regular room, it is a sign that his body has built up enough defences against any intruder. Typically, this will occur three days after surgery.

But the most important organ that needs to recover is the mind. The body is a wonderful interdependent ecosystem, a machine that operates efficiently and smoothly as long as each part is working properly. The lungs pump oxygen into the heart vessels that then send oxygenated blood to the other organs, where it is exchanged with carbon dioxide to be expelled as waste. If one cog in the machine fails, then everything else will fail slowly but surely. The brain, or rather, the mind, is part of that ecosystem. It drives everything else in the body. If it gives up, so will the entire corpus.

After the first operation, we noticed that Dad was withdrawn. He hardly spoke and didn't seem interested in watching television. I brought him books and magazines, including his favourite *Popular Science* and *Popular Mechanics*, but he barely touched them. Instead, he spent a lot of time staring out of the window, his face thin and drawn, the rims of his eyes red. He hated physiotherapy, thought it was torture and gave a grumpy face to his physiotherapists every day. He had no appetite, and his nutritionist could not get a smile out of him with her recommendations for a healthy yet seemingly dull diet.

Then one day I arrived at the hospital to find him asleep and no one around, not even Mum. Since Dad was admitted, she had been staying in the hospital and rarely left his side, including in the ICU where she would sleep in a chair wrapped up against the freezing air-conditioning, 'in case he needs me at night.' One night, dead asleep, she rolled off her chair onto the floor and suffered a twisted arm. But that afternoon, a nurse told me that Mum was in a meeting with the doctors in another room downstairs. Sensing something wrong, I entered the room to find a whole bank of Dad's doctors, including Mr Yahya Awang, at a conference table facing Mum, looking universally grim.

'We found the source of the fever,' Mr Yahya said, 'There's pus underneath his stitches. It means he has an infection.'

I looked at Mum. Her lips were pursed, the corners of her eyes turned down behind her glasses. The doctors were proposing opening up Dad's chest again.

It was one thing to subject Dad to open heart surgery when he was relatively well, it was another to once again make him go under the knife when he had already been severely weakened. This second operation was potentially more dangerous than the first.

The doctors lay the options before us as gently as they could. 'If we don't treat the infection, his fever will get worse. Antibiotics alone may not be enough,' they said.

In my head, I went over the risks of putting Dad under general anaesthesia again, when his body had been so weakened. Would he be able to take it? I had known of people much younger than he who had not woken up again after being put to sleep before an operation.

As a medical doctor herself, Mum trusted the team of surgeons and doctors attending to Dad. They had operated on him during his first surgery in 1989 and again just two weeks before. Theirs were the most experienced hands in any operating theatre in Malaysia. She knew that they were more than capable of giving him their best.

Mum looked at me and my brothers. Ultimately, we always deferred to her when there are major decisions like these to make. Assured that we would back her, she turned to the doctors, all looking expectantly at her. 'Alright,' she nodded. My heart cramped a little when she said that.

However, the patient had to consent too. This was arguably the more difficult hurdle to get over. Given his silence over the past two weeks, we didn't know what Dad was thinking. He had seemed depressed and miserable, perhaps over his lack of progress in recovery. A new operation might only set him back again.

The doctors, Mum, my husband Tara, my brothers and I crowded around Dad's bed as Mr Yahya calmly explained the position Dad was in and what needed to be done. He knew Dad well and knew that Dad liked to be talked to as the doctor he was, rather than as a mere patient. Nothing had to be simplified for him. The rest of us tried to keep the emotions off our faces as we nervously watched his.

He stared at Mr Yahya and listened carefully to his explanation. When the surgeon finished, Dad turned his tired reddened eyes first at Mum, then my brothers and me. I suppose he could see the fear in our faces, the fear of both the operation and that he would say no. Finally, after what seemed like an aeon, Dad turned to Mr Yahya and with a hoarse whisper, said 'Okay.'

If the first operation was tense, the second was even worse. It was set for the very same evening after the *maghrib* prayers where Mum and I fervently prayed for its success. It was already Ramadhan then, a time when people devoted more time to spiritual matters but we didn't want to tell the public yet about this new development. I had been blogging almost every day since Dad entered the hospital and realized that the thousands of Malaysians who followed my posts hung on to every word and had become emotionally invested in Dad's progress. I was afraid that telling them about this latest operation would open up more questions than we could really answer just yet. I decided I would only report after surgery, when I had time to process everything. We each kissed Dad, trying hard to control our tears, and watched him being wheeled into the OT yet again.

This operation, not as long as the first, was also successful. The infection was cleared up, the wound sewn close and Dad was returned to the ICU. But if we expected him to rebound immediately now that we had identified and solved his problem, we were mistaken. His body had been intruded on twice in a short space of time. That would fell anyone, regardless of age. For him, it was another long painful process of getting all his organs to work in tandem again. Most importantly his lungs had to function on their own, because they powered everything else. It did not matter if his heart was now perfectly repaired; if his lungs did not blow oxygen into his blood vessels, his heart could not do its job.

Intubation is a truly horrible word. It means sticking a long tube attached to an oxygen pump into a patient's throat and down his or her windpipe to help get air to the lungs. The patient's chest rises and falls in rhythm with the machine. Stop the pump and unless the body takes over immediately, the chest stills.

Ideally, soon after an operation, this tube is taken off because the patient starts breathing on his own. For a heart patient this is crucial. Not only must the patient breathe without any help, but he must also breathe deeply so that his blood is fully oxygenated. That oxygen is what brings life to his entire body.

The tube was taken off after the operation but Dad's breathing remained shallow and he still needed oxygen pumped through his nose. Besides the lungs, this phase of recovery, as before, requires the cooperation of the mind. Dad needed to want to get better, to put his entire willpower into his recovery. Nobody else could do it for him.

As each day passed by, it was clear that he was not trying. He lay there weak, exhausted and unmotivated. Traces of the same depression that we saw after the first operation started appearing. He rarely spoke and didn't want to eat to regain his strength, read or be entertained by anything. The doctors began to worry.

One afternoon, about a week after his second operation, it is my turn to sit by Dad's bed. The room is quiet, Mum is resting in another room. Apart from the humming of the machines constantly beeping and monitoring him, there is no other noise. Somewhere outside I hear people talking, a trolley rattling along, probably carrying meals to another patient. I pull a chair and sit close to his face. His eyes are closed but the lines on his face are creased, as if he is thinking of something serious, not having a nice dream.

A groan. He is awake.

'Hi Daddy, are you okay? You want some water?'

'No.'

'Something to eat, maybe?'

'No.'

I look around to find something, anything, to lift his mood. Someone, probably Mum, had brought a large CD player with discs of what we children call 'Mum's whale music', ambient music meant to soothe you as you rested. Lately we had decided to bring in something livelier and more familiar to Dad.

'Shall I put some music on? Nat King Cole maybe?'

'No.'

My, he's grumpy. He shouldn't have been in pain anymore; it has been a week since he came out of the operating theatre. His eyes squeeze tighter and his mouth turns down. That means he is unhappy. I frown. Then his bloodshot eyes open and look directly at me.

'I want to die.'

I forget to breathe for a second.

'You want to die?'

'Yes.'

Does heart surgery make people have these thoughts? Is it the drugs?

Should I ignore him and talk about something else? No, I had to confront this head-on.

'Why, Daddy?'

'I hate all this. I hate being here.'

The machines continue to beep and wheeze, giving me no information on what is in his mind. In the past few weeks, I have learnt to understand some of the numbers on the LED screen of the machines monitoring his heart and the oxygen levels in his blood. I know that they aren't good enough, that his body is not performing to the optimum levels that it should have by now.

'You can't think like that if you want to recover and go home.'

I hope my voice is soothing, not trembling the way my knees are.

'I don't care.'

'Why not, Daddy?'

'I just don't.'

The outline of his body, thin and fragile, lies still under the blanket. His eyes are closed again, the lines between them crunched up as if he is thinking only of misery. I take a deep breath. I have to say something. But how do you talk back to a parent when you've been brought up all your life to hold your counsel? I let the seconds tick by and then decide to go for it.

I take a deep breath and plunge in.

'Your time will come, Daddy, but just not here, among these machines in this cold hospital room. When you go, it will be somewhere better than this, with all of us around you. You know this is not how you want to leave us.'

It all comes out in one breath. I watch his face and brace myself for his reaction.

Dad's eyes flutter open and turn to me. I hold his gaze. I don't know whether he is cross at my impertinence or simply turning over what I had said in his mind. Finally, he sighs and closes his eyes again. The little dot on the screen keeps bouncing.

* * *

In the next few days, without any improvement in Dad's health, the doctors were concerned enough to ask my mother, my brothers and I for a meeting to discuss the situation. We sat in a little sunny corner of the VIP ward as Dr Mohamad Hassan Hj Mohamad Ariff, the senior consultant anaesthesiologist, explained the problem. Dad was just not breathing in enough oxygen to revive his cardio-vascular system. If he did not perk up, the possibility loomed that he would need to be intubated again.

Listening to him in silence, my brothers and I did not at first comprehend what he was saying. Dr Hassan, usually with a friendly smile, looked serious and worried. The doctor in Mum probably grasped the situation better than all of us lay people. 'We have to be prepared for every eventuality,' she began to say.

Fear sneaked into my bones as my mind began to understand what Dr Hassan was trying to say. Re-intubation was a bad sign. It means the patient is unable to breathe on his own or is unwilling to. It's rare for a re-intubated person to come off it, start breathing on his or her own and then recover. Re-introducing a tube into a patient's throat is a sign that we're headed down the path to death.

My brothers, eyes widened and silent, seemed to have understood at the same time as me. 'What we need you to do,' Dr Hassan explained, 'is to encourage him to try harder, to breathe on his own, to want to live.'

I thought back to my conversation at Dad's bedside and realized the truth of the doctor's words. Dad had to want this for himself, nobody else could breathe for him.

Looking at my brothers and Mum, I spoke first. 'We need a plan to motivate him. Maybe he needs a change. Maybe we can bring in people to talk to him. Maybe he's just tired of only seeing us and doctors and nurses.' My maybes poured out as I tried to clear the frightening fog in my head.

Mum perked up a little, seeing a ray of hope. Perhaps, the eventuality we had to prepare for was not quite what she envisioned just then.

After going through a list of possibilities, we decided to invite two people who could sit by Dad, cheer him up and encourage him. We were clear we didn't want any politicians or anyone who might agitate him. They had to be people who would talk about things he liked to hear, positive stories about what was going on in the world outside the sanitized corridors of the hospital. We finally decided on a young progressive religious scholar who, like Dad, was sometimes at odds with establishment thinking, Dr Mohamad Asri Zainal Abidin, the Mufti of Perlis state. Raja Iskandar, one of Dad's horse-riding friends, a naturally upbeat person, was another. He talked about their past horse-riding excursions, gave updates on their fellow riders and where they would go riding next when Dad was well enough to get into a saddle again. Dr Asri spoke not of matters of spirituality but about how Malaysia still needed him and how everyone was praying for his recovery. There was still much to live for.

Somehow these small injections of friendly diversions did the trick. Perhaps he was really sick of all of us, who only talked about getting better, taking medication and sticking to his physiotherapy schedule. From then on, his vital signs improved, and his appetite returned. The doctors encouraged us to get him to eat high calorie foods, including ice cream and Japanese fruit jellies. One time someone had the bright idea to bring him some *dadeh*, a dessert from our home state Kedah made from buffalo milk similar to pannacotta, and he ate pot after pot of it with nostalgic joy.

Fifty days after he entered the IJN for his surgery, Dad was well enough to be discharged. He had lost a lot of weight, but he was well on the road to recovery, body and mind. Dressed in a neat shirt and dark pants, we wheeled him down to the ground floor in the lift, accompanied by Mum, my brothers and Dad's entire team of doctors. At the ground floor we stopped. Slowly, he gathered his strength to get out of the wheelchair. We knew that around the corner were masses of photographers and reporters waiting to catch their first sight of him. Previously the only photographs of him they had seen were those that I posted on my blog. Dad was determined that he would not be photographed like a patient but like the former Prime Minister he was. Taking a deep breath, he put one foot in front of the other, walked, turned the corner and faced the media. The cameras flashed, reporters shouted, 'How are you, Tun?' as he walked the short distance to the main entrance of the hospital. To the photographers' irritation, I walked in front of Dad, acting somewhat like a minesweeper, determined not to allow anyone to come too close to him. Somewhere amidst the pack, incongruously I saw Ibrahim Ali, a politician given to many publicity stunts. 'Keep him away!' I hissed to my brother, pointing to Ibrahim.

Slowly Dad made his way to the porch where his car was waiting, waving and smiling to the reporters and the curious onlookers in the hospital lobby. Both he and Mum got into their car and quickly, without much ceremony, they left. I turned to one of his surgeons who had cared for him for the past seven weeks. His eyes were red. After almost seven weeks, we had gotten to know all the doctors and nurses in IJN very well and gone through the emotional troughs and crests of Dad's sojourn with them. Before we left, I had arranged for small gifts for everyone involved in Dad's care but those could never substitute for the gratitude we felt for saving his life, not once but twice.

For the next few weeks, Dad recovered at home, visited often by his doctors to check on his progress. He continued physiotherapy and a nutritionist taught his cook how to prepare healthy food. With his trademark discipline and determination, Dad returned to his old self and even went back to riding horses.

Who knew that slightly more than ten years later, he would be back in a different saddle as the seventh Prime Minister of Malaysia?

15

Easing Out of 'Normal'

It was probably too much to ask for Dad to retire like everyone else. He was not about to sit on a rocking chair doing nothing. His hobbies were action-packed—horse-riding, driving fast with his long-time driver Shawal nervously at his side. He doesn't garden, nor play golf. His retirement routine included going to his office every day at the Perdana Leadership Foundation, set up as a centre for the 'preservation, research and dissemination of information on the past Prime Ministers of Malaysia' where he would meet all sorts of people, ranging from foreign diplomats, businessmen, and even curious children. Or, as advisor to the national petroleum company, Petronas, he also received visitors at his 86th floor office in Tower One of the twin towers. Those guests would be shown to two large wooden doors that would silently slide to the side revealing Dad at his desk, a view of almost all of Kuala Lumpur behind him. I used to call it his Dr No office after the James Bond villain.

He would entertain all sorts of requests, not always from people in the political or business field. Dad is a naturally shy person who doesn't enjoy small talk, but occasionally I would ask if he would meet people he might find interesting, or who he could give a morale boost to. Soon after his heart operation, he hosted Tee Hui Yi, the fourteen-year-old girl who had received a heart transplant during the time he was in IJN, as well as a group of Timor Leste orphans I had befriended after raising money for one of them, Melina, to repair a hole in her heart. Another time, he agreed to meet the father of a friend of mine who was celebrating his 75th birthday. It turned out that the frail old man who had just recovered from surgery was an avid historian and had written many books and produced documentaries on the history of Malayan freedom fighters. Dad had a very enjoyable chat with him. Needless to say, these were the only types of people I would try to arrange meetings with him.

He was of course also meeting with other people. After the 13th General Elections in 2013 when the government under Najib Razak lost the popular vote, disgruntled members of UMNO were also beating a path to his door. He never talked about who they were, but they came with the same grouses: the leadership was not listening to the complaints of the grassroots, the GST was hurting people, people were suffering.

In those days of relative 'normality', I would often meet people who would tell me that they missed Dad and wanted him back. I found the idea ridiculous; why on earth would anyone want to have a leader who had already resigned? Besides our family was not about to let him go again. But still, while out shopping and at lunches and dinners, I kept bumping into people, often total strangers, who kept saying, 'Please ask him to come back'. I knew things had gotten bad under Najib Razak, but I thought surely people had more imagination than to simply want the same person back as their leader. Was there really no one else?

Dad too was getting the same feedback. Visitors increasingly brought news of many abuses that the top leadership, including the Prime Minister and his wife, were allegedly doing. This included the siphoning off of large sums of money meant to be used for developing the country. Stories of extravagant shopping sprees and jetting off on exotic holidays, including a trip to Hawaii to golf with President Obama, abounded. Meanwhile, Malaysians were facing calamities like floods and the much-disliked Goods and Services Tax that added an extra six per cent on top of every purchase. The contrast between Najib's lifestyle and that of ordinary Malaysians was becoming increasingly stark.

The mainstream media in Malaysia has always toed the government line. As Dad became more critical of the government, the media began to ignore him. Frustrated with this censorship and silencing, Dad realized that the only way to get his views heard was online, through a blog. I had already begun mine in 2006 in the nascent years of blogging. At the time the community of bloggers was very much pro-Dad and anti-Abdullah Badawi. I was part of a tight group of bloggers who met every Tuesday for lunch to discuss the issues of the day. But when Najib Razak came to power, a change came over the community. Some bloggers suddenly received honorary titles and new cars. The tone of their blogposts changed from criticizing the government to supporting everything Najib did, even the things that Dad criticized.

As soon as Dad began blogging, people flocked to read his thoughts. His followers eclipsed mine by several million, a fact that did not really worry me. In his habitual plain language, he would list out in point form his criticism of several issues, mostly those that had more than a whiff of financial malfeasance. One of his biggest bugbears was the Forest City development in Johor Bharu, a 1,370-hectare project that planned to build 700,000 residential units on reclaimed land. The problem was, Forest City was being built by a mainland Chinese company, using mostly their own nationals as labour, and geared to be sold to Chinese citizens. Complaints about its environmental impact abounded; not only was it altering currents in the Johor Straits, it also affected the livelihoods of local villagers and fishermen who depended on the fish and shellfish in those waters for their food and income. Government safeguards against such damage were sidestepped. There were rumours that Forest City's local connections were responsible for it riding roughshod over red tape.

When the 2013 elections gave Najib's government the shock of losing the popular vote, the pressure on him stepped up. His reaction was to stoke the racial fires by asking, on the front page of the Malay-language UMNO-owned newspaper, Utusan Malaysia, 'What else do the Chinese want?'

In Malaysia, everyone takes direction from the top. Just as how Trump enabled and emboldened white supremacists to show themselves, so did Najib's words encourage Malay supremacists to emerge, confident that they would be protected. Various non-state actors, organisations that claimed to be independent, began agitating against anyone they perceived were against the authorities, both secular and religious. Rumours ran that they were paid by the government.

Malaysia's non-Muslim citizens were besieged by attacks from these radical groups. Already, since 2009 when Najib took over, racial and religious-linked incidents had begun to appear. A group of Muslim men protested against the building of a Hindu temple by carrying the decapitated head of a cow, an animal sacred to the Hindus. Several churches were firebombed, after the Malaysian courts ruled that Catholics could use the word 'Allah' for God in their Malay-language publication. A woman called Jill Ireland took the government to court for banning the import of Malay-language Christian compact discs that used the same word.

Non-Muslims were not the only ones under attack. In 2008, Muslim Women and the Challenge of Islamic Extremism, a publication by Sisters in Islam, an advocacy group for justice and equality for Muslim women, was banned for allegedly being 'prejudicial to public order'. In other words, the contents of the book, a collection of academic papers from a conference, were likely to cause those who read it to take to the streets. I had joined Sisters in Islam in the same year and in the five years it took to get the ban lifted, I became very familiar with all levels of the Malaysian judicial system. In 2013, my colleagues and I finally could celebrate the end of the case, when the Federal Court, the highest court of the land, dismissed the government's appeal and the book could then be freely sold again.

And then there was 1MDB. Almost as soon as Najib Razak came to power in 2009, he set up 1 Malaysia Development Berhad (1MDB) as a government investment vehicle. Nobody paid much attention to this until 2015 when Sarawak Report, a website run by an Englishwoman Clare Rewcastle-Brown, and the Wall Street Journal revealed that they had received a cache of emails and other correspondences that showed that 1MDB's funds were siphoned to several personal accounts. Among them, allegedly, was Najib's.

The US government called the 1MDB scandal the largest case of corruption in the world. It had racked up some RM42 billion in debt and RM2.6 billion had wound up in Najib's personal account, a sum he claimed was a donation from the Saudi king. His collaborator Jho Low, a twenty-eight-year-old high-living man famous for cavorting with celebrities at over-the-top parties, became a household name. Photos of Najib's wife Rosmah, carrying expensive crocodile bags by the French house Hermes, began to circulate.

Everyone read these stories with their mouths agape. Never had there been such opulent greed, paid for by taxpayers' money. As the story circulated around the world, Malaysians who travelled overseas, including me, found themselves embarrassed by these revelations. From being a proud Southeast Asian success story, we were suddenly overshadowing even the worst excesses of the Marcos regime.

Najib's name had already been tainted by the murder case of Altantunya Shaaribuu, a Mongolian woman who allegedly had a relationship with him as well as his aide Razak Baginda. The case was convoluted and confusing, bringing in a French submarine sale scandal along with the use of explosives to shatter the woman's body. Two policemen were accused and found guilty of the deed, but no motive had been established.

I remember going with my Malaysian AIDS Foundation trustees to meet with Rosmah at her house to brief her on the year's programmes. Over a lavish tea, out of the blue she mentioned Altantunya. 'She's just a prostitute,' she declared as the rest of us kept our eyes firmly on our food and gave no comments.

With all these cases hanging like a cloud over the country, Malaysians became restless. Dad was one of them. He detests corruption, but he used to say that as long as it remained hidden, it meant society still stigmatized it and it could be managed. But when those in the highest office in the land were blatantly corrupt, and unashamedly displaying the spoils of such grand theft, what was previously petty had metastasised into a virulent cancer that threatened to kill the entire country. Everything he had done to develop the country would be undone.

The 1MDB scandal was probably the largest motivation for Dad to step up his criticisms of the government, and of Najib. And as Dad always does, he made headlines. Increasingly, he became an irritant to Najib who sent various emissaries to try and get Dad to shut up, 'for the sake of his legacy'. This was not the best tack to take with Dad, who does not care how history will judge him. He continued speaking, ever louder.

In the family, we didn't pay much heed to what Dad was saying. Like everyone else, we felt he had a right to speak. We should have known that he would eventually decide he would have to do more than speak and write.

Part 4

The Return (2011-2018)

16

Only the Dirty Fear the Clean

Yellow is the colour of Royalty in Malaysia.

It is also the colour of democracy, just one of the many ironies that make up Malaysian life.

On 10 November 2007, a sea of yellow appeared in the middle of Kuala Lumpur at the historic square Dataran Merdeka to protest against the Election Commission for its role in allegedly skewing elections to favour the ruling Barisan Nasional. Organized by a nascent movement calling itself Bersih, the Malay word for Clean, it was a mix of political parties and civil society that successfully turned out a crowd that numbered anywhere between 10,000 and 40,000 people.

As demonstrations go, it hardly filled a football stadium. But it was the biggest show of protest Malaysia had seen since 1998. Predictably enough, the government responded in its reflexive way: The Federal Reserve Unit, otherwise known as the Riot Squad, blasted out water cannons and shot tear gas. Thirty-four people were arrested but the heads of the opposition political parties succeeded in handing a memorandum to the Yang di Pertuan Agong with a list of their demands to level the electoral playing field.

In the 2008 General Elections, the BN lost its supermajority for the first time, a wound directly attributed to Bersih 1. This meant that it could not amend the Federal Constitution without bipartisan support since they would need two-thirds of the Members of Parliament to vote for it. Astoundingly, the BN also lost the states of Penang and Selangor to the DAP and PKR respectively for the first time. These losses led to the ousting of Prime Minister Abdullah Ahmad Badawi and the rise of his deputy, Najib Razak.

I did not attend Bersih 1, not because I didn't agree with electoral reforms but because I was wary of being in the company of political parties of any kind. But I watched with concern the reaction of the authorities to what was essentially a peaceful protest. A reaction like that would only do one of two things: scare people off, or anger them enough to make more want to join in.

In the next few years, the government under Najib did very little to meet any of the demands by Bersih 1. NGOs and activists decided that the movement had to regroup as a wholly civil society movement and be non-partisan politically. The former head of the Bar Council Ambiga Sreenevasan was elected Chairman and under her leadership, the group began to coalesce into a dynamic organization that was not only able to mobilize people in Malaysia but also in cities around the world where Malaysians resided.

Bersih 2 was scheduled for 9 July 2011. By then I was getting disappointed and angry with the government for not reforming the electoral system to make it fairer and cleaner. I could not see the honour in winning an election that was stacked against opponents. Stories abounded about dead people being still on the rolls or the numbers of voters with the same address far exceeding their houses' capacity. The time came for pressure to be put on the government with another protest.

I had never attended a demonstration before. Malaysians generally rarely protested, certainly not spontaneously. They had to be organized in some fashion. Government propaganda against protests as well as the show of force in previous ones in 1998 and 2007 had had the effect of making people wary of taking to the streets. On Facebook and Twitter, there were arguments about what it would do to businesses in central KL, as if that mattered more than the rights of people to choose their government fairly.

In the days before the demonstration, the government did everything they could to deter us. They offered a stadium as a way of mitigating any possible damage to property but when Bersih accepted and applied for permission, they were rejected. The organization then declared it would go ahead with the street protest. The authorities proceeded to lock down the areas of central KL where the protest would be held, effectively disrupting the same businesses it claimed Bersih would affect. Ninety-one persons, deemed the leaders of the movement, were barred from entering central KL.

All these restrictions began to grate on my nerves. My daughter Ineza had announced she was going to attend Bersih 2 and I worried about her and her friends. For days I pondered restlessly what I should do. I spoke to friends who were part of the Bersih movement, and they all said that the time for action had arrived, that we could not sit on our hands fretting about our weak democracy when the entire system was stacked against anyone except for the BN. Frankly I was afraid of the possible violence. On TV there were scenes of army trucks being moved around KL. It raised the spectre of an even more forceful response from the government than just water and gas. My stomach churned at the thought of facing our own soldiers and police.

But thinking of my daughter and all the young people who were determined to go and voice their anger at the electoral system made me pause. If they were willing to face being hosed and gassed, and arrested possibly, how could I in all conscience remain safely at home?

I told my husband that I had made up my mind that I would go. He knew I had thought it through and would not change my mind but felt he should stay away, not being Malaysian. Concerned for my safety however, he asked a friend if he would act as my 'bodyguard'.

The next morning our friend Leong, who lives in central KL, arrived to pick me up. My neighbours, Siva and Tony, and I packed into Leong's car and we headed cautiously downtown. We were dressed as if we were going hiking, with comfortable sneakers, hats, water and pouches of salt which we had been told would be useful if we got teargassed. The police had said they would arrest anyone wearing yellow t-shirts, so we obediently wore none.

On our way to Bukit Bintang where Leong had his apartment, we passed some policemen. Like a bunch of spies, we pulled our hats down over our foreheads and tried to look nonchalant. Obviously, we did not look as odd as we thought; they hardly looked twice at us.

After a quick bathroom stop at Leong's, we walked down to Berjaya Times Square mall where we had heard people were going to rendezvous before heading to the Stadium Merdeka area for the protest which was due to begin at about 1 p.m. Berjaya Times Square is a gigantic, red-marbled mall owned by the millionaire Vincent Tan. At its entrance, facing the main road, Jalan Imbi, is a two-storied Starbucks, where we decided to wait until it was time to walk to the protest site. Almost everybody else had the same idea. The coffee chain made a lot of money that day because every seat was taken by people dressed just like us, biding their time sipping iced lattes.

We sat there in air-conditioned comfort, saying hello to our fellow travellers. It hardly felt like the beginning of a revolution. As we chatted, outside the double-storied floor-to-ceiling glass windows a police truck drew up and young men in the navy-blue uniforms of the Royal Malaysian Police jumped out, readying themselves to deal with the supposed hooligans who were going to riot that afternoon. If they had only entered the Starbucks, they could have stopped a good number of the 'rioters' before we had even begun chanting the first slogan.

When the clock struck one, almost as a single body, every cappuccino-filled body in that Starbucks rose and made their way into the street to walk the 300 metres or so to the stadium area. Walking along Jalan Hang Tuah in the blazing afternoon sun, we had to pass the Kuala Lumpur Police Headquarters, a tall rectangular building painted white with a wide diagonal swathe of navy blue across its front, facing Pudu Prison, the jail built by the British in 1895 but by then largely unused. We walked nervously past the police buildings, sure that they would be on the lookout and ready to stop us. But luck seemed to be on our side: there was an event going on within the police grounds, under some striped tents, and nobody took heed of the streams of people walking in the same direction, in an area where people rarely walked.

There was no mistaking what was going on when we got to the street in front of Stadium Negara, one of the two stadiums within the complex. As a child visiting my grandparents in Kuala Lumpur during the school holidays, my brothers and I would often be taken to play in the grounds of Stadium Merdeka, the open stadium where Tunku Abdul Rahman had declared independence from the British on 31 August 1957. Stadium Negara was built five years later in 1962, the first indoor stadium in the country. As an adult I had been there several times to attend pop concerts by the likes of the singer James Ingram and exhibition tennis matches by Bjorn Borg.

On that day in 2011, Jalan Stadium was filled with people sitting patiently on the pavement, an air of nervous expectation hovering above us. In one corner, stood a bunch of lawyers in black suits who were monitoring the protest for any human rights violations by the police. We hailed friends and strangers, bonded together by this exercise of our Constitutional right to protest and express our dissatisfaction with how things were going. But mostly we didn't quite know what the programme was.

Soon we heard loud noises coming from the Chinatown area nearby. It sounded like a large crowd moving to a drumbeat of 'Bersih, Bersih'. With that cue, we moved downhill towards the sound hoping to join the chanters who seemed to be heading our way. Just then the steamy heat gave way, the skies opened up and it began to pour, and we dove into some five-foot-ways to shelter. I had not counted on rain and was prepared with neither an umbrella nor a raincoat. My thin t-shirt, meant to keep me cool in the sweltering heat, was getting sodden and I was in danger of looking like a pudgy wet t-shirt model. Seeing my dilemma, Siva took off the windbreaker jacket she was wearing and covered me with it.

By this time, my fellow demonstrators recognized me, looking a sight in a red jacket and damp lank hair with my left arm in a cast to protect my newly fractured wrist. Just a few weeks before, I had shattered the bones in my palm and wrist falling while trying to kick a ball in a futsal game and had a titanium plate inserted in my hand to help mend it. Most people were smiling, pleased to see me there, although one person did remark that I was wearing the wrong colour. Red was the colour of the counter-protestors, those who opposed the yellow-shirted Bersih crowd.

I must say that I have always been lucky in these demonstrations. In both Bersih 2 and Bersih 3 in 2012, I managed to evade the worst of the government's violent reaction to the demonstrations. At Bersih 2, although I saw FRU stationed in the lanes near Chinatown not far from us, they remained on standby, even smiling when we waved to them. But further down the hill on Jalan Pudu, another scene was playing out altogether. Demonstrators were chased by the FRU down to the Tung Shin Hospital, trapping them there and unleashing the full force of the water cannons and tear gas on them. Many were injured, coughing and choking, their eyes burning from the sting of the chemicals. Later I learnt some friends were in that unfortunate cluster. To my relief, my daughter was not among them.

Bersih 2 was an eye-opener for me. I saw that, far from the government's demonized portrayal of the demonstrators, participants were from all walks of life and all ages. There were old people and young ones, Malays, Chinese, Indians and everyone that make up our Malaysia. Some were KL residents but there were also many who had come from other states. I saw an elderly couple helping each other walk along, the husband with a cane, the wife in a hijab. Ordinary folk no longer felt helpless in the face of injustice. There were also lots of young people, some of whom were singing and dancing as if at a carnival. I recognized many as the children of my friends, even the children of government Ministers, happy to join their peers in protest against their parents' government.

In Malay, the phrase for 'demonstration' is 'tunjuk perasaan', literally to show your feelings. It seemed incredible to me that people would travel so far, even from more rural areas, just to show what they felt about the government. And what they felt was anger especially at elections that seemed to be stacked against anything but the BN.

The sight of seeing my fellow Malaysians undeterred by government threats surprised me but also made me feel happy and secure in the warmth of solidarity. Not for a minute did I feel unsafe where I was. The sounds of the chants were so thrilling, I had to call my friend Ivy Josiah at the time away in the US to let her listen to it too. Were we reaching a turning point of some sort in our lurching democracy?

Leong, true to his promise to protect me, walked me home all the way to Bangsar later when the crowd had finally dissipated. The streets were completely empty of vehicles except for FRU trucks, around which sat the riot squad eating packed food and ignoring us. At a bus stop near Muzium Negara, a family of foreign tourists stood looking puzzled at the lack of transport in any direction. I'm sure they would have understood when they found out why later.

* * *

The following year when Bersih 3 was called, once again I went, this time in a bit more organized fashion. My friends and I carpooled to the Central Market, the gathering point for demonstrators that time. We listened to Ambiga and the Bersih committee exhort us to march peacefully and not provoke anyone, and to keep the streets clean. Then we walked towards Dataran Merdeka. Again, it felt like a carnival, waving flags, shouting slogans and hailing familiar faces from the year before.

On Leboh Pasar Besar, near the river confluence that gives KL its name, we came to a barrier of razor wire strung across the road, about 200 metres from the square. On the other side, some policemen stood casually watching us. Somebody had put a sign up on the barrier that said, 'Welcome to Tel Aviv', the wire an unusually unfriendly sight for our city, a sharp barrier meant to stop citizens from accessing a space that was usually open to everyone. I stood just behind it, looked across at the policemen and asked them why, pointing at the razors. They merely shrugged and gave a sheepish smile.

It was, as always, a steamy afternoon, with the ever-present threat of rain. Unable to go further, all protestors behind the barrier sat down on the road, sipping from water bottles and wiping sweaty brows. In the front row, we took care not to get too close to the razor wire, which could slice our skin like a knife through a ciku fruit. The policemen stood nearby watching us cautiously.

Suddenly a phalanx of FRU, with their red helmets, batons and shields, appeared and lined up in a row facing us. Behind them were the ominous tank-like trucks they used for transport. We started at the sight, unsure of their intention but knew there were likely to be water cannons on top of the trucks. But as much as the razor wire stopped us from getting nearer Dataran Merdeka, so did it also stop the FRU from charging us as long as we remained behind it. They were not wearing any armour. Instead, they did nothing except stand shoulder-to-shoulder across the street, unmoving but nevertheless menacing. It was almost pitiable. On our side, we could sit down and drink water. They, on the other hand, had to stand immobile in the heat, their heads enclosed in suffocating helmets, their heavy shields in their left hands.

It seemed like a standoff until somebody said we should retreat and let others come and sit in the front. As we walked off, we heard that the call to end the protest had come. The Bersih leadership had declared that the rally would end at 4 p.m. Hearing that, I turned round and with my friends, found my car and went home.

It was only when I was safely home that my mobile phone lit up with news of what had happened afterwards. My daughter Ineza had been with me at Central Market; she and a friend were taking videos of the rally and they went off to find good shots. An hour after I got home, she called me to tell me that she had been caught in the melee when the FRU fired water cannons and tear gas at the crowd. On Jalan Tun Perak people had gotten much nearer to Dataran Merdeka than we had on the parallel street. All of a sudden, the police who had been guarding the square had retreated, only to be replaced by the FRU who, without warning, began blasting the water cannons and throwing tear gas canisters at them. The crowd, including Ineza and her friend, ran in the opposite direction down Jalan Tuanku Abdul Rahman, a mass of frantic bodies screaming in fear, their eyes tearing and almost blinding them. It's a wonder that nobody was trampled in the rush; Ineza said people helped to pick up anyone who fell in a gesture of terrified solidarity.

It was all that I feared but miraculously, neither Ineza nor her friend were seriously harmed, though they were badly shaken. Many others though were injured, both from the riot-dispersing weapons as well as being roughed up after some of them were arrested. There were sightings of policemen without name or serial number badges, leading to allegations that these were meant to hide abuses. Rumours of provocateurs abounded.

But Bersih 3 was an astounding success from the viewpoint of the organizers. Aerial views of the streets around Dataran Merdeka looked as if they had been coloured with yellow marker pens, so clear was the colour of the protestors' shirts. Again, all levels of civil society were there, united against a government that was increasingly oppressive towards its own people. Many of those who came to Bersih 3 were first-timers, emboldened by the largely peaceful experience of Bersih 2. My dentist, for example, told me that his aged parents had insisted he take them to the rally. They did not want to be left out.

It should be said that unlike pro-government rallies, Bersih did not have to organize transport for people to attend it. People came out of their own volition and paid their own way, whether it was to come from the nearest neighbourhood, or, as in the case of the group protesting against the Lynas company for its environmental pollution, all the way from Kuantan on the East Coast. By this third edition of the demonstration, overseas Malaysians calling themselves Global Bersih had organized similar rallies in thirty-four cities around the world, sending photos of yellow-shirted groups holding up Malaysian flags and banners supporting electoral reform from iconic sites like Sydney Harbour or Trafalgar Square. It was the most incredible people's movement the country had ever seen.

Despite his increasing criticism of the government, Dad did not take part in Bersih 3. For most of his political life, Dad had disapproved of demonstrations and protests, perhaps because most of them, as with the 1998 Reformasi protests, were against him. Like many of his generation, he believed that students should be studying and not marching in the streets. He was not convinced when my daughter tried to tell him that most students failed because they were partying, not protesting.

Still, it could not have escaped his notice that Bersih was a growing people's movement that was taking a stand against the government of Najib Razak. In the 13th General Elections in 2013, when Bersih's demand for indelible ink was met for the first time, the BN had again won the Federal Parliament with 133 seats but by the smallest majority it had ever had. Worse, it had lost the popular vote; more voters had voted against than for it. If it were not for gerrymandering, one of Bersih's biggest complaints, the opposition Pakatan Rakyat would have won. Each constituency, no matter its size, was represented by only one Member of Parliament. Their support in the urban centres with its large populations were negated by the BN's hold over the many more rural constituencies with smaller populations.

* * *

In 2013, Maria Chin Abdullah, a human rights activist and a colleague of mine in the women's groups, was made Chair of Bersih and Bersih 4 was held in August 2015. This time, instead of a one-day rally, it was to be held over the weekend, in several cities. Global Bersih had organized for rallies to be held in 70 cities around the world, marking the biggest show of solidarity by Malaysians for electoral reform in their home country. As it happened, I was in London at the time on holiday with my children and decided to join the march there.

In the UK I had no worries about safety since demonstrations are commonplace in that country. My two daughters and my husband were all going this time, along with some Malaysian friends we knew in London.

In the days leading up to the weekend, I kept in touch with friends back in KL on the progress of the preparations for the rally. At Dataran Merdeka they had planned not just speeches but music and performances for two days. Increasingly I began to wonder if Dad was going. He had become very vocal about his opposition to Najib especially when news about the 1MDB financial scandal in which the PM himself was implicated began to emerge. Bersih followers too were beginning to loudly criticise Najib. A convergence of causes seemed to be emerging.

Two nights before Bersih 4 was to take place, I texted Dad.

'Are you going to Bersih this weekend, Daddy?'

'I'm still thinking,' was the brief reply.

I thought that was encouraging, a big step from an absolute no.

Then on the eve of her first-ever rally, my younger daughter Shasha, then aged sixteen, wrote this on Facebook:

'Tomorrow will pretty much shift some tides in Malaysia. Although the government and anti-Bersih groups have gone through great lengths to

demonise the Bersih movement, it is, without a doubt, the greatest expression
I have ever seen of the true unity of Malaysians of all ages/genders/classes/
cultures/backgrounds coming together to empower, motivate, and support
each other—as well as push for much-needed change. As the year has gone
by, I have become increasingly aware of the many unanswered questions
and social injustices faced by the citizens of Malaysia—and although
I don't know everything—I am learning, and I am angry. I am angry
that as Malaysians, we do not have the democracy that we were promised,
and I'm angry that Malaysia is vulnerable to slowly regress into a close-
minded, conservative and narrow nation. Because that is not an accurate
representation of Malaysians. As a nation, we deserve freedom, we deserve
the right to question, we deserve the right to answers, we deserve the right
to make decisions collectively that can improve the country for everyone.
Bersih is for everyone.'

Apple. Tree.

I sent it to Dad with a note that said, 'This is what your granddaughter and many young people think.'

Whether she really influenced him to go to Bersih, I cannot say. But on that Saturday, he decided 'to have a look'. It is impossible for Dad to appear at anything so significant without everyone speculating as to his reasons. Whatever it was, his presence shook everyone up that day, from the participants at Bersih as undoubtedly also the government. When he returned to it the next day, taking an LRT with Mum and several other people, it was clear which side he'd laid his cap on.

Meanwhile it was a cool but sunny day in London on 29 August. My family and I, dressed in the yellow t-shirts specially brought from KL, intended to meet some friends for lunch before proceeding to the beginning of the march in front of the Malaysian High Commission in Belgrave Square. On the way we stopped at a stationery store to buy some cardboard and pens to make our protest signs. Running a bit late to meet our friends, I decided to go on ahead while the kids chose their protest materials. Which is why fifteen minutes later they arrived at lunch in a state of high excitement: on their way to meet me, they had bumped into Sir Jimmy Page, lead guitarist of the legendary rock band Led Zeppelin. He had declined to be photographed but had taken the time to chat with them, asking Shasha about the A-Levels she was taking. That encounter nearly overshadowed the other events of the day.

After lunch, which we spent writing slogans on our newly-bought cardboard, we took a bus to Hyde Park Corner and from there, walked the short distance to Belgrave Square, the leafy plaza built in the 19th century, one of the most expensive pieces of real estate in London. The buildings around the square, all uniformly white with tall porticos and balconies facing the gardens in the middle, house many embassies and institutions, including our High Commission at number 45. A wide road circles the gardens, and it was there that we met up with a large group of Malaysians waving flags and chanting 'Bersih, Bersih', facing the Malaysian flag fluttering from the balcony of our government representatives. Many of the participants were long-time UK residents but there were a few who said they had just arrived from Malaysia and had come directly from Heathrow airport to join in. Squeals and hugs came from friends I had not seen for a long time, as well as others who were also on holiday in the UK. A small number were students; most had stayed away for fear of being sanctioned for their participation and their scholarships taken away.

After a few spirit-rousing speeches, we began to walk from the square eastwards past the Mall where tourists take photographs outside the gates of Buckingham Palace, down towards the Houses of Parliament. As Big Ben loomed in front of us, we turned to the left to walk past Downing Street for a brief stop. We had hoped to attract the notice of David Cameron, then the British Prime Minister, but the security around No. 10 was very tight and we were told to stay away. Continuing our march, we finally arrived at Trafalgar Square, assembling in front of the National Gallery to listen to more speeches. By then the air had turned chilly, the clouds were grey and rain, the old English type, had begun to drench us. We were all better prepared this time, with windbreakers and umbrellas and although our group had thinned out, there were still the stalwarts who stayed for more speeches and chanting. Despite the weather, it had been a successful march; we were pleased to have shown solidarity with our friends back home. Our democracy is precious; we have to protect it from those intent on taking it away from us through corruption. As the poster that Shasha drew said: Only the *kotor* fear the *bersih*! Only the dirty fear the clean.

* * *

There are a few moments in my life when I have felt immensely proud of Dad. While there have been many areas of disagreement between us, when he does the unexpected right thing, something that aligns with my views, my heart swells so much I get teary.

That was what I felt when I saw a photo of him stepping off his flight on the morning of 19 November 2016 appeared on social media. He had been in Sudan at a conference of Islamic countries and I did not think he would return in time. But there he was looking fresh despite the long journey, smiling, wearing a yellow Bersih 5 t-shirt.

In fact, the foundation for his participation had already been laid in March of that year when Dad came up with the Citizens' Declaration, demanding the resignation of Najib Razak, for freedom of speech and a free media. What was remarkable about the Declaration was that it was signed by fifty-seven politicians and activists, including several former UMNO leaders as well as Dad's former rivals, the DAP's Lim Kit Siang and several of PKR's top leaders. NGOs and individuals then led a signature campaign that by May had garnered one million endorsements. I remember being at the first Citizens' Declaration forum at a hall in Shah Alam, Selangor and wondering if everyone else was noting the significance of seeing Dad onstage with people he had spent his entire career duelling with. In the case of Lim Kit Siang, Dad had even jailed him in Operation Lallang in 1987. But this common goal of ousting Najib could only be achieved if they worked together. The Citizens' Declaration was the first step towards building trust with one another to do just that. I watched them listen to each other's speeches as respectful equals and felt an excitement that I had never felt before.

Already the lead-up to the latest rally had been filled with activity. In the weeks before, Bersih had organized a 'road show' where members and supporters toured the country to persuade people to join the protest. For the first time I was asked to speak at a number of these small gatherings, mostly in Kedah my home state. I had never spoken at these types of assemblies before and at one session in Alor Setar, was a bit taken aback by the verve and passion of my fellow speakers, including Saifuddin Nasution of PKR and the young activists Adam Adli and Amir Abdul Hadi. When it came to my turn, the only woman speaker that evening, I decided to take a different tack. Lowering my voice to what I hoped was a steady calm, I spoke about my first experience of Bersih and why, as a mother concerned about the future of my children, I decided to go. The audience, which comprised of older men and women of all races, nodded but did not seem to respond very enthusiastically. Maybe it was just the Kedah reticence, but I had no idea if I had gotten through to them or not.

On 18 November 2016, the day before Bersih 5 was to take place, the police arrested Maria Chin under the detested Security Offences Special Measures Act (SOSMA) that allows detention, without charge, for up to twenty-eight days. Maria was a hardworking activist and had already successfully led one rally, following in the footsteps of Ambiga Sreenevasan. With the corruption scandals erupting all over the media involving the highest office of the land, the latest edition of the protest promised to be a big one. And we knew the government was scared of what it meant.

Typically, they reacted in the only way they knew how: through repression. My fellow activists got word in the afternoon that Maria had been carted off to the Petaling Jaya district police station and scrambled to go to her aid with lawyers. I heard the news while getting my hair done at a salon. That night I was to attend a dinner by *Prestige* magazine where I was to receive an award. Cutting my appointment short, I rushed to the police station to find media, lawyers and friends outside. We had no idea how long they would keep Maria for questioning. Her sons were concerned that she would need her medication but did not know how to get them to her.

Obviously, the government thought that cutting off the head of the movement would cause the body to fall away. But they had not understood that the spirit of Bersih resided in more than just one person. If anything, arresting Maria on the eve of the rally was exactly what would spur more people to attend it the next day.

That night I decided I could not go to the dinner. It didn't seem right to me to dress up and be feted at a five-star hotel when my friend was locked-up in a police cell. I had the awkward task of calling up Rubin Khoo, the editor of *Prestige*, to explain that I could not in all conscience attend that night. Thankfully, he understood and a friend of mine picked up the award on my behalf.

Unlike my first Bersih in 2011, I had no trepidation about attending Bersih 5. Despite threats from the government and attempts at intimidating participants by encouraging counter-rallies by the Red Shirts, an anti-Bersih group comprising primarily of UMNO members, people had become bolder. Going to protests had become normalized, at least in KL, something you do with your group of friends. Since this edition was to start near Bangsar, my party assembled at my house, took the requisite photographs, our thumbs held up in a gesture of togetherness and then walked the ten minutes to the starting point at the nearby LRT station. This time Tara came with us as our official photographer.

A large crowd had already assembled there, dressed in yellow and loudly chanting, cheering and waving signs. Activists such as Ambiga and politicians like Nurul Izzah Anwar, familiar faces from past protests, spoke. I was also given a speaking slot, but it was difficult to shout into a megaphone to make myself heard above the enthusiastic din. It didn't matter, we all knew why we were there.

The plan was to walk from Bangsar to Dataran Merdeka, the traditional destination for demonstrations in KL. We began walking the straight route to the square past the National Museum, the Moorish-styled KL railway station and the National Mosque, a distance of only three kilometres. At the junction where Jalan Bangsar met Jalan Travers, we were forced to stop. Ahead of us, flanked by the overhead pass on the right and houses and the Brickfields district police headquarters on the left, a squad of FRU trucks had lined up to block us. We heard rumours that their intention was to separate us from a Red Shirt group that was approaching from the other side. They too had lost their leader: Jamal Yunos, a young man with a penchant for newsmaking stunts, had also been arrested in the early hours of the same day.

Unable to proceed, and with no instructions coming from the online messaging service that Bersih had set up, we did what most Malaysians would do at lunchtime: we went to eat. Like a swarm of bees, the entire crowd turned right, crossed the small bridge over the Klang river into nearby Brickfields, an area famous for its banana leaf restaurants. Never had they been so full of people in uniform yellow filling their bellies with curry, rice and roti. Every table in every restaurant was occupied; people stood around waiting for others to finish eating so that they could have their seats. We managed to find a table and while waiting for further news, ordered lunch, chatting and laughing with people at the other tables. Demonstrations were obviously good for business. It felt like one big yellow party.

After we had been satiated with rice, curry and sweet hot tea, we received word that we were to head to the Kuala Lumpur City Center (KLCC), almost eight kilometres away. To get there, the choice was to either take a long hike or the Light Rapid Transit trains from Sentral station nearby. Walking to the station we bumped into Lim Kit Siang, the long-time head of the Democratic Action Party. He too was headed to the city center.

In the LRT station, long queues of yellow-clad people formed at the ticket booths. Somehow, we got our tickets fairly quickly and bundled into the packed coaches. They looked as if they were chartered for Bersih, so full were they of rally participants. When we finally got out at the KLCC stop, we saw people laughing and pointing behind us. Turning around, we too had to laugh. As the carriage emptied, the only person left was a young man in a red shirt, who tried his best to avert our stares. He needn't have feared anything: the Bersih crowd was a good-natured one and not inclined to violence.

Ascending the steps into the open air at the foot of the Petronas Twin Towers, I caught my breath as an amazing sight greeted me. Yellow-t-shirted human bodies covered every inch of ground around the Towers and on Jalan Ampang adjacent to it. Some were standing, some were sitting on whatever patch of ground that was available. Ahead of us, in front of Wisma Getah Asli, a tall glass-fronted office building, was a makeshift stage fashioned from the back of small truck.

Someone, I forget who, was speaking through a megaphone, the crowd roaring at every other sentence.

Tara and I headed for the stage. By then it seemed as if the organizers were making up the programme as it went but it didn't matter to the crowd who were relaxed and happy. Incredibly, there was no sign of any police, let alone the FRU. Perhaps the sight of what looked like 100,000 yellow shirts, sitting down peacefully on what is usually a busy road, at the foot of the iconic Towers, was too dramatic to do anything about.

By then I was wondering where my parents were. There were messages that they were coming to join us, but I had no idea how or when. With the roads fully occupied by protestors, no cars could come in. Discussing solutions with some of the Bersih committee, someone even suggested picking them up on motorcycles and bringing them to the stage. I had some difficulty picturing my Mum arriving in that way, although I'm sure she would have been game.

Then in the distance, at the junction of Jalan P. Ramlee and Jalan Ampang, I noticed a pickup truck with loudspeakers blaring out from above the driver's cabin. A tiny figure on it looked remarkably like Dad, surrounded by other people. Curious, I decided to make my way to it, picking my way through the protestors sitting on the road as if at a picnic. Halfway there, I came across Mum, sitting incongruously on a chair that had been placed in the middle of the road, my friend Ivy next to her. She looked as if it was the most natural thing in the world for a ninety-year-old woman, the wife of a former Prime Minister, to be calmly seated in the midst of thousands of protestors on a city road.

I walked up to her and, forgetting that she had just arrived from Sudan that morning, unceremoniously asked what she was doing.

'Oh, I'm just listening to Daddy. He's over there,' she said, pointing to the pickup, festooned with Bersih flags and placards.

'I think you'd better get into that pickup, Mum,' I said, 'because they're trying to move to the other stage.' Without a word of protest, she allowed Ivy and I to lead her to the car and gently help her into the cab. Dad was standing on the back, a megaphone held to his mouth by someone, surrounded by my brother Mukhriz and some burly men. I felt myself being pushed up onto it and slowly the pickup made its way towards the one I had come from, protestors cheerfully scrambling out of the way. Once we got within shouting distance of the other stage, I got Mum out of the cab and miraculously the chair reappeared, and she sat down.

With Dad on the second makeshift stage, and Mum safely seated next to me by the first, I got up to say a few words to the crowd. By then my voice had become hoarse and I couldn't think of anything inspiring to say. I choked up at the sight of the sea of yellow and could only congratulate the crowd for showing what Malaysia truly looks like, united for democracy and undivided by race, religion or class. I don't know if what I said reached Dad on the other stage. If it did, it would be the first time that we had both spoken on the same platform, a fact that didn't hit me until much later.

Meanwhile the sky above us was darkening and wind began to blow our hair onto our faces. I looked around, trying to figure out the fastest route to shelter that I could take Mum to if it started to rain. The buildings behind me were only accessible if I climbed over a fence; those were out of the question. Ahead of us was the KLCC mall. That was probably our safest bet, even though it would mean hotfooting it over the breadth of Jalan Ampang and crossing a plaza of fountains beyond it before arriving at the entrance of the mall.

The worry on my face must have been obvious; anyone could guess what I was thinking about. Just then, a woman rose from the crowd, came over and handed me a yellow plastic raincoat, folded into a little packet, and gestured towards Mum. It was one of the many moments of kindness that I have been privileged to witness at these rallies.

By the time it did rain some thirty minutes later, the entire rally broke up, scattering in all directions for shelter. A good number of yellow people wound up in KLCC mall, at various cafes facing the park, including my thirsty and tired friends. I needn't have worried so much about Mum and Dad because their security people made sure they got out of the rain and safely home. Drinking our hot lattes, I marvelled at how KLCC, with its expensive designer boutiques, had been taken over by a yellow wave symbolising equality that afternoon. Just another of those Malaysian contradictions.

That night I was invited by the Al-Jazeera TV network to speak on air about the rally. Along with me were two other commentators, one from Singapore and another from KL, who both said that Bersih 5 would have no impact on Malaysian politics, despite some 150,000 people, the largest number ever, having turned out to show their perasaan. My friends who watched the episode said that the incredulous look on my face as I listened to them was priceless. I had been there with the throngs, and so had Dad. If that was not a potent combination, I didn't know what was.

17

The 92-year-old Candidate

In the year after Bersih 5, I continued life as normal. My younger daughter Shasha had started school in England the year before, which meant that Tara and I had to show up for various parent-teacher days and other school events. In January 2017 her school messaged us to say that ShaSha, facing pressures as she headed towards her A-Levels, had said she didn't want to board at school anymore. As a minor she could not live on her own, so we had to ensure an adult stayed with her as she prepared for her exams. It was a difficult, not to mention expensive, few months for us as it disrupted all our plans. In 2017 I was turning sixty and had planned to give myself and Tara an adventure of a lifetime, a trip to Patagonia in Argentina. It was already paid for so we had to get Ineza to babysit her sister until we could return to take care of her in turns ourselves. It also meant that I was away from Malaysia for long periods of time including my birthday in June. But neither Tara nor I regretted it because our daughter needed us then. We were rewarded when she passed her exams with flying colours and got into the university of her choice.

In the midst of all this upheaval in my family, I didn't have time to keep track of what Dad was up to. I knew he was actively agitating against Najib through reading the news online and occasionally chatting with Mum but throughout 2017, I was not fully aware of his movements or who he was talking to. Chatter about impending elections was rife, competing with the increasingly mind-boggling scale of the 1MDB scandal.

I can't remember exactly when I caught up with Dad but it must have been a weekend some time in early 2018. Dad and I were seated at the long dining table at The Mines having tea. As always, he sat at the head of the table. I was seated on the right side of the table, a few chairs down. Mum had gone to her room upstairs, leaving Dad and I alone to chat.

In 2016, Dad had left UMNO for the second time and formed a new party Parti Pribumi Bersatu Malaysia along with Muhyiddin Yassin who had been fired by Najib Razak as Deputy Prime Minister after asking questions about 1MDB. I saw this as a move to attract UMNO members unhappy with Najib to leave the party for an almost carbon-copy party. I knew, as Dad saw it, the country was being raped and pillaged by corrupt leaders especially Najib Razak and something had to be done to stop them. I didn't understand then what he meant by 'stopping' Najib. I thought forums and petitions was all there was to do. But as he talked that afternoon as we sipped tea and munched on kuih, it began to dawn on me that he meant something more tangible than just shouting at the edges of power. Dad has never wanted power for its own sake, but he did and does believe that it's a necessary tool to change laws and policies that do not serve the country. Corruption was a constant theme; Dad felt that this time the rot had gone too deep, led by the 1MDB scandal. How would you expect the public to trust a government that was stealing its money?

It had not occurred to me until then that he was planning to stand for elections again. But as he talked about Najib possibly calling for elections soon and how Pakatan Harapan, the Alliance of Hope that his party had joined, needed to really go all out to win some seats, there was no mistaking the hints he was dropping. I stared at him as if he had just told me he was going to climb Mount Everest. Who on earth stands for elected office at age ninety-two? It was the most bizarre thing I'd ever heard of. But I should not have been surprised. Dad may have been in his tenth decade, but he was fit and healthy, with an upright back and a full head of hair. Most importantly, his mind was clear and lucid and nothing invigorates him more than a fight.

Still, the thought of him going on the campaign trail, with Mum inevitably trailing him, filled me with apprehension. Election campaigns require physical stamina like nothing else. I had followed my brother Mukhriz on just one given day in the 2008 campaign, the first time he stood for elections, and already I saw how taxing it was, rushing from one place to another, shaking hundreds of hands and making endless speeches so identical to one another you run the risk of zoning out mid-speech and losing your train of thought. It's hard enough for young men, what more a nonagenarian like Dad.

When the news spread within the family that Dad was going to stand at the next general elections, it sent a current of shock among the grandchildren. At the time, Dad's grandchildren were aged between thirty and eleven. When he retired in 2003, his oldest grandchild, my daughter Ineza, was sixteen and the youngest ones were not even born yet. It seemed inconceivable to them that he would be standing for elections again, with both the possibility of winning and joining the government again or losing and returning to normal life. The former wasn't the most desirable prospect for them, the latter, they knew, wasn't enough for him.

He said he had to stand because that would be the only way he would be able to lead the country out of the swamp of corruption it was then in. To do that, he had to win. That also meant that, given the odds, he had to campaign hard.

There's a reason why Dad doesn't like to tell us his most momentous decisions ahead of time. He hates being persuaded out of them, especially if we become emotional. This was why we didn't know he was going to announce his retirement in 2002. As it was, the fact that he had told me his intention to stand for elections in 2018 ahead of time was out of the ordinary. At the time nobody apart from Najib Razak really knew when the 14th General Elections would be held. I suppose, as far as Dad was concerned, given the uncertainties, it was as good as telling me at the last minute. No matter how much I screwed my face up in exasperation that day, there was nothing I could do to dissuade him.

I did not know then how that election was going to turn out, nor, for the first time ever, how involved I would become.

18

Nomination Day

If there was a way to gauge how shaky a government feels, the best would be to watch what tactics they deploy during an election campaign. The BN government was determined not to allow the Opposition, a coalition calling itself Pakatan Harapan (PH), the Alliance of Hope, the slightest chance of winning. Yet by doing so, it betrayed its own insecurities.

Ever since Najib Razak came to power, whenever friends and I talked about how terrible the political situation was, we inevitably circled back to the question of alternatives. The BN had ruled for so long it was hard to imagine another government that would have the experience to govern the entire country. Penang, Selangor, Kelantan and Terengganu had been ruled by Opposition parties with varying success but to rule at the Federal level was an entirely different proposition. Undoubtedly, there were popular Opposition figures but none really fit the bill as Prime Minister. By convention, the PM had to be Malay so Lim Kit Siang, even if he wanted to, was disqualified. Anwar Ibrahim had some Federal experience but he had been out of government for almost twenty years. Besides, in 2018 he was back in jail under another sodomy conviction. Every time this topic of leadership came up, we'd hold our heads in our hands in despair. Was there truly no one?

Already surprised that Dad was going to stand for elections again, I had not anticipated the next step, that he would be the Pakatan

Harapan candidate for Prime Minister. On the one hand, it was just crazy to have a ninety-two-year-old PM. On the other hand, it also made sense; he had more experience at governing than anyone else. For sure, not everybody in Pakatan Harapan welcomed the idea but they were hard put to name anyone who could bring the disparate parties together. For all the people who had beseeched me to ask Dad to return to the post, it meant a familiar steady hand.

Clearly the BN were unnerved by the prospect of the Pakatan Harapan being led by the man who had himself previously led them for twenty-two years. They knew he was a formidable tactician; after all he had led them to victory in five General Elections, most of them with strong majorities. They also knew that despite being now in the Opposition, Dad remains respected by many Malaysians, especially Malays. As much as they needed to treat him this time as an adversary, they still had to handle him with kid gloves.

These niceties get forgotten when you are desperate. Even before the campaign formally began, Pakatan Harapan held rallies called Jelajah Harapan, Hope Expeditions, all over the country. Stages, complete with backdrops featuring the faces of the PH leaders, were set up in any available outdoor space. The public would crowd into the area in front of the stages, standing or sitting on the ground, to listen to speakers they had never seen on the same stage before. There would be Lim Guan Eng from DAP, Azmin Ali and Saifuddin Nasution from PKR, the ever-popular orator Muhamad Sabu from Amanah and finally, always the last speaker, Dad.

The reaction to these 'expeditions' was raucous. Enthusiastic crowds appeared at each stop, encouraging the unlikely alliance of former enemies to challenge the incumbents. No wonder the BN government was nervous and began to put up as much hindrances as they could. First, in early April they de-registered Dad's Parti Pribumi Bersatu Malaysia 'temporarily', on the pretext of 'failing to furnish the minutes of meetings of its divisions and branches by the stipulated deadline'. Undaunted, both Dad and the Pakatan parties agreed to use the PKR logo, a white stylised eye against a bright blue background, as their common symbol. If anyone remembered that this logo was designed to symbolise the black eye Anwar Ibrahim got from the police after he was first arrested in 1998, they didn't mention the irony.

Next, the Election Commission decided that Polling Day would be a Wednesday, a move that drew howls of protest from the thousands of voters who had to take leave from their work to vote in their hometowns or villages. This was a move that I never understood. Surely having to vote on a weekday would also inconvenience BN voters. To this day, I have wondered how this was explained to their supporters. I suspect that the net effect of that decision was to further anger voters who saw it as denying their right to vote. Eventually, as often happens when they don't think things through, the government was obliged to declare Wednesday, 9 May, a public holiday.

Nomination Day, 28 April, spelled the beginning of a shorter-than-usual eleven-day campaign period. Dad was vying to become the Member of Parliament for the island of Langkawi, in our home state of Kedah, a place he had served as a young doctor straight out of medical school in 1955. Since he became PM the first time, he had focussed a lot of attention on the island, turning it from a lush but sleepy archipelago to a favourite holiday destination for both domestic and international tourists. During his retirement, Dad would spend many weekends on the island, driving his Toyota SUV and riding horses with his friends. It was a safe seat for him.

Candidates hoping to stand for a Malaysian election will find Nomination Day a nerve-wracking one. You have to turn up at the Election Commission office in the constituency you want to stand in with all your papers properly filled in, your proposers, seconders beside you, with RM10,000 as a deposit as well as an additional RM5000 to be used to clean up the mess your election posters and banners make after the campaign. What is most important is that you have your identity card with you. We Malaysians carry our National Registration Identity Cards with us wherever we go. Despite this, candidates have been known to forget them when going to fill in their nomination papers, as happened with one Pakatan Harapan candidate who left hers in a photocopying machine and only just managed to retrieve it in time. In 2018, people were getting disqualified for all sorts of reasons. The EC ruled for instance that Tian Chua, Vice-President of PKR, could not stand because he had been fined RM2000 in a court case, an odd ruling given that he had stood successfully in the previous election after having won a court judgment that allowed him to do so.

Dad was of course a veteran at filing nomination papers. But things could still go wrong.

My parents and those of us who were going to join him in Langkawi were due to fly to the island on Friday, 27 April, the day before Nomination Day, so that we would be fresh and relaxed the next morning. I had booked myself a ticket on the 1.25 p.m. Firefly flight to Langkawi and after accompanying my parents to file Dad's papers, was to leave for Penang to attend a rally there. Mum and Dad were flying with their entourage on a loaned private jet. At the last minute I was told they had a spare seat so decided to forego my ticket and join them.

I got to the Subang Private Jet terminal early at about 2 p.m. and sat in the waiting lounge for Mum and Dad to arrive. Our plan was to arrive in Langkawi at about 4 p.m. and proceed straight to the Election Commission office to check that they had all the necessary papers ready for the next day. The EC office was closing at 5 p.m.

Soon after my parents arrived, the pilot of the plane had a word with Dad. There was a technical problem with the plane which they were trying to fix. This would take some time and he was unsure when the plane would be ready to fly.

A major spanner was thrown into the day's plans. I had already missed my flight. The next commercial flight to Langkawi that day was at 4 p.m. or so, which would arrive on the island after the EC office had closed. If they could not fix the plane soon, the only option was to borrow another plane. Or drive.

Switching planes is not like switching cars. Even if there was one readily available, you cannot just roll out a plane from a garage, get into the cockpit and take off. You need to have a qualified pilot and crew, do all the necessary pre-flight technical checks and file a flight plan with the Department of Civil Aviation before you even start your engines. This would take at least an hour, if there was a plane and crew ready.

Driving to Langkawi was not a viable option either. It would take about seven hours to drive to Kuala Perlis, get on a ferry to do the one-hour crossing to Kuah, the main town on the island. By then it would be late at night and my parents would be exhausted, in no state to check important papers.

I'm not one for conspiracy theories but it did seem more than a coincidence that on the day that we absolutely had to get to Dad's would-be constituency, there seemed to be no way of getting there. None of us were qualified to know whether there was anything truly wrong with the plane we were using but we had to accept that, to all our intents and purposes, it was out of commission. As always, Dad remained calm while the rest of us paced anxiously about the room, making phone calls and discussing alternatives for transport.

We did know several people with their own private planes but either they were unavailable, or it would take too long to get one ready. Flying commercial was an option with Subang Airport right next door but as it was the beginning of the weekend, flights to the holiday island were full, and none would have gotten us there on time. As the afternoon wore on, we were running out of options.

At a time when Dad was persona non grata in the country, friendships are tested by situations like this. As she listened to all our worried discussions, my sister-in-law Mastisa, who was also scheduled to fly with Mum and Dad to Langkawi, looked up and saw a friend walk into the waiting lounge just then. A wealthy businessman, he was about to fly to Singapore on his own jet, a jet that was sitting on the tarmac ready and waiting to take off.

Mastisa leapt up and went to talk to him. She explained the situation, our urgent need to get to Langkawi that afternoon and our plane troubles. Listening to her and looking around and seeing Mum and Dad quietly waiting, he did not hesitate. 'Take my plane,' he said, 'I can go later.'

There were no words for our gratitude just then. The pilot of the friend's plane still had to file a new flight plan but at least he and the crew were ready. Within an hour or so, we were all seated and buckled in. I was still tense from the drama of the almost cancelled trip. Dad, on the other hand, dressed in a red shirt with the Bersatu stylised hibiscus logo embroidered on his left breast, his name beneath the Malaysian flag on his right, fell asleep immediately, as was his habit on any flight.

As we flew the one hour or so north to Langkawi, we did not know that there was more drama in the cockpit. Our pilot was being denied permission to land in Langkawi and ordered to divert to Penang instead, a clear attempt to delay us even more. My parents, my sister-in-law and I, exhausted from the drama before take-off were oblivious to what was going on. Only later, after we had landed safely in Langkawi, to be greeted by Dad's relieved staff and supporters, were we told what happened. I really don't know how it was resolved unless someone with a cool head and a conscience decided to ignore whoever issued the diversion order. Still the entire episode sent chills down my spine, the first time in my life that I had felt unsafe within my own country, knowing there were possible attempts to jeopardize my family's safety.

Good news greeted us upon landing. One of Dad's people had negotiated with the EC office to stay open late to cater to our delayed arrival. This was a good thing because Dad's itinerary also included a 'high tea' with the Chinese and Indian communities in a local hotel. The plan had been to attend it after checking his papers but now the schedule could be reversed. After a quick freshen-up at the hotel in Kuah, we entered the function room where a crowd of people sat at round tables laden with kuih and tea. At one end of the room, a small stage had been set up for Dad to speak at. Technically he could not campaign until the next day after filing his nomination papers so this event was merely to 'introduce' himself to his potential voters, even though most of them had known him for years. It's one of the many 'meet and greet' events that are obligatory for politicians. To my delight, I found that three of my cousins had arrived from Alor Setar, so it became a welcome family reunion for us.

After tea we took the short ride to the EC office, a small one crowded with staff readying themselves for the next day's event and the following eleven days' activities. I must say that the staff were friendly but stayed focussed on their work, professionals all the way. Their role to ensure free and fair elections would be so crucial in this historical event. They didn't make a fuss seeing their former Prime Minister sitting quietly in the office, his wife, looking wan and exhausted, in a pink floral baju kurung.

The papers were checked through to the most minute detail by Dad's lawyer and found to be complete. Only then could we finally get to our hotel rooms, relax and sleep.

* * *

The next morning, bright and early, I dressed in a blue baju kurung, the colour of Pakatan Harapan, and joined my parents for breakfast. Both were dressed in the bright red of Bersatu, Dad in traditional baju Melayu and Mum in a batik baju kurung, printed with giant versions of the Bersatu hibiscus accessorised with a Pakatan Harapan blue shawl and a simple string of pearls. In her hand, she held a folding paper fan. As a veteran of several Nomination Days, she knew what a necessary piece of equipment it was.

Before we left for the nomination centre, there were two things to do. One was to say a doa or prayer that things would go well and smoothly. The other was to check that Dad had his identity card.

'Show us your IC!' Mum and I insisted.

Dad looked at us aghast.

'I have it!' he said, irritated.

'Show us!'

We weren't satisfied until he took it out of his wallet and displayed it. We were not going to allow a missing IC to derail anything that morning.

The nomination centre was at the Langkawi District and Land Office, a large horizontal building with a pale orange tiled roof and a triangular peak jutting out from its middle, a typical government ode to 'local' architecture. It sits facing the main road, Jalan Pantai Kok, that had, that morning, been blocked and fenced off by the police to prevent party supporters from amassing in front of the building. A large tent had been set up in front of the office, from which the Election Officer would announce the names of the candidates.

On that sweltering morning, the plan was to gather some way before the nomination centre and walk to it, followed by cheering supporters, to show strength and confidence. Mum and Dad, due to their age, stayed in the car until we were a few metres from the centre while the rest of us walked alongside them. Already a large crowd of Pakatan supporters had gathered, wearing a variety of t-shirts with either the Pakatan logo, or Bersatu's. Some t-shirts even had Dad's face on them. I had been tasked to collect as many t-shirts as I could for archival purposes by the Malaysian Design Archive but apart from literally taking people's shirts off their backs, I didn't see how I could do this.

Mum, my brother Mokhzani, his wife Mastisa and I, with umbrellas, folding fans and sunglasses, walked beside Dad, trying not to get jostled by the eager crowd, until we got to the barrier on the left side of the District Office. On the far side, also behind fences was a crowd of navy blue, the supporters of the incumbent Member of Parliament, BN's Datuk Nawawi Ahmad. That year there was a three-cornered fight. Between the BN and our supporters, was a smaller group of green, those who had come to support the PAS candidate, Zubir Ahmad. Each crowd tried to outdo the other with chants and cheers, as if the louder one would get more votes. Amidst the cacophony, and it may have been just my imagination, I thought both the BN and PAS crowds quietened in respect when Dad turned up.

When we got to the barrier and only Dad and his seconder and lawyer could go further, he turned to Mum and gave her a big hug. They had gone to nominations many times, but both knew that this was different, that the stakes were much higher than all the previous elections. She clung to him as if he was leaving for a long time even though filing his papers would take no more than an hour. My brother, sister-in-law and I kissed him and then watched him cross the barrier and head on foot towards the District Office. It was my first time accompanying him on Nomination Day; I hadn't realized how humbling the actual process is, like putting in a job application where any imperfections on the form would be reason enough to spike it.

The sky was impossibly blue, and the sun was beating down on us. Rivulets of sweat started running down our batik-clad backs. I started wondering if we had to spend the entire hour or so standing out in the heat while we waited for Dad to return. I feared whether Mum would be able to do so, although always the trouper, she would not have complained.

Someone suggested that we retreat to a cooler place. As it happened, the nearest building with air-conditioning was just a few metres away. That was how Mum, my sister-in-law, I and some women accompanying us found ourselves sitting on some upholstered cane sofas, in a traffic police station. I'm not sure that the young policemen and women working behind the desks in that small office were entirely comfortable with us taking residence there, but they were polite and let us stay. They were not expecting much traffic complaints that day anyway.

We sat on those floral sofas for about an hour, glad to be out of the heat and off our feet, while outside we could still hear Dad's supporters keeping up their chants and cheers. It's funny but in a police station, even if you haven't committed a crime, you still feel you can't talk about anything more than the most mundane things. Certainly, we didn't feel right talking politics in what is supposed to be a neutral space. We were just grateful for the comfort. Just by the sofa, there was a transparent plexiglass box for donations towards a fund to upkeep a surau in the Langkawi police station. Mum decided a donation was a small way of thanking them for their hospitality. Eventually, the police personnel overcame their shyness and asked for photographs with Mum. It was not every day that a former (and possibly soon-to-be) Prime Minister's wife takes shelter in your office.

After about forty minutes, news came that they were about to announce the candidates' names for the Langkawi seat. Mum insisted on returning to the barriers outside the District Office again. With plenty of umbrellas overhead, we made our way back to the front of the crowd. In the distance we could hear someone testing the microphones from the tent that had been erected. Finally, we heard a voice, male, bureaucratically-dispassionate, over the loudspeaker announcing the candidates for the seat of P004 Langkawi. 42,697 voters would have a choice of three candidates, among them, Tun Dr Mahathir Mohamad. Dad.

A loud cheer rose up when Dad's name was announced. Before returning to us, he took time to walk to greet his supporters lined up with flags and banners behind the barriers. Their cheers alternated between 'Hidup Tun!' 'Long Live Tun' and 'Reformasi', two concepts that nobody could have foreseen being shouted together just two years before. Next to them, the PAS group tried to muster as loud a cheer for their candidate as they could. The two groups traded some good-natured bantering. Langkawi is a small enough island and everyone knew each other. Despite their support for different candidates, neighbours were not inclined to hostility towards one another.

Eventually Dad made his way back to us. Again, he gave Mum a hug. Her emotions were barely constrained, a mixture of relief and trepidation. Relief that his candidacy had been accepted, and anxiety at what lay ahead, a gruelling campaign with little of the resources that they had always enjoyed when they were in government.

A brief word about the disparity in resources between the government and the opposition during election campaigns. The government, and by that, I mean the BN government that had ruled for sixty years, had a huge advantage because they had vast resources to deploy every time they went to the polls. They had the money to print posters, banners, billboards and t-shirts and to pay volunteers. They had literally all the media to themselves, since they owned most of it. Their candidates had the support of a well-oiled campaign machine, with hundreds of volunteers ready to set up ceramah, or talks, knock on doors and hand out goodies to voters. On polling day, they were ready with cars and vans to ferry people to the voting stations.

On the other hand, the Opposition barely had any coverage in the media unless they said or did something scandalous or there was a novelty factor like Tok Mun, or Maimun Yusof, a ninety-four-year-old woman who stood in the Kuala Terengganu parliamentary seat in the 2013 General Elections. The entire government machinery was at BN's service, even though technically they are meant to be neutral. They also had planes and helicopters at their beck and call to travel to the remotest areas to campaign. In contrast, the Opposition had very little such resources, relying only on the generosity of supporters and volunteers.

In 2018, Dad worried constantly about money to campaign with. Even though people were volunteering their time and energy, there was still a need to pay for transport or sound systems or whatever was necessary just to get candidates in front of people. In a moment of quiet at home, long before the campaign, my brothers and I had just finished dinner with my parents when Dad started talking about selling his house in order to finance the Pakatan effort. I was startled: had it really come to that? But I understood why he felt the need for something so drastic. The wealthy donors who usually supported him in previous campaigns when he was the incumbent Prime Minister were shying away, perhaps for fear of reprisals from the BN government. No mainstream media would give him or any of the Pakatan candidates any time at all. The BN idea was to make the Pakatan Harapan invisible, so that voters would have no alternative. As the Malay saying goes, you can't love what you don't know.

But this was the age of the Internet. If you can't get on TV, there is always YouTube and Facebook. The Opposition Manifesto and any other messages could be passed on WhatsApp and Twitter. The former proved to be particularly effective, as Pakatan messages were viralled from one person to another, from one chat group to the next at a dizzying speed. I have no idea who those volunteers were who created videos, posters and memes that could easily be passed around through social media. I suspect that only a few of these originated from PH headquarters, the rest were organically created and spread by their supporters. One of my favourites was a meme that showed a photo of Dad and the caption: Please PM me. If nothing else, Pakatan had plenty of wit.

I have to say I liked the rawness of the Pakatan campaign. Although someone had certainly devised a corporate look and format for the rallies and money was found to build the stages and sound systems for the big ones in Melaka and Putrajaya, I went to the small ones where people made do with whatever was available. It felt more sincere and heart-warming. People volunteered because they wanted to, often using their own money to pay for whatever was needed. Stages were fashioned out of the backs of lorries, on top of vans, balconies and whatever was deemed suitable. The Pakatan campaign was truly a people's campaign.

* * *

Campaigning officially began as soon as the candidates were confirmed. For Dad, his first campaign stop was immediately after finishing at the nomination centre. We headed straight to a local hotel to attend, bizarrely, a wedding. Or rather, a double wedding. A son and daughter of a local grandee were having a wedding reception at lunchtime. Thankfully, they provided us first with a room to rest in, one that was dominated by a large double bed with barely any space to move in. All five of us, Mum, Dad, my brother, his wife and I, were grateful to have about half an hour to ourselves, a respite from the crowds and heat. As usual, Dad took a power nap while the rest of us sat with Mum on the bed and chatted about the morning's events. It was a brief moment of normalcy and intimacy, without anyone else watching over us, where we could let our guard down, take off our shoes, for a little while. These moments are precious for those of us involuntarily thrust into public life. While our smiles in public are genuine, it still feels good to not have to smile at strangers all the time, to not be stared at and scrutinized every second of the day.

After that short merciful break, we went down to attend the reception, with Mum and Dad still dressed in their red nomination outfits. In the ballroom, a stage with two pelamin, decorated with lots of pink and white flowers, had been set up. Both couples, who looked so alike it was hard to tell who the siblings and who the in-laws were, sat on the double daises to be photographed with family and friends. In true modern Malaysian style, one bride, dressed in an ice blue gown with a tight-fitting bodice and a skirt that flared out to the floor, a toning hijab with a tiara on top of her head, sat next to her new husband in a matching blue suit that looked rather rumpled. The other couple were all in white; the bride also in a flowing long gown with a peplumed top, a matching white hijab and tiara on her head, a bouquet in her hands, her bespectacled groom looking lost in his white suit that fitted a teeny bit too tightly over his middle. Somewhere in the room, a gaggle of young girls in matching outfits and hijabs had earlier done service as the bridesmaids in the bridal entourage, a modern innovation modelled after Western weddings.

We ate the traditional Malay lunch, took photographs and after an hour, could return to our hotel to rest. I had to pack to leave for my flight to Penang, where my own campaign adventure would begin.

19

The Campaign

I stood on the stage, my eyes prickling as if I had rubbed them with onions. Before me, on the grassy field in the middle of Georgetown, Penang known as The Esplanade, one hundred thousand mobile phones lit up and waved side to side creating white arcs of light, dizzying in their multitudes. Gigantic flags bearing the logo of the People's Justice Party, or its Malay initials PKR, fluttered and flapped high above the heads of the people filling every inch of the field that fronts the Georgetown City Hall. Cars in the surrounding streets honked in support. Vuvuzelas, those horns ubiquitous during the World Cup in South Africa, screeched their loud piercing screams. Hawkers selling local street food, the fragrant scent of fried noodles breezing faintly towards me, called out to the throng to fill their stomachs and quench their thirst while waiting.

Behind me, the waves of the Straits of Malacca lapped at the sea wall backing the stage. The night was cool but perhaps it was my nerves that made it seem warmer than it was. Eager faces, more than I had ever faced before, smiled up at me, waiting. My heart began to beat twice as fast as it normally does, my knees began to wobble, I could feel a trickle of sweat make its way down my back beneath the cotton of my baju kurung. Would my voice even make its way from the pit of my stomach out of my mouth? What could I possibly say to all these people?

Just an hour earlier that evening, Dyana Sofya from the Democratic Action Party (DAP), my assistant Chao, and I had been stuck. Our black MPV, with its comfortable cream leather seats, had sped us from Butterworth on the mainland only to come to a grinding halt on the narrow streets of Georgetown, choked by what seemed like thousands of cars and motorcycles. Ahead of us, the other MPV in our convoy also stopped and its door slid open. Lim Guan Eng, incumbent Chief Minister of Penang, hair permanently slicked down as always, leapt out and ran over to us.

'I'm going to get on a motorbike and go on.' he announced.

I looked at him aghast. Dressed in my prim floral baju kurung, I could not picture myself riding pillion on a motorcycle. Besides, whose bike would I be on?

'I can't do that!' the amateur campaigner that I was whined. It was the first day of campaigning for the 14th General Elections and we had already spoken at one rally on the mainland and were due to speak at a second at the Esplanade.

The rally at Butterworth, across the narrow strait from Penang island, was the first one I had spoken at. Ever. I had gotten up onto a small wooden stage ablaze with light, the light blue PH logo behind me and what looked like a dark sea of anonymous faces stretching out in front. It was my debut and as debuts go, by my standards, I was just acceptable, managing to say some words in Bahasa Malaysia, without my brain freezing up too much. Still, voters had never seen me on the campaign trail before so perhaps for them I was a novelty. In the twenty-two years and five General Elections that Dad had been on, I had never once gone on the hustings.

There were many reasons for this. Firstly, I had an aversion to politics, especially party politics, believing it to have too many rules and the possibility of excommunication if you broke them. Secondly, with the Barisan Nasional in power ever since we achieved independence in 1957 and seemingly impossible to topple, there did not seem any compelling reason to campaign for the party that Dad led. At the same time, as a non-governmental activist working on human rights issues, people often thought I was more aligned with the Opposition, but I was not interested in campaigning for them either. I didn't particularly trust that coalition of strange bedfellows, Islamists, Socialists and former defectors from Dad's party UMNO. I could just see the sort of headlines that would scream across the front pages the next day: 'Mahathir's daughter rebels, campaigns for other side', 'Daughter vs Father: Who Will Win?' I didn't want to spend my time explaining myself to the public via the media.

And finally, Dad had never asked me to come along when he went campaigning. Perhaps he knew I did not have the heart for it. Or perhaps he thought I might not be an asset. Either way I was unfamiliar with the campaign trail, what it felt like, what it sounded like, what makes people come out to listen to those they would vote to rule them.

* * *

When Dad stepped down in 2003, I felt only relief. For more than two decades, not only did I have to share my father with the entire nation, but I was also put in the spotlight. Not so much because I was his daughter but because I was his daughter as well as a newspaper columnist and an HIV/AIDS and women's rights activist. My fortnightly column did not always directly confront him, but it was clear that there was more than one occasion when my opinion on issues such as sex education, condom distribution, gender equality and freedom of expression and speech put me on the opposite side of the government. In a country where the government was personified by Dad, in the public imagination my honest and direct opinions also put me at odds with him. So curious was the public about this seeming conflict between Dad and I that it became the stock question that I had to endure in every interview I faced. I would reply truthfully that in fact, Dad had no time to read my columns and therefore was not particularly aware that I was supposed to be this unfilial daughter. But still those questions persisted.

When I finally stopped being 'The PM's Daughter' in 2003, I also came to a sudden realization. Never having gone campaigning at any of the previous general elections meant that there was a huge gap in my life experience. If I were inclined to write a book about those years—I am known as a writer after all—how would I ever describe those campaigns which impacted so much on my family's life? What would

I ever have to say about them? All I could talk about with any authority was the aftermath.

As an adult, I often sat with my parents and other party members in the Operations Room where the results came in. In 1982 when I was still a young writer at *Her World* magazine, I went along to what was then Rumah Malaysia on Jalan Ampang, before it was sold to the Brunei government, on Election Night. In those days, security was more relaxed, and my face was all I needed for clearance to enter. The media could mill around, talk to whoever was there and take photos whenever they wanted. At one point I went to talk to Dad and his Deputy Musa Hitam as they sat on a sofa together watching the results come in. The photographers immediately raised their cameras and that photo of my head behind the sofa, the two leaders turning back to talk to me, became one of the many illustrating that winning night.

Since then, I had been at every polling night venue, watching the computers and cheering—mostly cheering, but occasionally grieving—as the results came in. In the later years, the media was not allowed to so freely wander in, observe the VIPs watching the results and partake of the grand buffet with all sorts of the spicy and, quite honestly, stodgy food invariably laid out in the adjoining dining room. This was particularly true in 1999, the year of the economic crisis, the sacking of Deputy Prime Minister Anwar Ibrahim for alleged sodomy and the beginning of the Reformasi movement in its wake. The Barisan Nasional was not as certain of a win so Dad and his colleagues decided to wait out the results on their own, without the media present, in case it was not as good as it usually was. Only when it was clear who had won, would they go downstairs to the media centre to give a press conference. 1999 was not a great year; although the Barisan Nasional still won, they had not fared as well as before, losing for the first time two of the thirteen states, Kelantan and Terengganu. Still, at the Federal level, Dad remained firmly in power.

After Dad stepped down, I decided that I should make up for my lack of campaign experience at the next general elections. In 2004, the Barisan Nasional under the new Prime Minister Abdullah Ahmad Badawi had a landslide victory. Again, it had seemed inevitable and I did not see the point in following the campaign. But in 2008, my youngest brother Mukhriz, until then a businessman, decided to stand for a Parliamentary seat in our home state of Kedah, the first of my six siblings to take an active part in politics.

While Dad had been in office, he had never expressly prohibited us, his children, from joining his political party. I had no interest in joining any party at all, being averse to such organized politics, although many people did not seem to realize this. I was at a meeting in Washington DC once when someone from an American think-tank asked me what my role in UMNO was. I stared at him puzzled for what seemed like a full minute before I replied that I wasn't even a member. Mirzan and Melinda were also uninterested. Mokhzani was the only one who joined the party and had served as treasurer of UMNO Youth for five years, an appointed post. But any ambitions he might have had were extinguished when, amid claims of nepotism, Dad forbade him to stand for elections anywhere. Mukhriz was all of seventeen, too young to even vote, when Dad first became Prime Minister and it was only after Dad retired that he finally applied to join the party at the branch that Dad had last headed, in Kubang Pasu, Kedah.

Expecting to contest in Dad's old constituency of Kubang Pasu, he was instead placed in nearby Jerlun where he knew almost no one, and where they certainly did not know him. Party workers tend to welcome local candidates and not a young slickly-dressed scion who had been educated in Japan. The previous BN candidate from Jerlun was also not pleased at having to give way to Mukhriz, regarding him as a 'parachute candidate', an outsider dropped into a place where nobody knew him. He was a senior member of that local branch and his workers were loyal to him.

The only saving grace for Mukhriz in 2008 was the head of the Wanita UMNO in Jerlun. It turned out to be Maznah Hamid, a businesswoman who had gained fame for Securicor, the successful security company she founded, a flamboyant woman whose publicity photos showed her holding a gun, James Bond-style.

Maznah, in her mid-50s, was loud and dressed in bright richly-embellished clothes even when campaigning in the villages. Not only was she a loyal party member and a local Kedahan, but she was also supremely well-organized, having spent most of her career training and barking orders at male security guards. Realizing that the novice candidate needed help, she rolled up her sleeves and set her ladies to work, organizing the teams that would go house to house campaigning, making sure that banners and posters were in place, and ensuring food and drinks at every campaign stop.

It was against this backdrop that I decided to observe my first election campaign. My other brothers had already done their stints following their youngest sibling around so one Thursday I flew up to Alor Setar with Tara, my husband, to join Mukhriz as he campaigned in the villages in his constituency. Kedah state is known as the Rice Bowl of Malaysia for good reason. From the air, its flat landscape is a chequered pattern of the padi fields that produce the most rice in the country. In the rural areas, most people are Malay farmers although there are also small pockets of Chinese rice-millers and Indian labourers.

Campaigning in any election takes stamina. In Malaysia where election campaigns only run for two weeks at most, candidates have to be prepared for long days, little sleep and lost voices from the multitude of speeches at every stop. They also have to learn the art of eating just enough to not offend their hosts and at the same time not fill their stomachs too much at the many meals offered at every village community center or town hall they visit. Candidates in rural constituencies have to be prepared to travel long distances to meet their voters, and to nod, smile and speak at each of these stops.

Arriving in Alor Setar, I was driven in an SUV to join Mukhriz and his campaign team in a small village, a short walk into the padi fields not far from the irrigation canals that make those fields so productive. I had been advised by Mum to dress conservatively with a scarf to cover my hair, so I wore a cotton baju kurung and a light scarf casually draped on my head and around my shoulders.

The routine is the same in every village: first we eat the meal prepared by the local womenfolk, usually featuring a speciality of the area, sitting under a tent set up for such a purpose. It is hot and muggy and veteran female campaigners, which I was obviously not, know to bring folding fans along to keep themselves cool. After the meal and perhaps a short break to say prayers, the speeches begin.

The same protocols are observed at each stop. First the party branch head speaks, then it's the candidate's turn. I worried in case I might be asked to say something, an older sister's endorsement of her kid brother perhaps, but nobody asked, to my relief. Mostly I busied myself with the women, fascinated by how dedicated they were to supporting candidates in the most tangible, and stereotypically female, ways: preparing food and drink and clearing up afterwards. But they are also the engine without which no election campaign can succeed. The women I spoke to knew exactly the lay of the land in their constituency: who will vote for their candidate, who will definitely not and who can be persuaded. Like corporate executives, they had whiteboards charting their daily strategies and whose doors they needed to knock on. Even if we may not have agreed on some issues, I came away with a healthy respect for these grassroots women, whose hard work is often forgotten until time for another election.

Then it is off to another village and another before a short break for dinner and a quick freshen up. In the evening there is usually a gathering to meet the local Chinese leaders; the next day, to join the local Thai community in their annual Songkran or water festival celebrations. On and on it went for fourteen days, village after muddy village, shaking hands, smiling until your cheek muscles ached. I stayed for only twenty-four hours and it was more than enough to persuade me that no sedentary unfit person should ever stand for office. Not if they valued their health.

* * *

'You stay in the car, OK? It'll take you another 40 minutes to get to the Esplanade,' Guan Eng said, just before speeding off on the back of a motorbike, driven by a party supporter.

I got back into the car with Dyana and Chao and we slowly made our way through the traffic. The driver knew his Georgetown streets well. He found gaps in the traffic he could squeeze the MPV through and soon the traffic cleared and in twenty minutes we arrived at the large field in front of the white colonial-era buildings that housed the Penang City Hall.

Some Penang party members from the Democratic Action Party (DAP) were on hand to meet us. The DAP had come into power in the state in 2008 in Pak Lah's disastrous second General Election where he managed to lose the two most prosperous states, Selangor and Penang, to two of the Opposition component parties, PKR and DAP. Despite constant conflict with the BN-ruled Federal government especially after Pak Lah was forced to resign and Najib Razak took over as Prime Minister, Penang had thrived under Lim Guan Eng and the DAP. Penangites were prosperous and felt some level of freedom to promote their own diverse cultures. Mustering them to come to the Esplanade that night was no problem for the DAP.

As I got out of the car, I could smell the excitement in the mugginess of the night, heard what sounded like a carnival in progress, a loud voice shouting something unintelligible over the speakers. My stomach started rumbling, whether from hunger or nervousness I wasn't sure. I wondered if there were clean bathrooms within the vicinity.

'Come with us, come with us,' the party officials said, as they led us towards the stage set up on one side of the field, facing the city away from the busy waters of the Straits of Malacca. I followed them unsure of what was happening and what I was supposed to do. Nobody had really briefed me on the programme for the evening, other than that I had to speak twice, once in Butterworth and once on the island. As in the first event, I expected to be taken to seats set up in front of the stage and to wait for my turn to speak.

To my surprise my hosts led me straight up the steps of the stage. It was brightly lit and there were a number of people seated on chairs placed on it including Guan Eng and some others who looked vaguely familiar, smiling at me in greeting. I heard my name being announced:

'*Tuan-tuan dan puan-puan, beri tepukan untuk tetamu utama kita,* Marina Mahathirrrrrr!!!!'

'Ladies and gentlemen, please put your hands together for our main guest, Marina Mahathirrrrr!!!'

And I found myself at the front of the stage facing the crowd.

I stood there speechless, moved beyond words. In the two previous election campaigns in 2008 and 2013, I had gone to a few rallies to listen to Opposition candidates, but they were mostly in cramped fields in between public housing flats or in small village halls. Never had I seen a crowd this big at a rally, stretching from just below my feet to the furthest reaches of that huge *padang*, where people normally congregate to play football, fly kites in the sea breeze or just to stroll in the evenings. In fact, neither had any politician of any party during any election campaign in Malaysia. People had never been this interested in elections before; there had never been any point in the previous elections. Malaysians had been resigned to the BN winning over and over again.

But something was different about this one. Perhaps it was sheer weariness at sixty years of the same old, same old; the same people, the same policies, the same sense that nobody was listening, the same tactics of pitting us against each other by race and religion. Perhaps it was the unbelievable greed of Najib Razak and his wife Rosmah, with their luxurious lifestyle, their expensive clothes and handbags, their playing golf with world leaders and celebrities while their people suffered under rising costs, seemingly uncontrolled crime and unnatural disasters like floods caused by deforestation which left the poor and the not-so-poor alike homeless and living in shelters for weeks on end. Perhaps it was the blatant attempts at stacking the odds against the Opposition by gerrymandering the constituencies, arresting anyone who openly dissented with the government, even by declaring polling day on a Wednesday, a workday. Whatever it was, this election campaign seemed to have electrified people, roused them from a deep depression and given them the tiniest spark of hope. And so, they turned up.

Once I got over my shock at the raucous reception the crowd gave me, I started reaching into my bag to look for my phone. As a novice campaigner, I wanted to record the moment. Guan Eng looked at me bemused. The 'professional' politicians had assistants and official photographers recording these events for them. I only had Chao, and at that moment I couldn't see her. After several awkward seconds I fished out my iPhone and set about videoing the sight in front of me. The crowd roared again, delighted. Gigantic light blue, red and white flags, symbolising Pakatan Harapan, waved, several hundred flashlights went off.

It was not yet my turn to speak, that was only to introduce me to the crowd, to show them that I was there, all the way from Kuala Lumpur just to speak to them. After the usual protocols were followed with local politicians speaking first, I was called up again.

What was I to say to all those eager faces? There they were, men and women, young and old, representing all of Malaysia's diverse communities, looking up at me expectantly.

It was probably just a few seconds, but it seemed a lifetime before I remembered that although I was born sixty miles to the north in the neighbouring state of Kedah, I did have Penang in my blood. My great-grandfather Iskandar had landed here from India in the 19th century, and my grandfather Mohamad was born and brought up on the island and had taught at that august institution, the Penang Free School before he was appointed headmaster of the Government English School in Alor Setar and settled there. Penangites are indeed my people and they are not unaware of this family history.

'*Apa habaq* Pulau Pinang? How are you, Penang?!' I finally called out in my best northern dialect, the dialect I had grown up with.

'*Baikkkkkkk*! Good!!' came the response from what sounded like a hundred thousand of my family members, delighted that I spoke the same language as they, with its distinctive flat 'A's and its implied consonant word ending, an accent difficult to fake. I was at home.

I am not a politician, I have no stock speech, no promises I can make. Instead, I decided to tell the story of how, instead of enjoying his retirement playing with his grandchildren, my father had decided to return to politics to save the country from those who, through greed and corruption, were destroying it. I told of the incident the day before when Dad's plane flying him to Langkawi island where he was to file his nomination papers 'suddenly' had technical problems and we had to find alternatives at an impossibly short notice in order not to miss the filing deadline and how, miraculously, a friend had offered his private jet. I talked about how the ruling party had thrown every obstacle at us, from delineating the electoral boundaries to give them the advantage, to hastily passing the Anti-Fake News Act aimed at any criticism of their government, to attempting to ban Dad's new political party, to declaring polling day on a Wednesday. These were the acts of a party that was afraid of its own people, I said. The rakyat, the people, should therefore not be afraid to show them who is really boss.

If you have never spoken to a responsive crowd in a political rally, like I had not before then, then you would never experience that feeling of being in total communion with people who, as long as you treated them with respect, will do everything they can to encourage and support you. I'm sure not everybody in that gigantic crowd had ever read my columns or knew what I had been doing before this night. Perhaps some of them even disapproved of the stand I have taken on human rights or my support for the most vulnerable people in our society, those who most people did not or would not see, like sex workers, drug users, LGBT communities and people with HIV. But that night we bonded like people in love, feeding off each other's energy. I could feel a tingling in every atom of my body as I looked at the thousands of mobile phone lights, the smiles on the faces of those nearest to the stage, sitting on the grass, fanning themselves in the sweltering moistness of the island heat, the waving flags and banners that simply said *Ubah*! Change!

'This is crazy,' I thought. 'I've never done this before, but they seem to like what I'm saying.' It all felt oddly natural to me. I felt safe, I felt comfortable. And I heard a little voice inside me say, 'You know how to do this, my girl!'

Malaysian crowds come to campaign rallies not just to listen to political promises but to be entertained. I don't know how I knew that, but my instinct told me that I had to tell a joke or two. It was nearing midnight and I was slowly becoming aware that I had not had any dinner. Guan Eng was still to speak after me.

'Friends,' I said, 'I should stop talking now.'

'Noooooo!!' they roared.

'Guan Eng has to speak after me and you know how he is!'

'Yessss!' they laughed.

'If I don't let him speak now, you'll never get to bed at a decent hour!'

'*Betulllllll!*' they agreed.

'So, I will stop now and give him a chance. Okay?'

'Okayyyyyy!!!!'

I ended with the chant that I had heard the politicians use and which people were responding enthusiastically to.

'Pakatannnnn!' I shouted, punching my right fist high into the air.

'Harapan!!' came the thunderous reply.

* * *

How did I find myself addressing the crowds on the 2018 campaign trail? I had not envisioned such a role at all when it became clear that a general election was on the cards early that year. Campaigning had begun soon after the Pakatan Harapan coalition was announced with Dad as their Prime Ministerial candidate. 'Jelajah Harapan' rallies were organized, mostly in any open space that could fit a stage and had room for people to gather. These turned out to be the outdoor areas in between local council flats and carparks.

I went to my first rally one Sunday night in late April 2018 at the Danau Kota flats, in the Setapak suburb of KL. Accompanied by my friend Ivy Josiah, I was there just to observe but what I saw made me shiver with excitement. Whatever happens on polling day, this was an extraordinary moment in Malaysian history, one not seen perhaps since 1998 when the Reformasi movement began. I had been in large rallies and protests before beginning with Bersih 2 in 2011 all the way until Bersih 5 in 2017 and those had been inspiring and exhilarating, even with the government reacting with teargas and water cannons. But this had a special spark in it, probably because of the previously unlikely coming together of Dad with his former political rivals.

The momentousness of this was not lost on Dian Lee, a young friend of mine who, like many of her generation, took a great interest in what was happening in the country. Earlier that day, she had called me with a simple question: should we not document this on film for historical record? I replied that of course we should, and she quickly set up a meeting the very next day with a videographer Sean Lam. His job, we briefed him, was just to follow Dad around and film him during the campaign. It may well be his last campaign and for that reason alone, regardless of whether he won or lost, we should document it.

Dian and I were to produce it together and since it was so hastily put together, we had to not only act as co-producers but also co-financiers. The idea was that every day we would film Dad and then in the evening interview him on the events of the day. I was given the task of talking to him on camera about how the campaign was going.

Sean dove into the job without hesitation. His previous experience was in filming weddings but there's not a lot of difference between filming the hubbub of nuptials and those of an election campaign. He already had a crew and equipment. All he needed was the schedule and whatever permissions necessary.

Just a day later I accompanied the video crew to Bersatu headquarters at Bangunan Yayasan Selangor in Petaling Jaya to film the PH Presidential Council in a meeting. I had to inform all the Pakatan leaders and others that this crew would be filming them not just in this meeting but wherever else they might be meeting or speaking. They had to go about their business as usual and ignore the cameras so that they looked natural and unself-conscious.

While waiting for the meeting to begin, I was standing outside in the corridor when Dad and the other leaders, Muhyiddin, Guan Eng, Kit Siang, Mat Sabu and others arrived. We stood chatting while the cameras rolled and it was there, as they were laughing and joking, that Guan Eng turned to me and invited me to speak at his rally in Penang the following Saturday.

'Whaaattt? But I've never spoken at a rally before!' I said.

'You can lah . . . just come and help us.'

I had expected to be behind the camera throughout the campaign, not in front of people. I had also never spoken at a political rally, not being a politician.

'But that's what we need! A non-politician!' Guan Eng replied, in his usual earnest way.

I was sceptical but finally I agreed to attend, with no idea what I would talk about. The Saturday coming up was Nomination Day and I was scheduled to be in Langkawi to support Dad when he filed his nomination papers. After that I would fly to Penang for Guan Eng's rally.

A funny thing happened once I agreed to speak at Guan Eng's rally. One rally in Penang became two, one on the mainland and one on the island. Suddenly word got round that I was available to speak at campaign rallies and other candidates began to request me to speak for them too. Theresa Kok of Seputih, Fahmi Fadzil of Lembah Pantai and several more. I began to feel overwhelmed and confused about how to manage these requests. Unlike these politicians, I did not have a team to help me coordinate these schedules. Plus, I was working with Dian on this video.

Panicked, I called my friend Karim Raslan and asked for help. Karim has a consultancy firm filled with young people whose job is to keep their ears to the political ground and help their clients manage their public profiles. I asked if he could spare anyone to sort out my growing campaign schedule and advise me what I should talk about at these rallies.

This was how a young woman called Lee Chao Wee came to work with me. Tall and fashionably turned out, Chao had worked with Karim for a few years and followed him on his trips in Indonesia and the Philippines. Helping me on my little schedule would be easy because it would be nowhere near as frantic as the politicians'. The requests were coming in from various Klang Valley candidates as well as those in Pahang and Johor. Chao had to not only work out how I was to get to those places but also brief me on the candidates and the constituencies they were standing in.

As Chao fielded these requests for me, a problem arose. How was I supposed to interview Dad every day for the video if I had to be elsewhere? He had an even more frantic schedule traversing the country and although Dian was already going to follow him as much as she could with the crew, someone else also needed to cover for her.

That's when we remembered my daughter Ineza. Ineza had studied film and TV production in Australia and had worked for a company in KL that produced documentaries for the History Channel. She certainly knew all the technical aspects of video production. The problem was convincing her to take on the job.

Ineza is the first of my parents' grandchildren and now at thirty-four she is a bright young woman who, besides being a filmmaker, is also a human rights activist. As a little girl I took her with me everywhere when I was president of the Malaysian AIDS Council. I even took her with me to New York when I was asked to speak at the United Nations General Assembly's special session for World AIDS Day in 1996. She thus spent her formative years immersed in the NGO activist world and my colleagues had watched her grow up from the quiet little girl to the slim outspoken woman she now is. Today she still works with some of them.

Her work means that she has opinions of her own about the human rights situation in the country. This sometimes means that she doesn't always agree with her grandfather although she adores him and vice versa. For this reason, when I first called her to ask her to stand in for me doing the interviews, her first instinct was reluctance.

'But you only need to ask him about his day, that's all!' I pleaded. She was not required to debate him.

Her unwillingness also stemmed from her disappointment that her Grandpa was again the Prime Ministerial candidate. Like her cousins, Ineza had enjoyed having Dad back as an almost fulltime grandfather for the last fifteen years. He could attend her birthday parties and even fulfil a promise to visit her at school in Melbourne. Now she had to give him up to the Malaysian public again.

But even more, like many of her generation, she was disappointed that, as much as she loved her Tok Det, Pakatan Harapan could not come up with a PM candidate who was younger. For her and her friends, they could not see how a ninety-two-year-old PM was going to understand and represent their views. Many of them thought they would not even vote in these elections. Indeed, some young people began a boycott of the elections that, if it gained major traction, might have caused PH to lose.

After much pleading from me, Ineza finally agreed to do the daily interviews. Neither she nor I would realize at that point how so much more involved she would get in the project. We filmed over ninety hours of footage that eventually was edited to become the documentary *M for Malaysia*, directed by Ineza and Dian, the first documentary feature ever shown in Malaysian cinemas and was our entry for the Academy Awards in 2020.

20

Election Day

The 2018 election campaign may have been the first I ever truly participated in, but it was more exciting than I could ever have imagined. I attended some of Dad's rallies where crowds of Malaysians gathered at open fields, car parks and badminton courts to listen to the lineup of politicians that they hardly ever saw or heard on their TV screens. At one rally in the Desa Pandan suburb of KL, I sat with friends under umbrellas as the rain poured. It deterred no one. The full crowd sat or stood wherever they could, clapped and cheered at each speaker, slotted money into donation boxes that were passed around and bought souvenir t-shirts from stalls that had popped up.

I was also asked to speak at many rallies where the same electric atmosphere was present. In Johor, I did a marathon relay with Ambiga Sreenevasen speaking at three small towns in one night. In Pahang I followed Young Syefura, a hijabed DAP candidate, on a walk around a housing estate handing out campaign leaflets, and then was whisked off to another two rallies with a short dinner break in between. In KL, Fahmi Fadzil in Lembah Pantai, the constituency I vote in, and Teresa Kok in Seputeh also recruited me to speak to multiracial crowds, sometimes with heavy garlands around my neck, in Malay and English. It was exhilarating and exhausting but I discovered to my great surprise that I could rouse the crowds as well as any politician.

These PH rallies were in huge contrast to the BN ones that often were smaller, more sedate and often relied on people being bused in. In the previous election in 2013, I had hoped to support a BN woman candidate in Segambut, Jayanthi Devi Balaguru, because I had heard that even though a novice, she had a good track record of community service. But her campaign was so lacklustre; her so-called rally was manned by listless campaign supporters who couldn't even give me her biodata. I left before she even arrived. Instead, I went to the Opposition's rally at Kelana Jaya stadium which sounded like a rock concert, with an exuberant cheering crowd. It was clear that something was in the air and indeed that was the year that BN lost the popular vote.

In 2018, for the first time in my adult life, I voted where I lived.

I was previously in the Segambut constituency, in Kuala Lumpur. When I turned twenty-one and hence could vote, I was living at 3, Jalan Tunku with my parents—our home came under Segambut. They had made sure I was registered to vote and every five years or so, I would trot down to the Sekolah Sultan Hishamuddin Alam Shah across the road from Bank Negara to mark my ballot.

Segambut had been a DAP stronghold since 2008; but I had always voted for the BN candidate, more out of habit than anything. It is a very large constituency, with more than 77,000 voters ranging from the working-class neighbourhoods of Segambut and Kampung Kassipillay to the middle-class enclaves of Taman Tun Dr Ismail, Bukit Damansara and Bukit Tunku. We rarely saw our Member of Parliament, I suppose because we never really needed him. I had always voted for the BN but by 2013, my loyalty was faltering. The Najib Razak government was in power and I had attended several Bersih rallies for free and fair elections.

In the 14th General Election of 2018, a woman was finally voted in to represent Segambut. Hannah Yeoh already had a track record as a member of the Selangor State Assembly and then as its Speaker. A personable young woman, she swept to victory with 82 per cent of the vote and a majority of over 45,000 over two male candidates.

Unfortunately, I did not get to vote for Hannah. In 2017, I decided to change my voting address to the constituency where I have actually lived for over twenty years, Lembah Pantai. It is a quirk of the

Malaysian election system that you have to vote in the constituency you are registered in, which may not necessarily coincide with the area where you live or the address on your identity card. This is the reason why there is so much movement of people in the days before polling day, when voters have to make their way to wherever they are registered, usually their villages and hometowns. Not that it is difficult to change your registered address as I found out: it is just a matter of going to the Post Office and filling up a form. It is also the reason why elections are held on weekends, so that working people need not take leave to travel to their polling stations.

On the morning of 9 May 2018, I was hoping to go with my neighbours to the local school to vote. But it turned out that almost everyone on my street, eight houses in all, voted in different constituencies. One was even voting in Johor and had driven there the day before. Alone, I decided to walk to the Sekolah Bukit Pantai, my new voting station, at about nine in the morning.

There, I found that long queues had already formed. Voters from all walks of life were in snaking lines around the school buildings, patiently waiting for their turn to enter the classrooms, dip their fingers in purple ink, pick up their ballot paper, mark against the candidate they wanted and slip it into the transparent box placed squarely in the middle of the room. There was a cheery atmosphere as people chatted with one another and greeted neighbours. Some older people pointed out friends they said they had never seen at a polling station before, suggesting that those were voting for the first time. An undercurrent of excitement was in the air; everyone knew that this election was going to be different. We were already hearing that the scene was the same at every polling station in the country. The Opposition's call for as big a turnout as possible was being heeded.

Still, I dared not hope too much. I left the polling station with my violet-coloured index figure, an indication that I had done my civic duty, and went home. Later in the afternoon, my husband and I went to shop for groceries at Publika, an upmarket mall in the Hartamas neighbourhood. As we walked around the aisles, Tara remarked that very few people seemed to have dyed fingers like me. Had they not voted yet? Or were they not going to vote? My heart thudded wildly in fear. I only consoled myself that the mall was mostly frequented by expatriates, who would not have been able to vote anyway. It was not yet time to worry.

Meanwhile though, the PH campaign was beginning to become concerned. Polling was to close at 5 p.m., yet many polling stations were still seeing long lines of voters waiting to vote. What if they did not get to exercise their right by 5 p.m. as looked likely? Surely, in a democracy, they ought not to be denied, especially if they had travelled far to do their duty.

At about 4 p.m., Dad, still in Langkawi, held a press conference requesting the Election Commission (EC) to extend voting hours. It seemed like the logical thing to do, or else hundreds of voters would be locked out. But the EC, an organization that seemed to be doing the bidding of the Najib government then, declined. They would shut the doors promptly at 5 p.m.

The 2018 general election was significant in how there were so many attempts to thwart voters' rights. From the shorter-than-usual 11-day campaign period, to the unheard-of Wednesday polling day to the refusal to extend voting hours, the government through the EC did everything to make sure that the voters they assumed were going to vote for the Opposition would be at least hindered from doing so. I have never understood this strategy. Surely their own voters would be just as hampered by these decisions. Unless they already knew that the tide was turning very much against them, it didn't make much sense.

After polls closed, there was nothing to do but wait for the results. I showered and changed into jeans, a t-shirt with Dad's face a la Che Guevara on it and a red hoodie to keep warm and headed with Tara to the Sheraton Hotel in Petaling Jaya to await the results with the rest of the PH crowd. Dad and Mum had returned from Langkawi and would appear later. Meanwhile, Pakatan Harapan members and supporters were trickling into the ballroom of the hotel where big screens and banks of computers had been set up to track the results as they came in. Outside the ballroom, a buffet had been set up for hungry campaigners to nourish themselves. If we were going to lose, at least we were going to lose in style. But the atmosphere was hopeful. Already, many of the folks there were getting reports from their supporters around the country, people who had witnessed the counting of the votes, that PH was winning. And not just winning, but winning big.

As the hours ticked by, with people constantly holding their phones to their ears to get reports from around the country, I remembered one of the first rallies I attended in Kuala Selangor. Dad and several of his PH allies were speaking then. But I particularly remembered what Azmin Ali, then a member of PKR, had said. In that strident voice of his, reminiscent of his boss then, he made a prescient prediction: if the results came in early, that meant that the BN had won. But if the results trickled in late, then the chances were that PH was winning. The later it got, the bigger the likelihood that PH had won.

I remembered that because that was exactly as it happened on the night of 9 May. As we sat in rows facing the giant screen, even molasses moved faster than the way the results came in. The EC began by announcing the confirmed results from the east coast states of Kelantan and Terengganu, both of which had been won by PAS, then in alliance with the BN. Then they stopped.

Meanwhile, we were hearing reports that the heads of the polling stations, most of whom were appointed by the EC, were refusing to sign Form 14, which confirmed the votes and the winners of each station. Without their signatures, the winners could not be confirmed. I was getting calls from friends who told me they were rushing to various polling stations to assist people trying to safeguard the boxes of votes and to ensure that the Form 14 was signed. There was palpable anxiety in the air that the election would be stolen from us.

The ballroom, even with so many people in it, was freezing. I walked around it to chat with friends in case they had more up-to-date news. As the night grew later, we became alternately hopeful and worried. Would we actually be allowed to win?

Dad and Mum had arrived earlier. While Dad was busy huddling with his PH colleagues, Mum sat in the ballroom, a shawl wrapped around her, exhaustion clearly on her face. My sisters-in-law and I tried to get her to take a rest upstairs in a room reserved for her. She swatted us away, irritated. Whatever happened, Mum wanted to be there just like the rest of us.

On TV, the chairman of the EC denied that they were delaying the results. In the ballroom, we booed him. TV analysts and commentators were getting visibly agitated at not being able to say much about the results.

By 10 p.m., we were getting impatient. I sat between Mum and Dad watching the giant screens broadcasting the tiny portion of confirmed results. Anxiety and anger began to seep in my veins. Malaysia has had 14 general elections: surely the EC had mastered the intricacies of tabulating and confirming results?

At almost midnight, Dad made a decision: he would call the vote. He trooped downstairs with his entire squad of PH allies to face the media. Unable to get into the lifts, I ran down with my mobile phone to find reporters surrounding Dad, a thicket of microphones and cameras in his face. Being short, I could barely see anything above the bodies crowding him so I held my phone up as high as I could above my head to record whatever it could see. Dad announced that PH had won; his campaign knew this from the reports being phoned in by supporters all over the country. It was only up to the EC to confirm it.

Returning back upstairs, we watched as Karim Raslan, the political commentator, suddenly lost it at the EC on national TV. He said it was disgraceful that they were refusing to release the results and if they did not like the heat in the kitchen, they 'should just get out'. That outburst and Dad's declaration seemed to add to the pressure on the EC. Within an hour, well past midnight, the dam finally broke.

Soon a deluge of results came in, confirming what we already knew. PH had won decisively in almost every constituency they had contested. Incredibly, they had also won eight out of the thirteen states in the Federation including Johor, the birthplace and bastion of UMNO. All the PH leadership, including Dad, had won.

As we watched the now-speedy results, with a lot of backslapping and congratulations for those who had won, the next obvious step, the conceding of the results by Najib and the declaration of the winner, was yet to come. At about two in the morning, Dr Wan Azizah, the president of PKR, received a call from Istana Negara to present herself before the Agong, at the time the Sultan of Kelantan. It was a bit strange by any measure but unable to refuse a summons from the King himself, she had to go. Mum and I looked at each other in surprise. 'I don't like this,' she said. I held her hand, more to calm myself than to reassure her. She was the veteran in these things, I was not.

Wan Azizah returned about an hour later. By that time, most of the results were in and it was very clear that history had been made. Sixty years after independence, for the first time, Malaysia had voted for a government that was NOT Barisan Nasional. Even the PH was startled. In the ballroom, the new MPs hugged and cheered. I sat watching the results with my palms clasped over my nose and mouth, unable to believe what had happened. My activist colleagues and friends could barely keep from dancing around. We took 'we-fies' to record the occasion, as if we could ever forget it. My husband put his arms around my shoulders, gave me a squeeze and then said, 'Congratulations! But be careful what you wish for.' I grinned, too happy to heed his words.

One of the strangest things that happened that night was the sudden appearance of soldiers complete with what looked like automatic rifles at the periphery of the ballroom. The presence of any guns makes me nervous, but these looked especially lethal. Still, there were only about four of these soldiers in a room of about hundred people and it didn't seem like the beginning of a coup. They stood silently by the doors and just watched us. After a while, it dawned on us that they were a signal, a sign that we had most likely won because they had been sent to protect us.

It's interesting how government transitions work in not-so-subtle ways as acknowledgements that power has been transferred even without formal swearings-in. When Mum and Dad left the Sheraton to go home at about five in the morning, their car was escorted by a full police motorcade, as a sitting Prime Minister is entitled to. Although as an ex-Prime Minister, Dad had a small security detail, it was clearly beefed up in those early hours of 10 May. These were the small ways in which a peaceful transition of power happens, even when some people still refused to accept it. The streets, however, were lined with people who knew exactly what had occurred. As the motorcade passed by on its way to my parents' home in Sungai Besi, they cheered, whooped and clapped, knowing very well it was a victory that they had made real.

In normal times, the swearing-in of the newly-elected Prime Minister would happen first thing the next morning. Dressed in their best formal clothes, Dad and Mum would go to Istana Negara to take his oath of office before the Agong. Still hyper from the night's excitement, I barely slept. At first light, I gave up and got out of bed, eager to hear news about the swearing-in ceremony. But there was nothing.

I texted my brothers and they told me that there was no word yet about the ceremony. Even I knew this was highly unusual. Worried, I dressed quickly and rushed to the Sheraton, where I knew the PH leadership would be. Few people were in the lobby but there was an air of anxiety around it. I tried not to breathe it in as I made my way to the 15th floor where I was told they were convening. The door to the suite was closed but there were a few people standing around outside it. Thinking that it was a confidential meeting, I sat on the floor outside to wait, my heart drumming hard. I was fearful that after all the euphoria of the previous night, the victory would still be snatched from us.

After about twenty minutes of sitting there texting everyone I knew for news, the door to the suite opened and my Dad's aide-de-camp's head popped out. I looked at him enquiringly, gesturing that I wanted to go inside. Thankfully, he let me in. The first person I saw was Mum, beautifully dressed in a flowery formal baju kurung and *selendang*, her hair and makeup immaculate.

'Why are you so dressed up, Mummy?' I asked, thinking that it seemed a bit surreal, given the uncertainties of the moment.

'Well, I was expecting to go to the Palace.' She replied with a shrug and a smile, looking fresh despite her late night.

Around her, people milled about, talking in soft whispers. Lim Kit Siang, Wan Azizah, Mat Sabu, Lim Guan Eng, Muhyiddin Yassin, Azmin Ali and of course Dad stood around in groups, busy discussing this unprecedented situation. Most of them were poring over a letter that had been drafted to confirm that all of them agreed that the PH candidate for Prime Minister was Dad, as they had promised during the election campaign. The uncertainty had arisen after Wan Azizah had been called to the palace the previous night. The King was apparently of the impression that as leader of the party with the biggest number of seats, she was the Prime Minister-elect.

This was puzzling, because PH had made it clear from the very beginning who their candidate was. Dad's face was on every banner, despite Najib's attempts to have it cut out from all their campaign materials. How could the King have thought otherwise?

Things became clearer once Najib appeared on TV to concede defeat, a first for any BN leader. He would abide by the people's decision, he said in a sombre tone, his Deputy and other UMNO leaders beside him. 'However,' he added, and here he released the poisoned arrow that was truly the first shot in the battle to retain power, it was 'unclear' who was the new Prime Minister because 'no party had gained an absolute majority in Parliament'.

This was disingenuous. Just like Barisan Nasional, Pakatan Harapan had stood as a coalition. The number of winning seats should be counted as a whole and not by individual parties. Pakatan had won 113 seats, one more than the 112 required to win the 222-seat Parliament. Along with its partner Warisan in Sabah and its eight seats, they had a very secure 121 seats. Even though Parti Keadilan Rakyat (PKR) won the greatest number of seats, 47, in the coalition, they had campaigned on the platform that Dad was their PM candidate.

Listening to Najib twist the logic of coalition politics triggered a memory. During the campaign, a friend, well-connected and knowledgeable, had called to ask me to pass a message to Dad. He had heard on good authority that, should PH win the election, there would be an attempt to thwart the victory, not through violent means but through a novel and equally unconstitutional way: by getting the King not to acknowledge and accept the new Prime Minister. As with the Trump refusal to accept Biden's win, democracy depends on a peaceful transfer of power to whoever won the most votes. I was alarmed at this information; it seemed to me that this was a step towards chaos, should this happen. It also seemed to me, given that there was such a contingency plan, that the BN, especially Najib, was feeling exceedingly insecure. Nevertheless, it was a frightening thought and I passed on the message to Dad. In his typical way, Dad received the information with calmness, as we sat at lunch in Alor Setar where I had gone to support him. I wonder if he remembered that warning when it seemed to be coming true that 10 May.

All the PH leaders stood around the television in that Sheraton suite watching Najib's announcement with some unease. As soon as he was done, they sat down in a circle as Wan Azizah explained what happened when she went to the Palace the previous night. She had insisted to the King that the PH agreement was that Dad would be the Prime Minister should the coalition win. Among PH there was no conflict about this but still they felt that they needed a watertight document to support it, hence the letters that each coalition party had to write to affirm their choice of leadership. By then there were already rumours and fake news appearing online. I was even sent a news clipping claiming that Dad had said he was fine with Wan Azizah being Prime Minister.

The tension of that morning overrode the fatigue and lack of sleep from the night before. I watched as Dad and his colleagues busied themselves with their lawyers, talking through the constitutional arguments for claiming their victory. As veteran politicians, Dad and Lim Kit Siang were a vortex of calm while the others swirled around them, trying to sort this unprecedented challenge out. Nurul Izzah was hoarse from the eleven days of campaign speeches. I went over and gave Dad a tight squeeze, I think more to comfort myself than him.

By late morning, when there was still no word from the palace as to the swearing-in ceremony, Dad and the PH leadership decided to hold another press conference. As the most experienced person there, the one who had been in government the longest, Dad emphasised that the country could not be left without an administration for too long. Already, it had been ten hours since PH was declared the winner of the general elections, and it was very unconventional to not swear in the new Prime Minister by the next morning. With Wan Azizah and Lim Kit Siang by his side and all his new colleagues around them, he held up the letter that confirmed that the entire PH had agreed that he should be the new leader of the country. I sat on the floor in front of their table, surrounded by a whole congregation of media, both local and international, marvelling at the scene. Who would have thought this would happen, that Malaysians had voted out their old government and elected a new group? Undoubtedly, Dad was a familiar face but that assured people that at least one person had the experience to guide the newer ones on the intricacies of governing.

As the day wore on, news about the timing of the swearing-in was slow in coming. My father's office alerted my siblings and I that we were invited to the ceremony. Since it was a formal occasion, we would all be expected to wear black.

This presented several dilemmas for me. Tara and I were due to fly to Dhaka in Bangladesh that night for a meeting of the Board of Advisers of the Asian University for Women, an institution that I have been involved with since 2008. Our flight was at eight-thirty in the evening which meant that I had to check in by seven at the latest, leaving the house by 6.15 p.m. to catch the KLIA Express to the airport.

Word reached us that the ceremony was to be at 4.30 p.m. I had to make a choice. Should I dress up in formal black baju and selendang, with Tara in a suit, to attend the ceremony and then rush off to KLIA, to change in the loo there into our travel clothes? I actually had nothing suitable to wear; my black bajus are reserved for funerals. After going over my options repeatedly, I decided the schedule was too tight and despite its historic significance, I would have to forego the ceremony. Instead, I would watch what I could on TV and then dash off to the airport.

It turned out to be the wiser choice. My parents' car drove past the Istana Negara gates at just before 4.30 p.m. and entered the Palace accompanied by my suitably-dressed brothers and their spouses. And then they waited.

As did I, my TV at home tuned to RTM ready to watch the ceremony live, my bags hastily packed for my two-day trip. Time wore on and nothing happened. My brothers texted me that they were all in a sitting room with my parents waiting for the ceremony to begin, yet there had been no word at all as to when that would be. The TV too showed nothing much, only the *Balai Rong Seri* with chairs set up for the ceremony, facing the throne where the Agong would sit as his new Prime Minister took the oath of office. All over the country, Malaysians too were doing the same thing I was, sitting and waiting. But at least they could be dressed more casually, sitting relaxed in their own living rooms or gathered with friends at a coffee shop, their teh tariks in front of them. At the Palace, dressed in their formal bests, Mum, Dad and whoever else was invited were forced to sit calmly and quietly, waiting for the country to finally have a government.

By 5.30 p.m. my parents had been in the palace for an hour and still there had been no progress. My brother texted me that they still didn't know what was happening but that there was a rumour that the ceremony would take place only at 9.30 p.m. Would they be able to leave first and return later? No, it was only a rumour and it would be terrible if they left and then had to scramble back or miss it altogether.

I too had to make a decision. If it was true that the ceremony was delayed until 9.30 p.m., it meant that I would already be on the plane to Dhaka and wouldn't know what occurred until I landed some three hours later. Resigning ourselves to that fact, Tara and I headed to Sentral station to catch the KLIA Express fast train to the airport.

Already exhausted from a lack of sleep, Tara and I could barely keep awake as we headed for the airport. We had hardly pulled out of the Sentral station when my phone began to vibrate with messages. Rumours were circulating that the King was not going to swear in the new Prime Minister despite Pakatan Harapan's decisive win in the polls. People were beginning to gather at the palace gates, anxious that their will was about to be denied.

I began to feel uneasy. Could I really go abroad if something terrible happened and the victory we had worked so hard for was seized from us? My brother sent me photos of my parents patiently waiting, dressed in their formal clothes, without much to eat except for some curry puffs.

By the time we reached the airport, there was a deluge of messages about the delay. As Malaysians are wont to do, all sorts of speculation arose as to what was causing it. I turned to Tara, 'I can't leave while it's so uncertain. I don't think we can go.'

He agreed and instead of disembarking the train, we remained onboard and took it back to KL. Meanwhile I had messaged my daughter Ineza, who was with her camera crew filming as much of the day as possible, to pick me up at Sentral. Together we would all proceed to the palace gates.

The new Istana Negara, completed in 2011 to replace the more centrally-located one, has three entrances: Gates A, B and C. We chose to go to Gate C on a narrow street in Damansara Heights down the road from some office buildings. There were a few people already gathered there, waving giant blue, red and white flags and chanting 'Reformasi!'.

Some young boys on motorbikes rode up and down the street whooping and cheering. The mood was still jubilant.

I got out of the car and found my friends Ivy Josiah and Vivienne Lee. The air was warm and humid and dressed in clothes meant to keep me warm on the flight, I began to sweat. That brought with it a feeling of nausea as fatigue began to roll over me. I sat down on the curb and put my head down. My stomach rumbled. I had forgotten that I hadn't eaten much all day.

Dian Lee, whose camera crew was continually filming, suggested we go to the office building nearby where her husband owned a restaurant. We could have a quick dinner there.

By the time we returned to the palace gates less than an hour later, the crowd had swelled up. Young people gathered around waving flags, singing *Negaraku*, our national anthem, chanting and laughing. The atmosphere was friendly and festive, but I could feel an undercurrent of anxiety running through it as people waited for the ceremony to begin.

By then it had been four hours since my parents entered the palace and as far as I knew, they hadn't had dinner. As 9 p.m. approached, there was still no news of when the King would summon them into the gilded Throne Room to formally accept my father as Prime Minister. I kept texting my brothers, but they had no further news.

Various friends appeared at the gates, smiling and hugging each other. It seemed as if nobody wanted to miss this historic moment, even those who I was fairly sure did not vote for Pakatan Harapan. But no matter, the mood of the crowd was inclusive, that this was a moment for all Malaysians regardless of party loyalties.

Eventually we got word that the ceremony would be broadcast live online at 9.30 p.m. People huddled around, the light from their mobile phones illuminating their faces as they watched Dad, solemn and sombre in his black baju and *songkok*, place his right hand on the Quran, raised his left hand and promised to uphold the Constitution and govern as best as he can. Then he sat down and placed his signature on his letter of appointment while the 15th Yang di-Pertuan Agong, Sultan Muhammad V, watched from the throne, his large mobile phone very clearly outlined in his breast pocket. As soon as it was confirmed that Dad was the seventh Malaysian Prime Minister, having last been the fourth for twenty-two years, I shouted to the crowd, 'Ladies and gentlemen, we have a Prime Minister! And we have a new government!'

Cheers and applause broke out. My husband, daughter and friends hugged me and each other. Dian stood on the sidewalk, tears flowing down her face. With the task of filming the campaign, the last fortnight had been gruelling for her. The relief combined with fatigue to release all her emotions. Around us, people danced with a carefree joy, a scene that was repeated at the other gates to the palace as well as all over the city.

Despite the long day and late hour, we got word that Dad was headed back to the Sheraton hotel for a press conference. Quickly we made our way back to our van, pausing to take photographs with the crowd and shaking hands, and rushing across town back to the ballroom where we had spent almost all of the previous night. On the way social media lit up with lots of messages of congratulations. At the same time, learning that Dad was still going to speak to the press, concerned people on Twitter begged him to go home and rest, that we could all wait until the next day to hear what he had to say.

But Dad was not deterred and gave a short press conference about the delayed swearing-in, although he did not dwell on the reasons why. And finally, he left for home, escorted by the same police motorbikes that had magically appeared the night before.

The scene at the Sheraton hotel that night was a sight I had never seen before, nor since, and will never forget. In the ground floor glass-enclosed lobby, thousands of people had converged to celebrate with one another and simply exult in a moment that had not been seen since independence in 1957. Outside, thousands more gathered, waving gigantic PH flags, singing and dancing as if they were at a carnival. Later, we would see videos of the people lining the streets cheering as Dad's car passed them by. In all his political life, he had never seen exuberance like this. Nor had any of us.

What was truly extraordinary about the crowd that night was the sheer diversity of the people, all races, creeds and ages. What they had done together, oust a government that had ruled for sixty years and only a year before had seemed immovable, was nothing short of miraculous. The victory belonged well and truly to the people who backed an under-resourced David against a deep-pocketed Goliath, who refused to fall for the false promises and in some cases actual handouts of cash if they voted Barisan Nasional, who disapproved of the insults hurled towards the leaders of Pakatan Harapan. For the first time, people recognized the power of their vote, that by coming together they could do the unimaginable. They could prise a solid boulder from its perch on the mountain and roll it crashing down the rocky slope to the ground. Democracy had prevailed in Malaysia, without a single drop of blood being shed.

In our euphoria, we did not know that the exhilaration would not last, that we would all come down to Earth with a very hard thud.

21

Six Hundred and Sixty-One Days

Waking up on 11 May 2018 felt different. The sun seemed to shine brighter, the air was cleaner, and people walked around with a smile for friends and strangers. Something heavy had been lifted from our shoulders.

On TV, broadcasters threw off the millstone that had hung around their necks for decades and began to talk about real issues. Suddenly news programmes and talk shows became worth watching again, asking hard questions and no longer forced to stick to safe subjects anymore. We began to see faces we had never seen before on the screen; different opinions being voiced side by side.

With this atmosphere of newness came an expectation of the government that weighed heavily. Dad's first task was to form the Cabinet. On 10 May, he appointed Dr Wan Azizah as the new Deputy Prime Minister, the first woman in the post. Two days later he announced three Cabinet posts for the leaders of the Pakatan Harapan component parties: Muhyiddin Yassin of Bersatu as Home Minister, DAP Secretary-General Lim Guan Eng as Finance Minister and Muhamad Sabu of Amanah as Defence Minister. At the same time, he announced the setting up of a Council of Eminent Persons, a circle of sages comprising a former Finance Minister, former Governor of Bank Negara, a tycoon, a former President of Petronas and an economics expert who had served at the UN. Their task was to advise the government on economic and financial affairs.

Dad pledged to compose a smaller Cabinet than the previous governments. But here the burden of anticipation hung over his head. Each party expected a certain number of portfolios that had to be carefully balanced among each other. There were already some murmurs of dissatisfaction about who the most prestigious posts were going to. If the new government hoped to match Ministerial portfolios to the actual talents and skills of the party candidates, this didn't prove easy.

During the campaign, amongst other promises, Pakatan Harapan had pledged that they would fill 30 per cent of the Cabinet posts with women. That would mean eight women Ministers, a record for Malaysia. But this didn't gel well with the number of portfolios available, nor the names submitted to him to select. Furthermore, with Wan Azizah also taking on the Women, Family and Community Development Ministry, it meant greater competition between the male and female candidates for the 21 posts that were left. In the end, he appointed four more women as Ministers and four Deputy Ministers. For women's groups this was not nearly satisfactory. But Dad's choices were limited to the names nominated by the political parties. As there were more men's names than women's, it was impossible to meet the manifesto's pledges.

Be careful what you wish for. For many of the Pakatan Harapan parties who had spent most of their lives in the Opposition, it had perhaps become a habit of promising policies that they knew they could not fulfil. But they won, and voters expected them to make good the 203-page manifesto known as Buku Harapan or Book of Hope. It included ten promises they would undertake within the first hundred days and another sixty within the next five years. Some of it, such as introducing term limits for the Prime Minister and Chief Ministers and lowering the voting age to eighteen were undoubtedly necessary and doable. Some others, including abolishing the much-hated Goods and Services Tax and replacing it with a 'much fairer' sales and services tax and a 'people-friendly and entrepreneur-friendly tax' seemed like oxymorons.

As for me and many activists, the victory of Pakatan Harapan presented a dilemma. On the one hand, we were happy that the Barisan Nasional was no longer in power. It had not been an easy six decades for alternative viewpoints on the state Malaysia was in. The previous ten years had been especially hard, with the passing of laws such as SOSMA that curtailed freedom of speech and expression even more than previous laws already had. So, we welcomed the new government with open arms. After all many of us had also worked to support its campaign.

On the other hand, our role as civil society is to keep the government honest. We had to ensure that it kept to its promises, improved Malaysia's imperfect democracy and supported justice and equality for everyone within it. There could be a grace period while the new government found its feet, but we also expected them to do the work of learning their jobs very quickly. The last government may not have cared that we were watching, but this one, by definition, should.

The dilemma was that we also didn't want to be in the uncomfortable position of giving the new Opposition any mud to throw at the government. For once we could not side with the Opposition because by no definition were they underdogs. UMNO especially was still well-funded and after so long in power, had allies everywhere within the system who could work to undermine their new bosses. They still stood for everything that we were against including racial, religious and gender inequality.

In the end we need not have worried. The Opposition, instead of reflecting on the reasons for their losses, simply continued their old formula of inciting racial and religious conflict with added fervour. Everything the Pakatan government did was seen through a racial lens and twisted to mean the opposite of what was intended. They were not overly interested in demanding accountability of the new government in the way civil society was. Not that they were beyond hypocrisy of course, calling out the government for alleged wrongdoings that they themselves had committed.

Every time the Opposition protested against a government initiative or policy, such as ratifying the International Convention for the Eradication of Racial Discrimination, it reminded me of the Trump administration. The populist nationalist rhetoric sounded so similar, they could have been the same people if it weren't for skin colour and language. This is the odd thing about populist movements everywhere in the world. They think they have nothing in common just because they come from different countries. But in fact, they're often mirror images of one another. In Malaysia, the new BN Opposition was determined to be the worst kind of Opposition. Even their former leader, under 42 counts of corruption and money-laundering charges related to 1MDB, walked around freely and shamelessly, with a new image-building campaign calling himself BossKu.

I wish I could say that Pakatan Harapan handled it all with finesse and polish. I know it was hard to learn the ropes of governing so quickly. Even for the most experienced persons in Cabinet it was not easy. Having been out of government for fifteen years, Dad no longer knew the top civil servants he had to work with. Some Ministers who had been in the previous government were now in different Ministries. Others came in with set ideas about how things should be done and were impervious to advice from the more experienced. And some did little work at all.

Not that there were not good Ministers in the Pakatan government. People like Yeo Bee Yin who headed the very lengthily-named Ministry of Energy, Science, Technology, Environment and Climate Change and her Deputy, Isnaraissah Munirah Majilis, were well-suited for their jobs. Hannah Yeoh, Deputy Minister of Women, Family and Community Development, was sensitive and sensible.

But some arrived with baggage from their Opposition days or slid comfortably into their new roles in much the same way as their predecessors.

For many of us on the outside, frustration grew. Some, like me, felt that they were doing a poor job of communicating to the public, allowing the Opposition and their many social media cohorts to dictate the narrative. I felt that too often, the government was being defensive, reacting too much to whatever the Opposition threw at them. Instead of touting what good they had done, they responded to charges of poor work hurled at them by the other side. Worse still, internal conflicts within some parties spilled over into the public space.

I wish I could say that the six hundred and sixty days that Pakatan Harapan was in power was as exhilarating as the elections. They had come in on a wave of goodwill but soon became bogged down by problems, some of which were of their own making. For me, they had a major communications problem that they either did not recognise or just did not have the skilled personnel to handle. Or perhaps, in retrospect, that was the way some people wanted it. Every single thing Pakatan did was picked on, whether it was black school shoes or a new sales and services tax or the more ridiculous things like a flying car. They spent a lot of time being defensive against attacks by the Opposition, aware that a substantial number of Malays, about 70 per cent, had not voted for them. In October 2019 Dad spoke at the Malay Congress, a convention of Malay nationalist groups, but he faced criticism from all sides. Non-Malays thought his attendance marked an endorsement of the views of the Congress. The Malay nationalist groups on the other hand didn't like his scolding of them; they thought it gave a bad image to Malays. There was no winning that.

Two attempts at ratifying international agreements were effectively torpedoed by the Opposition who misrepresented what they stood for. In March 2019, then Foreign Minister Saifuddin Abdullah had signed the Instrument of Accession to the Rome Statute of the International Criminal Court (ICC), set up in 1992 to try perpetrators of the most serious crimes against humanity including genocide, war crimes, crimes against humanity and crimes of aggression. The ICC would have made it possible to try the Myanmar military for the genocide of the Rohingyas for example. Malaysia had nothing to lose by ratifying it. Yet the Opposition, as well as some Rulers, distorted it to mean a loss of sovereignty for Malaysia as well as the possible loss of Malay privileges. Incredibly, it sounded as if some people were saying that they wanted to be free to commit crimes against humanity. The blowback was so great that the government was forced to withdraw the accession, putting it alongside other recalcitrant countries including the United States, China, Russia and India. A self-inflicted international humiliation.

The same reasoning, that it would cause the loss of Malay privileges, caused Malaysia to reverse the ratification of the International Convention for the Elimination of Racial Discrimination (ICERD). The convention does allow for affirmative action programmes such as the New Economic Policy but again, Malay nationalist groups and UMNO and PAS insisted that ratifying it would mean the death knell of Malay rights.

These two losses were carefully orchestrated by the Opposition to manipulate the public with misinformation. They could have been won by a better managed strategy by the PH government to educate the public first with a good communications programme. Indeed, there were many professional communications experts who were ready to assist the government then, but they were mostly brushed off as unnecessary, because they already had Bernama, the national news agency, and Radio Television Malaysia, the government broadcasters. For a government that was full of former opposition politicians and activists, it was astonishing that they forgot that the people mistrust the government propaganda channels.

In short, the entire fiasco was handled in a chaotic and amateurish way and it was often left to Dad to explain when things turned turtle. At times it seemed as if he was the only one who would take the bull by the horns. International treaties and conventions come under the purview of the Foreign Minister. It is astounding to me, given his track record, that that Minister then became the Minister of Communications and Multimedia.

Perhaps had they been given time, Pakatan Harapan would have gained enough savvy to know how to manage these issues in a more professional way. But fighting fires all the time was not only wearying but distracting.

Slowly the goodwill that had been hard-won after the 14th General Elections in 2018 eroded.

22

Taking a Breather

When 2018 began, amidst the swirling politics and uncertainties around me, I was making plans of my own. For years I had been wanting to study creative writing. Although I had written my column in *The Star* for more than twenty years by then, I was beginning to feel it was limiting me. I yearned to write a book from start to finish, rather than just compile my columns as my three previous books had been, but I had no idea how to do it. I would press every writer I met on how they did it, even though most wrote novels instead of nonfiction like me.

After listening to my hankering for so many years, in 2017 for my sixtieth birthday, Tara gave me a present. He would pay for me to go to school to learn how to write a book. It was an incredibly generous offer, wholly supported by my children. They knew I had to get it out of my system.

Tara's idea was for me to do a course that would take a few months. I knew of some well-known creative writing courses in the United States but none of their timings suited me. Either they were too long or were split up in inconvenient ways, taking several weekends. I was also not keen to travel to the United States while Trump was in the White House; I felt the environment there had gotten too ugly to be safe for a brown Muslim person.

My research was slow, making my family impatient. They began to doubt I really wanted to go. But one day my friend Bernard Chauly suggested I look at the University of East Anglia's Creative Writing courses. There I found what seemed to be perfect: A Master's degree in Biography and Creative Non-Fiction.

The only problem was it would mean I had to be away for an entire year. Uncertain if that was what I wanted, I sat on it.

Sometimes when you're hesitant about a big step in your life, the universe has a knack of pushing you. Mine came in the form of strange coincidences that I took as signs. In January 2018, I was invited to Bangkok to speak at a festival of culture and literature called Bangkok Edge.

My schedule was fairly light and one afternoon I went to listen to a panel of international journalists. One speaker was Anjan Sundaram, an Indian journalist who had written a book on the destruction of free speech and the rise of dictatorship in Rwanda—a harrowing account of how reporters became silenced under the rule of President Paul Kagame. But what really interested me was that Anjan had done a PhD in Creative Writing at the University of East Anglia. After his talk I asked him about the course and told him about my intention to do my Master's there. His advice: forget the Master's, do the PhD, a thought that was quite terrifying for me.

In early March I was in Singapore and one evening I went to a cocktail reception hosted by one of my fellow Asian University of Women Board members at her home. The university is a project dear to my heart ever since I visited it in Chittagong, Bangladesh in 2008. Its aim is to provide tertiary education with a liberal arts curriculum to young women from all over Asia who might not have had a chance to go to university otherwise. Students come from all over the continent, from remote villages in Afghanistan to as far away as Palestine. At the reception, several of the students and Board members were to speak in the hopes of gaining more support from Singaporean benefactors.

The reception, in one of those renovated old houses with colourful tiles and high ceilings, was small but very convivial. I was standing by a staircase next to a woman I did not know and in an effort to make conversation, I asked her what she did. 'I just finished my Masters in Biography and Creative Nonfiction at the University of East Anglia,' replied Chan Li Shan. I could hardly believe my ears. Not only had I met two people who had been to the same university I had been surveying within a month of each other, but by sheer chance I was standing next to someone who had completed the very subject I was interested in.

The signs were clear that I should apply. Li Shan proved to be very helpful, giving me tips on the approach I should take for my personal statement. It was not the time to be shy and reticent, she said, I really had to sell myself. With good reason too. The UEA Masters course is a very well-known one. On the Fiction side it has produced two Booker Prize winners, Ian McEwan and Anne Enright, and a Nobel Laureate, Kazuo Ishiguro. Although the Non-Fiction side is not as well-known, every year it accepts only a limited number of students for the Master's programme.

I sent off my application along with a long personal statement and an essay to give them an idea if I could write at all. Then I forgot about it in the excitement of the election campaign in late April and the inauguration of the new government in May. In June, UEA emailed me to say that they wanted to interview me. I was at a week-long workshop at a resort outside KL and with birds singing in the background, over Skype I managed to convince them that I would be a good addition to their course. A week later, they offered me a place beginning that Autumn.

This was a bit more than Tara had bargained for. Instead of going away for a few months, I was going away for a year. When I told my friends of my plans, some of them were shocked. 'How can you go now?' Ambiga Sreenevasan asked me. I had hesitated myself, afraid that I would miss out on all the exciting things that I assumed would happen under the new government. But post-elections I had not felt I was needed for anything important in KL. Life for me had gone on as usual with work on the travel website I founded, Zafigo.com, as well as my NGO work and other interests.

I was also a bit worried about being far away from my parents at their advanced age, even though I know they are both extraordinary specimens for elderly people. Still one can never be certain; each day they are still healthy is to me a blessing.

But I reasoned, if I didn't go then, when would I have another chance? At sixty-one by the time I enrolled, I would be one of the most senior in the class, if not the oldest. I had to seize the opportunity to do something I always wanted.

My family accepted my decision with equanimity. Mum was a bit sad at the thought of me being away for so long, but I promised her that I would be home every three months or so during the holidays. Much like my undergraduate years four decades earlier, Dad did not have much to say. He had a new government to run.

In late September, I arrived at the UEA campus for my first class. The university, just outside Norwich in Norfolk, is built in the brutalist style: stark grey buildings with a long open-air pathway connecting them amongst more than fifty acres of parkland surrounding a large lake. The central focus of the campus is a stepped plaza where, in good weather, students sit to chat, eat and sometimes play music. On one side is the student union building where I sometimes retreat to a lounge specially for post-graduate students, cafes, a bookstore and other shops. If you walk along the elevated open-air pathway past the zig-zaggy pyramid-shaped student accommodation known as the Ziggurat, you get to the Sainsbury Center, a public art museum designed by the renowned architect Norman Foster that houses a permanent collection of tribal artefacts and art collected by the Sainsbury family. It became one of my favourite places to hide out and work because it has two lovely cafes and a small gift shop.

Tara, who had accompanied me for my first day back at university, videoed me as I headed for my first class. The nervousness showed on my face very clearly. It had been so long since I last attended a university class, that my confidence had dwindled to almost nothing. What if everyone is much younger and smarter than me?

To my relief, my class consisted of a wide range of ages, from new graduates in their twenties to retirees in their sixties. There was also a good mix of nationalities, mostly British but also some Americans and Asians. I breathed easier. Maybe I could do this after all.

My year at UEA was only nine months; three terms of three months each. I had two classes per term, both of which were at the beginning of the week so that those who commuted from London or elsewhere needed only to stay on campus for two nights at most.

I had decided not to stay on campus, reasoning that with most residents in their late teens, I would not enjoy it as much as I did in my undergraduate days. I had a place to stay in London so every week on Monday I worked out a routine. At 9.30 a.m., I would cross the road from my apartment building to the bus stop and take the bus to Notting Hill Gate station about fifteen minutes away. Then I would take the Central Line underground train ten stations east to Liverpool Street station and get there by about 10.10 a.m., with just enough time to buy myself a coffee and something for lunch. At 10.30 a.m. my train would leave for the almost two-hour ride to Norwich, during which I could do some reading for class.

When I got to Norwich, I would hop on the bus to the campus that waits just outside the station. The ride takes about twenty minutes, and I had about an hour to check into my room at the campus guest lodge, have my lunch and head to class at 2 p.m.

My second class would be the next afternoon, after which I would make the reverse trip—bus, train, Tube. By the time I arrived back at Notting Hill Gate station in the evening, I was so tired that I would indulge in a taxi for the short ride home.

This was my routine every week during the term and most of the time it would go like clockwork. But occasionally there would be hitches. The most common one would be delays or even cancellations caused by 'jumpers'. Mondays tended to be the day when some poor person decides to jump onto the rail line in a suicide attempt. The railway company is very discreet; they never reveal what the actual cause of the delay is, but we soon figured out what it meant. In my nine months, there must have been at least three times when we had such delays. It often meant quickly switching to another train taking a longer route, but somehow, we rarely missed classes. Not only did half my class commute from London but some of my tutors did too.

As tiring as the weekly commute could be, I truly enjoyed the routine, so different from my life in KL where I have a driver and rarely used public transport. I didn't miss any classes at all, even when in January I came down with a cold, as did several of my classmates. Once, I returned from KL to London early in the morning, and still managed to get to my flat, have a shower, pack my books and other necessities for class and did my usual bus-Tube-train-bus journey to make my class. During Ramadan in May 2019, I would break my fast with a sandwich from Marks and Spencer's on the train back to London.

Being a mature student was quite a revelation. I realized very quickly that I was at a severe disadvantage for having not studied English Literature. Although I had read Shakespeare, Dickens and such classic writers at school, I did not study them in any depth. Every week we had to read at least two books, mostly biographies, memoirs or other nonfiction books. My first shock was having to read St. Augustine that first week. My second was in seeing how my classmates analysed our reading material. They asked questions I would never have thought of, such as about the motivations of the writers or referring to their similarities or differences with other writers of the same genre. I understood then that I had come from a school system where I was never taught to think critically. I tended to accept whatever the writers wrote and was confused when others saw their writing from entirely different angles.

This facility for critical thinking became even more crucial when we 'workshopped' our work. Every week two of us had to write an essay and send it to the rest of the class to read. When we came to the next tutorial, we had to comment on their pieces.

Although our tutors told us beforehand that comments should be respectful and constructive, the first time my piece was to be workshopped, my nerves began jangling even before we all took our seats. Once we got going however, it became clear that not only were the comments delivered in the gentlest of ways, but they were also helpful in improving my essays. Having a different set of eyes look at your work gives you perspectives that you might not have thought of. It is deeply humbling but also educational. Ultimately, your work comes out all the better for it. As someone who rarely showed anyone, not even those nearest to me, what I write before it is published, this was the biggest lesson I learnt.

Living in London was also an exercise in discipline. I had to put my studies first and so had to spend time reading and writing. But the city has its distractions. Apart from the many museums, theatres and events that it is famous for, I soon discovered that it is almost literally true when people say that London is a 'suburb' of KL. Almost every week a friend would arrive from KL and call me up for lunch or dinner. Which was lovely of course but it did sometimes make me feel as if I had not left home. Some friends came to stay which was lovely for the companionship especially if they are the independent types who can explore the city on their own.

Others turned up for work or on their way elsewhere. My parents came three times, once on their way to New York for the UN General Assembly and twice for Dad's speaking engagements at Oxford and Cambridge. I broke fast with Dr Dzulkefly Ahmad, the former Minister of Health and his wife once and my brother Mukhriz and his wife another time. Dr Maszlee Malik and Hannah Yeoh were kind enough to invite me to dinner with them when they were in town for conferences. It was hard to be lonely or to lose track of what was happening at home with this number of visitors.

True to my promise to Mum, I came home every long holiday, at Christmas and Easter for about three weeks, weeks that were a blur of seeing family and friends for lunches, teas and dinners and trying to do my reading and write my assignments as well. A friend who had done a postgraduate degree later in life had told me that you do become smarter when you're older. She neglected to tell me that you also have more responsibilities that take up a lot of your time. Either I felt guilty at not hitting the books, or guilty at not giving enough time to those close to me.

Then in March 2019, I woke up in the early hours of a cold Monday morning with a silent scream. I dreamt that Mum had fallen down a flight of stone steps, outside a traditional Malay house. Frightened, I texted her to ask if she was alright.

I did not hear from her until several hours later when I was already on campus about to go to class. My mobile rang and Mum's voice came on, sounding chirpy.

'Hi *sayang*, how are you? Just wanted to tell you something.'

'Hi Mummy, I'm about to go to class. Anything?'

'Yes. I found a little lump in my breast and this Saturday they are going to take it out. And after they've done that, they'll give me some radiotherapy so that I won't have to do chemo later on.'

Lump? Radiotherapy? Chemo?

These were not words I was expecting to hear, not in her cheery tone of voice. I was too shocked to ask too many questions and after a few minutes Mum rang off and I went to class, pausing only to call Tara and tell him about Mum's strange phone call. My tutorial lasted three hours; I had a hard time concentrating, going over in my mind what I should do. There were my children to inform, but what would be a good time?

Class ended and switching on my phone, I found a whole slew of angry messages from Ineza, who was in Bangkok for post-production work on *M for Malaysia*. She had found out through my youngest sister Maizura and was furious at me for not telling her immediately. 'You never tell us anything!' she accused me, 'When were you going to tell us?'

Shasha was coming down from her university in Bristol on Friday to spend the weekend with me. I thought I would tell her then. In retrospect, that would have been too late. But I thought it was unfair of Ineza to rail against me without understanding that Mum's news had hit me like a ten-tonne truck.

I went to bed that night tossing and turning, with plenty of questions in my head. Who should I talk to? Should I take the next flight home? And the most dreaded question: what if Mum doesn't survive the operation?

The next day I managed to get hold of Dr Harjit Kaur, the oncologist who was treating Mum at Prince Court Medical Center. In a voice as calm as the lake in the middle of my campus, she walked me through Mum's diagnosis and the procedure she would be doing. She assured me that there was very little risk from the operation itself, but it needed to be done. Mum would be in very capable hands.

Once I could breathe a little easier, I remembered the one person who must be just as anxious as me: Dad. I texted his office to ask for a slot to call him. After a few hours I got an answer: I could call him the next day at 4 p.m. KL time, essentially the next morning my time. Once again, I received no priority as family.

Another restless night. Waking up in the morning, I decided to take a chance. I called up Dad's ADC, Tuan Zaidi, and asked him to give his phone to Dad. Unbelievably he was available.

'How are you, Daddy?'

I knew Dad didn't like me being emotional, so I kept my voice steady.

'I'm OK.'

Matter-of-fact as always. Was I keeping him from something?

'So . . . about Mummy's operation, are you OK with it?'

'Yes, I talked to the doctors, and I agree with them.'

I sighed. Could he stop being a doctor for a minute and be like any other husband of over sixty years?

'Okay. Should I come home?'

'No, no need.'

With that, he put the phone down.

I didn't know whether to trust my Dad on that but his calmness gave me hope that things would be alright. If he had given the slightest hint of breaking down, I would have caught the first flight out. Still, with Mum's operation scheduled for the following Saturday morning, I began plotting how fast Shasha and I could get home if it became necessary. If we took a flight on Saturday morning London time, we could conceivably be home by Sunday morning.

On Friday night, Shasha and I Facetimed Mum just before she was wheeled into the operating theatre. She was lying in bed with what looked like a shower cap covering her hair. Yet she was cheerful, seemingly bent on not worrying us. We sent kisses over the phone and told her we loved her. Dad had been to see her and then had left to attend a DAP function. Nothing stood in the way of work and duty for him.

After putting the phone down, Shasha and I had a good cry. I was glad she was with me. The week had been a terrible one in so many ways. Besides the news from Mum, there had been others that distressed me almost as much. A friend in Paris suffering from cancer was being taken off life-support. And on the Friday, 15 March, 2019, a gunman shot and killed 51 people at two mosques in Christchurch, New Zealand. I prayed and prayed that there would be no more.

To everybody's immense relief but especially mine so far away in London, Mum got through her operation with flying colours. At age ninety-two, she had survived breast cancer. True to her nature, she did not hide the fact, speaking about it at every opportunity in order to encourage other women to do breast self-examinations. Mum had found the tiny lump by herself and had been alert enough to contact her doctor right away. If more women did that, more lives would be saved.

I came home finally in July 2019, but I still had to hunker down and write my final dissertation. I had chosen to write about the lives of some transgender Malaysians and the problem of discrimination that they suffered. In the course of that, I had to interview several transwomen and transmen, including one in the UK. I had known of their problems before, from my work at MAC, but at these interviews, the discrimination they face every day really floated up to the surface; abuse during childhood, difficulties in getting jobs, trying to be their authentic selves. It's nothing short of tragic and I hope to write a book on it someday.

My dissertation was submitted at the end of August. I had not known before then that I could write anything as long as sixteen thousand words. If nothing else, that course taught me that I had the stamina to do it.

* * *

Sometimes I can be prescient. In late September 2019, Dad was going to speak at the United Nations General Assembly for the second time as the seventh Prime Minister of Malaysia. The previous year I had not been able to join him because I had to begin my course. This time I decided I had to go because I didn't know how many more of these he could attend. None of us were to know that it would indeed be the last time for Dad, or any government leader for that matter, to speak at the UN building in New York.

My parents were staying at the Ritz-Carlton, one of those grand hotels facing Central Park. I had booked a cheaper hotel nearby with a room so tiny I barely had squeezing space between the bed and the door. But it meant I could walk to their hotel for meals and be fast but not last for the ride to the UN.

Dad's speech was on a Friday afternoon. We gathered at his hotel, jumped into a convoy of cars and zipped through the traffic to the office of the Malaysian Permanent Representative to the UN office, on East 43rd Street, very near to the UN itself. There in the Banquet Hall we were treated to lunch—not New York-style sandwiches, burgers or pizza but Malaysian food, cooked by the wives of the mission staff.

When I look back at the photos of that trip, it's very striking how much things have changed. At the lunch, as is typical for Malaysians, we recorded these moments with group photos. There's one photo of me with four smiling women, dressed to the nines for the visit to the UN. Three of the women were Norainee Abdul Rahman, wife of Muhyiddin Yassin, then Minister for Home Affairs, Shamshida Taharin, wife of Azmin Ali, then Minister of Economic Affairs and Sheila Devaraj, wife of Xavier Jayakumar, then Minister of Water, Land and Natural Resources. I'm sure our then Foreign Minister, Saifuddin Abdullah was there too but I did not get a photograph with his wife.

After lunch, Mum and Dad were whisked by car round the corner to the UN building. My brother Mokhzani, his wife, and three of Mirzan's children who were studying in the US as well as other officials from our embassy walked in the sunshine up the busy New York streets, past some protestors, and onto United Nations Plaza by the East River.

Dad's turn was sandwiched between the leaders of two small countries, Cabo Verde and Saint Lucia. He spoke at a podium placed front and center in the cavernous General Assembly Hall. Behind him sat the President of the General Assembly underneath the giant logo of the United Nations set against a gold-coloured wall. On either side of the logo were two giant screens which allowed us to see Dad clearly since apart from Mum and the wife of our Permanent Representative to the UN who were seated in the hall near the podium, the rest of us were seated way up in the 'gods' in the guest area. From our perch, Dad looked tiny.

His speech though, calling out the UN for its inefficiencies and particularly the undemocratic nature of the Security Council, went down well enough with the almost full hall. He spoke for about twenty minutes, touching on many global issues including climate change. And then it was over and as is the usual practice, he was taken to a press conference room to speak to the international press with our Foreign Minister and Permanent Representative in attendance. I didn't follow him this time and instead headed to the UN gift shop in the basement to look for souvenirs. Doing my bit to upkeep the UN.

* * *

That September had been a busy month for me. After handing in my dissertation, I plunged back into work. The Malaysian premiere of *M for Malaysia* was set for 10 September at a cinema at Pavilion mall. It was the culmination of many months of hard work for Dian, Ineza and I, not least to even get it screened in our own country. Malaysian cinema chains rarely show feature-length documentaries because they believe that nobody would be interested in them. They were also wary of a politically-themed story, even though it was the tale of the government then in power. I think some theatre owners were afraid that the Opposition might make trouble, perhaps protesting in front of the cinemas. I was disheartened at their attitude at first but kept pushing until they agreed to show it in limited theatres for only four days.

I guess they hadn't counted on people's sentimentality. At the invitation-only premiere at the Pavilion mall, all the halls we booked were full. Dad and several Pakatan politicians came and some people, like Azmin Ali's wife, begged to be invited. Later some of them, including Saifuddin Abdullah, bought out entire cinema halls for their own guests. I suppose I can now laugh at the irony of that.

But what really brought people out to see it were the influencers we invited to the premiere. Vivy Yusof, the Fashion Valet entrepreneur with 1.8million followers on Instagram, did a 'story' immediately after coming out of the theatre with tears in her eyes and told the whole world that they had to see it. That pretty much did it. *M for Malaysia* played in the cinemas for a full unheard-of four weeks. Not only was it a unique success for a documentary, but it also qualified us to represent Malaysia at the Academy Awards.

There were certainly other Malaysian films that could have been submitted for the 2020 awards. But Dian, Ineza and I were convinced that ours was worth a try. And we really did try. Throughout 2019, *M for Malaysia* had been screened at film festivals in San Francisco,

Auckland and Busan to very warm receptions. In our own country, we had to beg for recognition and a chance to show it. It was not until the last minute just before the deadline for Oscar submissions that Hans Isaac, then Chairman of FINAS, finally gave us the go-ahead.

And then we were on our own. We had to scramble to find out what we needed to do. A friend in Los Angeles introduced us to a public relations consultant who helped us place advertisements in Variety and The Hollywood Reporter, the two biggest movie trade papers. He also arranged for some interviews of the two co-directors which were published in a story on women in film. The documentary was shown in some limited theatres in the Los Angeles area and we got our friends, Malaysians and non-Malaysians, to go see it. To help with promotions, Ineza and Dian flew to LA and presented their film at a number of forums.

For the most part we did it all on our own dime. We had entered the film in several categories: Best Film, Best Foreign Film, Best Feature-Length Documentary, Best Soundtrack and Best Song. We particularly had high hopes for the soundtrack and song which was composed by Rendra Zawawi, a Malaysian musician and composer who lives in LA, and sung by Yuna, the Malaysian singer already becoming well-known in the United States. The only sponsorships we got were some money from some Malaysian businessmen and the use of the Dewan Filharmonik Petronas to record the song. Tony Fernandes, the founder of Air Asia helped with airline tickets to some of the film festivals. Everything else had to come from our own pockets. It is no way to have a running chance at winning an Oscar.

In the end we did not make the shortlists, but it was also the year that the Korean film Parasite won for Best Film, so we were up against intense competition. Still, we were happy that an Asian film made it. Additionally, Malaysia had a small flag to fly when a short documentary called St. Louis Superman, about a young Black activist Bruce Franks Jr who stood for elections in that Missouri city, was nominated. Two of its producers, Poh Si Teng and Cheyenne Tan, are Malaysian.

Part 5

The End? (2020)

23

The Wedding, The Virus and the Coup

The end of 2019 was not going well politically in Malaysia. Against the relentless attacks by the Opposition, Pakatan Harapan had begun to fray. Party infighting especially in PKR were spilling out into the open, making many of us observers despairing at the lack of decorum. Shades of old dirty tricks—intimate videos, for instance—were making a reappearance. Dissatisfaction with the government among the public grew; at every coffeeshop you heard grumbles about almost everything the government did. There seemed very little they could get right.

But there was 2020 to look forward to. In 1991, Dad had introduced Vision 2020, a set of challenges by which he hoped Malaysia would become an advanced country economically, socially, educationally, politically and psychologically by that year. The concept had been so iconic that we assumed that it heralded a shiny new future for the country. Nobody could have foreseen how it actually turned out.

February 2020 was meant to be one of joy for us in the Mahathir family. We were celebrating the wedding of a pretty young granddaughter and her handsome groom. The bajus were ready, the invitations sent out, the flowers arranged, the banquets ordered.

My niece Meera Alyanna, known as Ally, the eldest daughter of my brother Mukhriz, was getting married to her young man Ezran Daud Cheah and had chosen an auspicious date, February 20, otherwise written as 20/02/2020, for her big day. As this was the first wedding for Mukhriz's family, they had planned an elaborate one, with the solemnization ceremony, the *akad nikah*, at home, a grand reception at the Shangri-La hotel ballroom and a black-tie party at the St. Regis hotel. A week later, in keeping with tradition, the groom's family would host a reception, the *majlis bertandang*, at lunchtime again at the Shangri-La. The following week, we were all to go to Alor Setar. After Pakatan Harapan won the state in 2018, Mukhriz had been appointed Chief Minister and he had planned a reception at his official residence, Sri Mentalon, for the benefit of our relatives in our hometown and Mukhriz's constituents.

Our family was looking forward to the nuptials in a year that was almost mythical to Malaysians. All of us, as well as close friends had been instructed to wear the wedding 'corporate colours'; emerald green for the akad nikah, dark blue for the grand reception and any colour we wanted for the other events. For the first time since my own wedding twenty-two years previously, I ordered several outfits from a young Malaysian designer to wear to all these events, reasoning that they may last me for some time.

I don't know if it was possible to see the storm clouds brewing so early in that long-awaited year, but we should have noticed the ill wind blowing. In January, the first thunderbolt had hit when Maszlee Malik, the Education Minister, quit after being able to do nothing right in the eyes of a public that had extremely high expectations. Many of us, including me, were shocked: Ministers rarely ever quit their posts, being loath to give up the chauffeured cars and the bowing and scraping from Ministry staff. Was he leaving on principle or to spare the government further grief?

In January too, the first news reports appeared that many residents in the city of Wuhan in China were falling sick with a mysterious illness and some were even dying. This raised a concern in Malaysia, given the number of Chinese tourists we received annually, that we might—at that time, the operative word was still 'might'—be next. Heeding the warnings of the Ministry of Health, we started to stock up on masks and hand sanitizers. I bought supplies for my house and office and briefed my staff on the precautions they should take. Still, it did not yet feel like a colossus that would steamroll over us in the next few months.

Borders were yet to close. My two best friends Ivy and Vivienne and I had long planned a trip to Kerala, India in early February, and we felt safe enough to not cancel it. On the flight, we were three of the very few passengers who wore masks, apart from the cabin crew. Our hand luggage contained plenty of hand sanitizers. In fact, the first case of Covid-19 in India actually occurred in Kerala just as we landed, but at the time we did not worry too much, despite the apparent lack of social distancing and mask-wearing there. We enjoyed our week, sightseeing, eating and shopping not knowing that it would be our last trip abroad for a long time.

Ally's wedding day arrived, and we all gathered to witness the ceremony, looking rather like the Wizard of Oz's disciples in our emerald green finery. As is traditional, the religious solemnization is held at the bride's house. The guest list was kept small with only family and close friends which allowed for an intimate ceremony. My parents revelled in seeing another granddaughter married, only the third so far. Ally and her bridesmaids, comprising some of her cousins and best friends, looked radiant and Dad's grandsons, in their green *baju melayu*, looked polished and sleek. Our family gatherings, being few and far between, are precious to us. Watching my nephews and nieces, I wished Shasha was home too but she had refused because she was gearing up for her finals at Bristol University.

Mukhriz and his wife were exemplary hosts. Among the guests were five couples who make up their closest cohort of friends, always at every party they host and who holiday with them every year. Among them was Faizal Azumu, known to us as Peja, and his wife Nomi, a paediatric cardiologist. Faizal was a political operative who had been by my brother's side ever since he first began in politics in 2008. He had always been the Alfred to my brother's Batman, not even a Robin, but after the 2018 elections he had managed to get himself appointed as Chief Minister of Perak state, a big step-up from his previous position as an aide. I had always been a little wary of Peja but I didn't know exactly why.

It is usually tradition in my home state Kedah to hold an akad nikah on a Thursday night because Friday is a public holiday in the state. As it happened, 20 February was a Thursday. The next day was a rest day for the couple and their families to prepare for the next reception on Saturday. But it was not a holiday for Dad.

On Friday, 21st February, the Pakatan Harapan leadership, known as the Presidential Council, met to discuss the timeline for Dad to hand over the reins of government to his ostensible successor, Anwar Ibrahim. It had been understood when the coalition was formed to fight the 14th General Elections that Dad would be Prime Minister for a limited time and then pass on the post to Anwar. But nobody seemed to agree when this would happen. Some people insisted it would be after two years. Dad himself would not say although he hinted that it might be after the meeting of the APEC countries in Kuala Lumpur in November. At the meeting however, the Pakatan Harapan leaders agreed that the exact date would be left to Dad to decide. This seemed to take some of the pressure off the speculations that a big fight was brewing in the PH government.

That day I was at work when I received an unexpected text message. A former UMNO cybertrooper—freelance paid social media trolls employed by political parties—known as Ratu Naga asked if she could make an appointment to see me the following week. Ratu Naga is the online nom de plume of Syarul Ema who had crossed over to join the People's Justice Party, known by its Malay acronym PKR, after being harassed by Najib's people for seemingly having gone rogue by writing a social media post critical of his government. That was traitorous for someone in his pay. She called because she had a programme to empower women that she wanted to run by me, she said. I was curious enough to agree to this unexpected request but not alert enough to wonder why she, of all people, would be running such a programme. I had never known her to be involved in any activity run by women's groups before.

The following night, Saturday night, was the grand reception at the Shangri-La hotel ballroom. As instructed, our family turned out in navy blue, to match the décor that featured flower arrangements in various shades of the colour and giant blue butterflies flitting up the walls and stage. The Yang DiPertuan Agong was attending solo as the Raja Permaisuri Agong was away in London. As we are from Kedah and Mukhriz is the Chief Minister of the state, the Sultan and Sultanah, the Crown Prince and his wife and other members of the Kedah royal family were also in attendance. Also invited was the entire Cabinet as well as our extended family and friends, some of whom had come from abroad.

Ally looked regal in a light blue and silver songket gown designed and made by a local designer, accompanied by her groom in a matching blue baju Melayu, and her eight bridesmaids, this time in pale blue sarong kebayas. Tara and I had a small role to play escorting my parents up the dias to bless the bride and groom. My job was to ensure Mum, with her poor eyesight, climbed the steps up the stage safely. I was more worried about tripping over the hem of my dress and keeling over in front of the VIPs. Thankfully everything went well and we could go to our tables to eat.

The ballroom buzzed as about a thousand guests, the women be-jewelled and be-gowned, greeted one another and congratulated the hosts. During dinner, I left my table to go to the bathroom. Just outside the heavy doors of the ballroom, I saw Azmin Ali, then Minister for Economic Affairs, on his mobile, talking animatedly. This was not particularly unusual for a politician, but the ballroom was full of the most important politicians in the country yet nobody else seemed to feel the need to exit it to speak on their phones. Dad was on the VIP table near his newly-married granddaughter, but I noticed he seemed distracted, barely speaking to the other VIP guests on either side of him. Perhaps, he was just tired from all the meetings of the past few days.

After the thank you speech by the host, and the cutting of the cake by the bridal couple, they headed to the ballroom doors to bid farewell to their guests. This was usually a signal to form long lines to greet the newlyweds and wish them the best, a traffic jam that some people avoid by choosing to leave by the other exit doors. That night, despite gentle pleas from Mum to stay for the requisite family photos with the bride and groom, Dad insisted on leaving immediately, saying that he was tired. Mum was disappointed but none of us felt we could persuade Dad when he was in that mood.

My brothers and their wives, my husband and I stationed ourselves at the lower lobby of the hotel where most guests were heading to wait for their cars. Dr Wan Azizah, the Deputy Prime Minister, and her husband Anwar Ibrahim were one of the first, after the Agong and Sultan, to come up the escalator and head towards the entrance of the hotel. This was the first time we had seen him since our wedding twenty-two years before. At the sight of us, Anwar immediately mentioned the *Time* portrait and Tara took the opportunity to ask if he could take another one. Readily, Anwar agreed.

As we chatted, Anwar jokingly complained about the protocol he had to endure as the husband of the second most powerful person in the government. 'They're always telling me I have to walk two steps behind her!' he laughed. Funny that he should mention that. More than twenty years ago, when he was still the DPM, I hosted a charity film show for the Malaysian AIDS Foundation where Dr Wan Azizah was the guest-of-honour. Unexpectedly he turned up as well and, in deference to his wife, walked behind her on the red carpet. I was discomfited by this, trying to escort her while at the same time not wanting to turn my back to the more important person protocol-wise. But he laughed it away then, confident that this reversal of roles was only going to last the evening.

Other ministers and guests also stopped by to chat before they left the wedding. Having fought that gruelling campaign in May 2018 with them, I was on familiar terms with most of the Cabinet. In the midst of the crowd, I managed to take a selfie with Siti Norhaliza, the singing star who had performed one song in the bride and groom's honour that night, at my mother's request.

My brother and his wife went to bed that night exhausted, but they could tick off the successful completion of another event in the week-long roster of their daughter's wedding. Again, nothing indicated the gathering storm clouds. Everyone looked happy and friendly with each other, including the politicians.

The next night, 23rd February, we had to get dressed once again for the third event in Ally and Ezran's wedding. A smaller reception was held at the St. Regis hotel for friends of the couple and close relatives on both sides. The dress code was black tie formal. Women were dressed in floor-length gowns and jewellery, and men suited up in dinner jackets although probably not as reluctantly as my husband. We gathered at the outside lobby for cocktails and photographs before we entered the ballroom where long banquet tables, set with silverware and bouquets of flowers, were set at an angle to the dance floor in the middle.

Prior to the party, we had been warned that we would all be required to check in our phones before we entered the ballroom. This was to protect the privacy of the evening, allowing the young people to relax and not have to worry that their every move would be put on social media. An official photographer was already booked so no one needed their camera phones to take souvenir photos. It was tough for those who were addicted to their devices, but they had no choice. If they didn't turn in their phones, which were put in Ziplock bags with ID tags, much like restaurant cloakrooms, they could not enter the dinner. The internet was not going to get live feeds of this party.

That Sunday, we had already heard that something was brewing in politics. Getting ready for the evening, I had not paid too much attention, being too busy to watch my Twitter feeds that day. My brother Mukhriz and his wife were again hosting, and he didn't look particularly disturbed by anything untoward. My parents were absent; I assumed they were probably tired and needed to rest or wanted to leave the young people to their fun.

Not having our phones with us meant that we were spared seeing them constantly light up with news. We ate our dinners, listened to the funny speeches and performances by the bridal couples' siblings and friends and a band and then took to the dance floor.

Well after dinner had been served and cleared, Faizal Azumu and his wife arrived. Dressed in a white dinner jacket, I noticed he was in an exuberant mood. By nature, he is a lively person, sometimes a bit too much in my reckoning, but that evening he seemed to be on a particular high. By then the dance floor was filled with swaying bodies and Peja and wife joined them, dancing with surprising enthusiasm and energy. It was not going to be clear until a few days later where he had come from and why he was late.

24

The Resignation

Despite the late night of dancing, I woke up on Monday morning 24 February fairly early. As I was sipping my coffee, a message appeared on my phone. It was from my uncle Hashim, my mother's younger brother who lived very near them. 'I was just with your Mum. She's very teary, worried about what's happening.'

I wondered if this had anything to do with them not showing up at the party. Or worse, was Dad ill? Politics had not quite occurred to me just then. I showered and drove straight to my parents' home at the Mines, a half hour away. My parents live in a bungalow they call Sri Cahaya overlooking a golf course where we once watched Tiger Woods play in a tournament. A giant cement tiger, a gift from someone who knew of Mum's fondness for the animal, greets visitors in the driveway. Inside, more tiger soft toys, in every size and pose, filled the sofas and sideboards.

I arrived and headed upstairs to the airy sitting room where my parents watch TV. Mum was sitting quietly on the sofa, looking worried and bewildered. Three of Dad's staff were handing him a piece of paper which he read while sitting at his breakfast table on the adjoining balcony. I greeted Mum and sat with her for a minute. But looking at Dad hunched over the piece of paper outside, I felt uneasy.

Walking to the balcony, I peered over Dad's shoulder. In his hand was a letter addressed to the Agong tendering his resignation as Prime Minister. He was reading it carefully but had not yet signed it.

'I knew you would do that,' I said evenly although I didn't know precisely why he had made the decision. It must have had something to do with the goings-on the previous day. I wished I had paid closer attention. For Dad to do this, it must be serious. Yet again, he had told us nothing.

From the balcony where my parents like to have their breakfast, we can see the large lake that had once been a tin-mining pool. From those humble industrial origins, the area had been developed into a gated community complete with a golf course, club house and shopping centre. It was an ideal quiet area for retirees like my parents.

Sitting in front of Dad in the cool of that Monday morning, I looked at his face. Despite his thick grey hair, as always Dad didn't look his ninety-four years. His eyes though were sad. His mouth curled downwards in a pout as he looked at me. I've seen that expression before. It's the look he gives me when he thinks I'm about to scold him, as if he's about to burst into tears.

In retrospect I wish I had scolded him, had asked him to consider his options more deliberately. Instead, I said, 'I'm okay with it.' Our family has never been bothered about what position Dad holds. We had greeted his resignation in 2003 with relief, having finally gotten our father and grandfather back. For the next fifteen years our time with him was not subject to his gruelling schedule. We could finally go on holidays together and he could attend our birthday parties and graduations. It had come as a shock when he re-entered politics in 2017 and then stood for elections once again in 2018. But we had resigned ourselves to his decision and had stood by him throughout the campaign, quietly working in the background. Then, against our wildest dreams, Pakatan Harapan won and he was once again in the driver's seat.

Seeing that I did not object, Dad's face relaxed. I didn't know my opinion mattered so much. He signed the letter and handed it over to his staff to deliver to the palace. Then we sat down on the comfortable old sofa in his TV room and I asked him why.

'They want me to join up with UMNO again.'

'Who does?'

'Muhyiddin and some of the Bersatu members.'

I didn't know that the afternoon before, while I was getting ready to go to Ally and Ezran's party, Dad was at a meeting of Bersatu, the political party he co-founded and chaired. It had been an emotional one as they debated the move to leave the Pakatan Harapan coalition and team up with the party they had defeated to form a new government. Dad was against it, reasoning that the PH had won the people's mandate by campaigning against a corrupt government. How could he possibly betray that mandate by allying with the losers?

I did not grasp at the time how deep his feeling of betrayal and how palpable his pain was. At the Sunday afternoon meeting, he had been shocked at the rudeness and defiance shown towards him. His own political secretary, Zahid Mat Arip, who he had appointed after losing to Najib Razak in Pekan, had shouted and pounded the table at him insisting they leave the PH coalition. Dad, very much of the old school, was affronted by this show of disrespect towards him more deeply than anyone could have guessed.

As we dined and danced on Sunday night, separated from our mobile phones, most of the guests at Ally and Ezran's party were unaware of what was going on outside. Only ten minutes away down the Federal Highway at the Sheraton Hotel in Petaling Jaya, an unusual gathering was taking place. Some top leaders from Pakatan Harapan Coalition parties, principally Bersatu and PKR, were meeting with UMNO leaders in the very same ballroom that just short of two years before Pakatan had announced its victory over Barisan Nasional. Faizal Azumu was among them and it was after that meeting that he had changed into his dinner jacket and come to the party. His energetic performance on the dance floor now made sense.

News travelled fast that Monday morning. Before long visitors started to arrive to speak to Dad. I wanted to stay by his side, but Mum discreetly asked me to join her in the bedroom to look at some material she had bought. It wasn't clear to me if she knew what was going on; Dad has made these big decisions before without telling her. But despite her poor eyesight, Mum often sees things clearly and her loyalty to Dad is total.

I sat with Mum in her room, my ears straining to hear what was going on outside. I had glimpsed Lim Guan Eng arriving and sitting with Dad in the TV room where I had sat just a few minutes before. 'I cannot be a hypocrite,' I heard Dad say.

After choosing the fabric Mum offered me, I grew impatient not knowing what was going on. Walking past the TV room, I saw Anwar Ibrahim in the chair opposite Dad, the latest in the line of visitors. Downstairs I found his wife, the Deputy Prime Minister Dr Wan Azizah, dressed in a light grey pantsuit and her customary hijab, about to leave in her official car, smiling as usual. She had already had her turn with Dad and did not look particularly worried.

Having received my urgent message, my brother Mokhzani was the first to arrive. Standing by the front door, I quickly told him what had happened. As we talked, trying to make sense of events, Anwar came down the stairs and joined us. 'I tried,' he said, a wan smile on his face. He put his head on my brother's shoulder. I noticed his shoulders shook a bit. Then he straightened himself, his face dry-eyed, bid farewell and left.

By this time, the rest of my siblings and my husband had arrived, and I quickly briefed them. They were all shocked; we had been so busy with Ally's wedding that we had not been fully aware of what was going on. Even Mukhriz, the only active political party member in the family, was caught off-guard. As the father of the bride, he had been busy hosting her receptions all weekend and had not attended the fateful Bersatu meeting that had left Dad so distraught.

Done with visitors, Dad finally came down to the living room downstairs where we had gathered. We surrounded him as he sat on the sofa with Mum and explained why he had resigned. He had been upset at his Bersatu colleagues' plans to team up with UMNO again and disappointed that they had refused to listen to him, had even been rude to him. If there's one thing Dad cannot abide it is discourtesy in any form, even if anyone disagrees with him. To remain as their leader when they were determined to go ahead with their plans was untenable. To him, he had no choice but to step down.

As a family we received his explanation with understanding. We had resigned ourselves to his decision to re-enter the political fray two years previously, had supported him fully during the campaign in 2018 and had rejoiced with him, as the nation did, when he won. Now we accepted his decision once again. It meant we had him back, like we did in those fifteen years when he retired the first time. But we were not to know that the transition was not going to be as peaceful as it had been before.

* * *

My parents' house features an open plan ground floor with large doors that lead up to a terrace facing the Mines Country Club golf course. When visitors arrive at the front double doors, they face an atrium with a rock garden and what looks like a giant polished marble globe that, when switched on, becomes a revolving water feature. When it was first built, this open-roofed atrium would soak everything and every person near it every time it rained. A roof was finally built over it and now the rock garden stays mostly dry, marble water features notwithstanding, and gets filled with the flower baskets that frequently arrive for Mum from friends and admirers.

When arriving at the front door, visitors leave their shoes outside as is the custom, step in and turn right past the portraits of my maternal grandparents and round the corner to the living room with its plump sofas and armchairs and a baby grand piano that Mum plays. Dad likes the English style of decor, with plush cushions, rugs and chintz curtains. But over time, with so many gifts received from friends and acquaintances, the decor style has gone awry and become a mishmash of eclecticism. Chinese screens clash with elephant tusks, Persian carpets with gaudy jars of Raya cookies. The sofas are home to so many tiger soft toys given to Mum as patron of a tiger conservation project that we are always obliged to either sit on them or move them aside to get a comfortable seat. The walls surrounding the living room are covered with a large-screen TV, glass display cases filled with knickknacks or photos of the grandchildren. If they could talk, they would surely tell us about the astonishing visitors who have come to visit Dad here, from presidents to entertainers to political friends and foes.

Turning left from the living room, you walk through a short passage. On the left is a large sideboard topped with family photos and more tiger toys. On the right is Mum's little cubbyhole, a bright nook with a desk and a Yamaha organ. Here she writes her diary and letters although these days these are almost impossible tasks due to her deteriorating eyesight.

Straight ahead is the dining room where Mum and Dad eat their meals, with a kitchen adjoining it. Beyond the dry kitchen via some swing doors is the real kitchen where their cook makes the simple Malay meals they eat every day. The dining table fits twenty, but it is rarely ever full except when we visit with all the grandchildren or at the once-a-year Hari Raya gathering for the extended family. Otherwise, it is a large expanse covered inexplicably with a glittery silver cloth on which sit more containers of cookies. My parents' friends have a habit of sending food gifts, most of which they don't touch. Behind the dining table is a ten-foot sideboard topped with more containers of cookies, gift boxes of chocolates, packets of dried fruit and bottles of vitamins and supplements. Every time we go to the house, Mum invites us to help ourselves to whatever is there, but the abundance never seems to deplete.

Before long on that fateful morning the house began to fill with people: Muhyiddin, Azmin, and the others who had gathered at the Sheraton the night before. They were shown straight to the dining room. Azmin arrived and saw me sitting with my brothers in the living room and unlike the last few occasions I saw him, did not smile. Zuraidah Kamaruddin, the heavyset head of Wanita PKR, in her usual long tunic and pants headed towards me. I had always been friendly with Zuraidah. She had a good grasp of women's issues and had supported the women's groups when we marched in protest against child marriage. I always thought she would make an excellent Women's Affairs Minister, but Dad had made her Minister of Housing and Local Government where she was doing well.

As she headed towards me with a smile on her face, I couldn't help but ask, 'Why are you doing this to Dad?' Her smile disappeared. Without a word, she turned and joined the rest at the dining table.

I could not believe the array of people who were arriving. Faizal Azumu arrived inexplicably with his wife who came and sat with Mum, a move that made us all uncomfortable. How do you talk to someone whose husband was about to betray yours?

Shortly after, Dad came down and sat grim-faced at the dining table facing the rebels. His jaw was set, his brow furrowed as he listened to their arguments. I was in the living room some five metres away but the only voice I could hear distinctly was Azmin Ali's. He seemed the one most determined to carry out the deed, to leave the government that voters had given the mandate to rule and team up with the losers.

By lunchtime they did not seem to have gotten anywhere with Dad and finally left. Dad went upstairs to rest.

At 1.26 p.m., I got a call from Saifuddin Abdullah. Unable to pick it up at that moment, I texted him to say I couldn't talk. OK, he said. About an hour later I was forwarded a media statement that said that eleven members of PKR including Azmin, Zuraidah and Saifuddin were leaving their party to form an independent bloc in Parliament. I forwarded it to Saifuddin with the query, 'You're leaving to join this Muafakat thing?' He replied that Azmin and Zuraidah had been sacked from Keadilan and this was to show solidarity with them. 'Yes, we are for the new coalition.'

I had known Saifuddin for close to twenty years, having met him when we were both sent to a short course for NGOs at the Harvard Business School in Cambridge, Massachusetts, when I was President of MAC and he was heading the Malaysian Youth Council. We became friends and I remember in one class, he complained about political interference in the running of his NGO. I had always known him to be a reasonable and open-minded person.

I asked him again, 'With UMNO and PAS?' He never replied.

In the afternoon, after the first lot had left empty-handed and we had lunch, another set of people arrived, this time the ones the rebels wanted to team up with. My eyes widened as Zahid Hamidi, the President of UMNO facing 47 corruption charges and Hadi Awang, dressed in his usual white turban and looking a lot younger than I expected, scurried in smiling, sure that they would be able to persuade Dad. They too sat around our long dining table facing Dad at the head of it, his face possibly looking more disgusted than before. The presence of these people made the house feel unclean; if Najib Razak had walked in then, I think I would truly have lost it.

My siblings, husband and I sat and waited in the living room, monitoring our phones. Outside, the world was abuzz with news that Dad had resigned and social media lined up on either side of the fence, those who condemned him and those who supported him.

Meanwhile I remembered that I had an appointment the next day. I texted Syarul Ema, the blogger known as Ratu Naga, if she was still coming to see me or had the situation changed things. She replied immediately, 'No, I'm coming to talk to you about this women's programme I'm organising.' I agreed to see her.

That afternoon at about 4 p.m., Dad went to the Palace to meet with the King. In his previous career, Dad had been Prime Minister to four Agongs including the father of the current one. The late Sultan Pahang had been close to Dad; when Dad had his first bypass operation, the Sultan was in London and had tearfully called his daughters to visit Mum in hospital and convey his best wishes. On my part I knew the King from when we were students in the UK. He and his younger brother Tengku Abdul Rahman had been at the same boarding school as my brother Mirzan. As young adults we had been at the same parties, along with the King's three older sisters. We remained friendly but not close, moving in entirely different circles.

By the time Dad returned, the King had appointed him Interim Prime Minister, a position normally reserved for an incumbent leader just before elections. His Majesty reasoned that there was a need for stability above all, to assure the public that everything would be sorted out. Dad would remain in charge until there was a new Prime Minister announced.

There has been much speculation about the sequence of events that day. Some say that Dad had betrayed Pakatan Harapan by not consulting the other component party leaders before he resigned. But I watched each of them after they came to listen to his explanation of why he did it. Not a single one, least of all Anwar Ibrahim and Wan Azizah, looked despairing after they heard him out. I believe that they all surmised that the baton would be passed over to the next likely leader, most probably Anwar. On the previous Friday, they had given Dad the mandate to choose when he wanted to leave. Although it was a lot sooner than they, or anyone, expected, it was still, in their minds, according to plan. Pakatan would still be the government but with a new Prime Minister.

But someone else must have come to the same conclusion and decided he did not like it. Azmin Ali also assumed that the new Prime Minister would be Anwar Ibrahim. That assumption was probably the catalyst for him to leave the coalition, a plan that, in retrospect, was there all along. With Muhyiddin also pulling Bersatu out, the government was teetering on the precipice. Not all of the Bersatu MPs, least of all Dad and Mukhriz, went with Muhyiddin so Pakatan still had the majority, albeit with 113 MPs, a very slim one. The question now was whether it could hold on to it.

25

Betrayals

Looking back, I should have seen the red flags.

Unlike Dad, who's had enough experience with betrayal that he can smell it a mile off, I am so trusting I cannot see the obvious even when it's staring me in the face.

The day after Dad resigned, I went to work as usual. I still had one appointment that day, with Syarul Ema the ex-cybertrooper. She arrived late with a wiry young man with greased-back hair who she said was her husband.

Ratu Naga is a big girl. Her long, blonde-streaked hair is worn pulled back from a plump-cheeked face and small eyes that dart around taking in everything. Although she had been one of Najib's most notorious social media hacks, she had fallen out with him and crossed over to join PKR. She claimed that she became disillusioned with Najib, wrote something critical and then had to suffer six raids on her home by people presumably searching for signs that would incriminate her as a traitor. When she joined the then Opposition, she told the world how the BN cybertrooping machine had deep pockets to employ social media hired guns, some from abroad, to run propaganda for them. In the 2019 Netflix documentary *The Great Hack*, on how the political consulting firm Cambridge Analytica used big data to undermine democratic processes in various countries, Najib Razak was mentioned as one of their clients. Ratu Naga's account squared with this.

The first red flag I should have seen was when Syarul's husband, prone to nervous giggles, said that up to the day before, he had been the communications person for Zuraidah Kamaruddin, the Minister for Local Government and Housing and one of the PKR people who had left PH and therefore caused its downfall. By that he probably meant he ran her own band of cybertroopers. But nothing yet caused my antenna to buzz. Instead, I sympathized with his job loss and then told him how I had reacted when she had approached me the day before. They had both nodded in understanding.

Syarul and her husband came to see me ostensibly to discuss a Women's Day event that she was organizing for one of the PKR women leaders. They presented me with a slick printed brochure filled with words and pictures showing an ambitious programme for the day, with talks, performances and a marketplace. They were looking for sponsors and wanted me to endorse it although it eluded me why I was chosen, being better known for feminist positions on women's rights that often did not sit well with the mainstream.

I know enough however to know that when events such as these are organized by political parties or those connected to them, their objective is less about empowering women than about recruiting new members or at least getting women so beholden to them that they would hopefully vote for them come the next elections. In my entire life working for women's rights in Malaysia, I had never known any political party women's wing advocating to move the needle even the slightest on change for women. It has always been a great mystery to me why they have never made bettering the lives of Malaysian women a campaign issue.

Anyway, I listened politely, made a few comments and then the conversation turned to the previous day's events. Their ears perked up with interest at my recounting of what happened at my parents' house, especially at what Anwar Ibrahim had said.

That should have been the second red flag.

Supposing they were PKR insiders, I asked about some rumours I had heard about Anwar, especially whether it was true he was living apart from his wife. They readily confirmed it. It did not occur to me at the time to wonder why they were so ready to dish about their own boss. I should have known that they had another boss.

It was a friendly conversation. I made it clear that I was sad about it all, but that Dad was firm in his decision, not so much because of PKR's internal problems but because he was disappointed with his own party Bersatu for its defiance of him, their Chairman. I made some suggestions for their project and then they left.

As events unfolded in the days after, I stayed in communication with Syarul. When Pakatan said they had appointed Anwar as their Prime Ministerial candidate because Dad had not turned up at their Presidential Council meeting, I asked Syarul to put out on her networks that Dad had stayed home because he no longer had any locus standi at the meeting, Bersatu having pulled out of the coalition. She willingly passed the message on social media without attributing it to me.

The red flag finally waved its blood colour directly in front of my face when on Saturday, 29 February, as I sat in the Shangri-La's ballroom for the reception hosted by my niece's new in-laws, Syarul messaged to ask me to 'do something, they're all fighting'. I assumed she meant Anwar's and Dad's supporters as by then, after the meeting at Dad's house the night before, Pakatan had reverted to naming Dad again as their candidate for Prime Minister. No, she said, the fights are between Dad's supporters and Muhyiddin's.

For a second I was puzzled. She worked for PKR, not Bersatu, why was she concerned about Muhyiddin's supporters? Then I felt the worm of suspicion crawl all over my scalp. She asked me, 'Won't Tun join Muhyiddin?'

'No,' I replied, 'Dad will never forgive him for what he did.'

'Then Bersatu will break up.'

The final red flag flapped loudly. Why was she so concerned with the fate of Bersatu? Unless she had crossed over to the dark side herself.

The shutters fell from my eyes. If she worked for PKR but had no loyalty to its head, it must surely mean that she worked for Azmin. The fact that her husband worked for Zuraidah should have alerted me. I had made all the wrong assumptions about people's loyalties, that they were permanent and principled.

As I sat amidst the pretty floral surroundings of that wedding reception, I quietly berated myself for being such a trusting fool. I tried to recall what I had said to them, to see if I had inadvertently said anything that could be used against Dad. At the long VIP table beautifully decorated with flowers behind me, Dad sat for lunch, having arrived a little late. He was not going to miss his granddaughter's reception for anything. But only he carried the burden of knowing what the political situation was at that moment.

I texted Syarul that I could not talk because I was at a wedding. That was the last time I communicated with the Dragon Queen.

* * *

If anything characterized the strange year that was 2020, it would probably be betrayal. In no other year had we seen so many shocking examples of political, public and personal betrayal, carried out blatantly and unashamedly by people who were trusted by their friends and colleagues. And it continues without end, as if the new normal means that to betray is the standard one should achieve.

I may be only on the periphery of Malaysian politics but I still felt the betrayal personally. Like many Malaysians who had invested so much hope in the Pakatan Harapan government, I had wanted it very much to work. Undoubtedly, I shared the despair of so many when several mistakes in policy and approach were made—the unnecessary battles over ICERD or the Jawi in schools controversy. Chiefly, I felt that they had not gotten their communications strategy right and had offered to assist. But nobody took me up on it.

Only about a month before the 'coup', I had sat with Ainon Mohamad, then in charge of Pakatan Harapan communications, to talk about ways to change the narrative in the public arena, a narrative controlled by the Opposition and which constantly placed Pakatan on the backfoot. Dad had asked her to talk to me, after I kept nagging him about their poor communications work. We sat in a Bangsar café for breakfast and talked through some ideas. I thought she sounded sincere and professional; after all she had been in the business of government communications for a long time, working as press secretary to Muhyiddin Yassin.

I should not have been surprised that when the backdoor government was led by Muhyiddin, she should follow him as Press Secretary once

again. It made me wonder about the nature of people. In 2019, I had
seen her in Cambridge when Dad was giving a speech; although she
was not on official duty then, she was there to ensure that the Malaysian
TV crew covering the speech were set up at the venue. I suppose people
just do what they do, not out of any conviction but only out of loyalty.
Even if your boss is wrong, betraying the voters' trust, you still remain
loyal.

Indeed, I find many people giving the same excuse. They have
been friends a long time. No they weren't paid. They're just loyal to the
person. But what does it mean when you have no loyalty to principles?

Perhaps the person I felt most betrayed by is Art Harun, now the
Speaker of the non-sitting Parliament. I met Art many years ago at
the behest of a mutual friend who thought we would find each other
interesting because we had many common interests. Indeed we did,
and became good friends. Occasionally, I sought his legal opinion on
some matters. But most of the time we would meet for lunch and just
chat about what was happening in the country. Before 2018, we both
despaired over the direction of the country and agreed that we had a
leadership problem under a corrupt government.

I had even met Art, his wife and children for lunch one cold wintry
day in London when we were both there at the same time. Every year
he comes to my Hari Raya Open House. One year he sat at a table
with my father eating satay. To make conversation, he asked Dad if
he played any musical instruments since he himself plays guitar. Dad,
with his usual wit, replied, 'Yes, a gramophone.' At my first Open
House after Pakatan took over government, Art and his family came
as usual. I had heard rumours that his name was up as head of the
Election Commission and asked him about it. He evaded answering,
but I wagged a finger at him and said, 'If they offer it, don't say no.
You'd be good there.'

Soon enough he accepted the post and topped it by bringing
our friend the law professor Azmi Sharom with him. He was very
enthusiastic about his new job. When we next caught up, he told me
that his staff at the EC were pretty good, and when empowered, had
some innovative ideas for improving the electoral system. For example,
it was they who suggested livestreaming the counting of votes at the

Cameron Highlands by-election, so as to be transparent to all. He seemed very proud of them.

In early March, soon after Muhyiddin's Perikatan Nasional government took over I texted him when his brother Idrus Harun was appointed as Attorney-General. I asked him what his brother was like and he said he was hardworking but conservative. He was one of the judges on the Federal Court who had dismissed the bin Abdullah case: the Court of Appeal ruling that Muslim children born less than six months after their parents' wedding had to be considered illegitimate and could not carry their father's name, thus condemning them to the stigma.

Then I asked him if his job at the EC was safe. The EC Chairman, Deputy Chairman and five members are appointed by the Yang Di Pertuan Agong, after consultation with the Council of Rulers, and on the advice of the Prime Minister. Members of the Commission retire at the age of sixty-five. He said that he thought his job and Azmi's were safe. Then he asked me about Dad, saying that he hoped he got enough rest and sleep. We chatted about the impossibility of keeping Dad still, and with the coronavirus around, safe as well. Then I made a remark about looking at the new Muhyiddin Cabinet in horror. He replied with an emoji depicting a person swearing.

In early April he texted me to ask how I was and we had a long friendly catch-up on how the lockdown was affecting us all. He said it was depressing. We talked about my daughter's studies and he said he wished he had the money to do a doctorate but he didn't think he would be able to until he's seventy. I remarked that it's never too late to return to the books; I had done it at sixty-one and he was still younger than me. He told me he was working from home and the EC was in the midst of election worker training online with interactive modules. Their ICT system, he said, was being upgraded to handle auto registration.

Over the next few months it went on like this, normal friendly chats about our health, everyday grouses. He always asked how Dad was; we share the same home state and I think Dad knew his father. Then on 30 June I posted the news that he had been nominated as the Dewan Rakyat Speaker with a one-word query, 'Really?'.

He didn't respond until the next day after I forwarded him the link to the Digital Parliament, an effort by young people to prove that it was possible to hold Parliamentary sittings online. Up to that point, Parliament had not sat, stating that it was dangerous with the Covid pandemic, an excuse that was nonsensical when several other countries had already had legislative meetings via Zoom. He did not comment on it but instead talked about how he was undergoing treatment for a bad shoulder. I sympathized but continued to push him on why he had resigned so suddenly from the EC. His reply was that he could not say much, but that there wasn't any pressure on him at all, as many had speculated.

I expressed concern about the EC without him but he insisted that he had installed a 'very strong checks (sic) mechanism in (the) SPR'. SPR is the Malay acronym for the Election Commission. I felt reassured especially when he said that Azmi was not leaving and told him I thought he would be a good Speaker. Again, he asked after Dad and we continued as normal. At the end of the conversation I told him that I was his friend and he could always talk to me. I wanted him to know that if he was troubled by anything, I was always there to listen.

Twelve days later Parliament sat for the first time since the change in government. Their first order of business was to get rid of the former Speaker, the esteemed former judge Mohamad Ariff Yusoff, whose term otherwise would only have ended when the House is dissolved. Only a two-MP majority, 111 to 109, ensured that he lost his job.

The appointment of a new Speaker normally follows certain procedures. A candidate for Speaker must be nominated and seconded by at least two MPs other than himself. This nomination process must be conducted at least fourteen days before the election of the Speaker, although there is precedent for shorter time periods. If only one candidate meets these conditions, he is automatically elected Speaker; otherwise, voting by secret ballot is conducted, with the winner decided by a simple majority. Two deputy Speakers are elected in a similar manner.

It was very clear to the most casual observer with even the slightest knowledge of Parliamentary procedures that this was not what happened. Not only was the former Speaker summarily dismissed in the most undignified manner, but Art replaced him immediately, without the formal nomination period when the Opposition would have been able to name their candidate and a vote.

On his first day as Speaker, Parliament descended into chaos with Opposition MPs demanding to know why nomination procedures were not adhered to. There was further ignominy when Batu Kawan MP Kasthuri Patto faced racist and sexist remarks from PN MPs and the Speaker said nothing to admonish them. He capped the day by booting out Shah Alam MP Khalid Samad from the House for 'causing disruptions'.

This was not the Art Harun I knew, the one who had done a series of YouTube videos called *The Art of the Matter* on, among other topics, how a Speaker is selected. He had a lot of admirers in his days as a commentator on politics, always siding with those with the most liberal views. His views on democracy were clear, aligned with those in the Opposition during the Najib era and then with much of Pakatan Harapan. These were the credentials that had gotten him appointed as the Chairman of the Election Commission. Undoubtedly public service paid less well than a private legal practice. But the opportunity to put right what was wrong in government is often the motivation for many to accept a public service appointment. I assumed Art was one of them.

I must have assumed wrongly. I did think that as a Speaker Art would be a good one, would keep some of the more rough and crude MPs in line. But his first day in the job proved otherwise. And little of what he has done since has made me see even the slightest shade of the old Art.

Art complained in an interview that many of his old friends do not speak to him anymore. It's hard to continue a friendship when you have lost trust. It's even harder when you no longer know who you're talking to.

26

The Leap Year Day

29 February 2020 began early for me. It was the day of the *bertandang*, or the reception hosted by the groom's family to receive their new daughter-in-law. As it was a lunchtime event, I had to be up early to have my hair done and makeup applied.

While I sat having my hair blow dried, I kept checking my phone. After a night spent persuading their party members, the Pakatan Harapan leaders were to report back to Dad the numbers they had. These numbers were then to be presented to the Agong as proof that Dad had the backing he needed to be named the PM again.

That morning, messages kept pouring in from various politicians' aides, mostly asking for help to get through the notoriously strict guards at the entrance to the gated community my parents live in at the Mines. I had to constantly message Dad's aide-de-camp to inform the guards to let various party functionaries in.

The message the aides were delivering was positive. Yes, they had more than the required 112, the simple majority in Parliament. All Dad had to do was to have an audience with the Agong.

As I pulled on my dress, a cheery cotton number I had had made just for this occasion, the messages abated. I assumed everything was alright and we could relax and enjoy the fourth part of Ally's wedding celebrations. Tara and I drove to the Shangri-La to meet up with my siblings and their families before we descended together to the ballroom as the bridal party. My nieces, with no official duties that day, looked more relaxed and beautiful in their long dresses. Mum and Dad were to arrive a little later, presumably after Dad had visited the Palace.

If February's extra day in a leap year is supposed to bring us luck, it wasn't with us that day. As we celebrated at the Shangri-La, only Dad knew that the Agong had refused to see him that morning. In fact, he was refusing to have any contact with any of the parties involved. Palace officials were either giving evasive answers or rejecting requests for audiences outright. There was only stony silence from Istana Negara.

Dad had entered the Shangri-La ballroom escorted by the hosts with a grim expression on his face. There was a smattering of applause as he walked, upright and steady, to his seat, Mum following behind him. As usual Mum was smiling to everyone even though with her poor eyesight, she could barely make out anyone's face. But no matter, this was her granddaughter's wedding reception, and she was happy.

In a few hours, we would find out that the wedding reception, a lovely flower and music-filled affair, would be Dad's last as the 7th Prime Minister of Malaysia, after only twenty-two months. It contrasted with his previous two decade long tenure as the fourth Prime Minister.

* * *

Dad had not been too surprised it had ended this way. The previous day, Friday 28 February, I had joined him at his office at the Albukhary Foundation, an office he used on Fridays because it was near the modern Sixties era Masjid Negara, or National Mosque, with its unique roof design based on a half-open umbrella. My brothers would usually join him for lunch before going to prayers together. Occasionally I and a couple of nieces would join them for the meal and keep Mum company while the men were at the mosque.

That day, still a few hours before the Pakatan Harapan leadership descended on him to persuade him to lead them again, he sat at his paper-strewn desk, a thoughtful look on his face. I had arrived early and sat in front of him and as is my habit, tried to read what was on his desk upside-down, an art I have almost mastered.

'Are you reading my papers upside down?'

'Yes, it's a very handy skill.' I smiled, glad to hear the almost upbeat tone in his voice.

He looked at me with a wan smile.

'I made a blunder.'

'You did?'

'Yes.' He sighed.

He did not elaborate. I watched his face. As always, he looked at least twenty years younger than his ninety-four years. Despite being battle-hardened after all these decades in politics, nothing, least of all failure, etched more lines in his face or added grey to his abundant head of hair. I have watched much younger politicians age quickly once they entered politics, stressed out by the many demands and long hours. But if I were to line up a series of photos from each year of Dad's life in politics, if he aged at all, he aged very slowly. He did not even turn grey until well into his eighties.

That day I gathered he was telling me that he had made a mistake by resigning. He had assumed that his Pakatan Harapan colleagues would re-nominate him as their Prime Minister candidate when they saw the danger signs. Instead, they had nominated Anwar, and almost immediately saw their supporters fall away. This was why they were now scrambling in desperation, trying not to lose the government.

I too felt a twinge of guilt. If only I had stopped him, as I watched his pen hover ready to sign his letter to the Agong just five days before. But all I could think of then was that I would back whatever decision he made. Whether he stayed or left did not matter.

But sometimes we can't predict the future no matter how close it is.

* * *

As my family sat on that Saturday afternoon dressed in our Sunday best at Ally's new in-laws' lunchtime reception, in a ballroom decorated like a garden complete with a pergola right in the middle of the room, we had no idea what black clouds were gathering outside.

I sat at a round table with my husband, my brothers and their wives, my sister and two nieces. Behind us was a long table for the guests of honour, the men at one end, the women at the other. Dad sat next to

Mukhriz, while Mum sat with his wife, Norzieta, vampishly glamorous in a red dress. Scattered around the table were people like Dad's first Deputy Musa Hitam and former Inspector-General of Police Hanif Omar and their wives. After everyone was seated, Ally, in a long white gown with a lace back and her groom Ezran entered the room in a procession of groomsmen and bridesmaids and seated themselves next to each other in the center of the long table.

It was in every way a joyous occasion. Despite the grand setting the atmosphere was casual and friendly. We were entertained by Ezran's Uncle Peter playing the saxophone and singing *Fly Me to the Moon* by Frank Sinatra. A bunch of his paternal Aunties and Uncles formed a choir to sing *Consider Yourself (One of Us)* from the musical *Oliver!* to welcome Ally into the clan, apparently a tradition that they perform at every family wedding. A whole troupe of Ezran's mother's friends lined up on the dance floor to perform a well-choreographed joget. The food was superb, and we rejoiced in this wonderful joining of two families as we greeted each other and took plenty of photographs to mark the occasion.

At about three in the afternoon, we finally dispersed. I have one photo with Dad where we were both beaming at the other guests. Anyone would think this was normal at a family wedding. Who could have thought otherwise?

Back home I was getting out of my dress readying for a nap when the messages started pouring in. The King has appointed Muhyiddin, they said. I sat on the floor in shock, unable to believe what was happening. Didn't the PH aides assure Dad and their bosses that they had the majority of Members of Parliament behind Dad? Shouldn't the King therefore appoint him as the Prime Minister? How could Muhyiddin, whom nobody considered a PM candidate, be the one he chose?

I texted my brothers and others who might know what was going on. One by one they all confirmed the news. Ally's wedding was indeed the last function Dad attended as Prime Minister of Malaysia, on leap year day in 2020.

* * *

My mind returned to the events of the last few days, which had been difficult and tense. After Pakatan Harapan had announced Anwar Ibrahim as their Prime Minister candidate, they quickly realized they would not have enough support among MPs to regain the government.

On the Thursday night, 27 February, as I headed to a friend's house for dinner, I received a text from Liew Chin Tong of the DAP. 'Marina, can you arrange a call with your dad? Kit Siang would like to speak to him.'

I was startled. Such phone calls had never needed to go through me before. Although Dad was still Interim Prime Minister, these calls were obviously not meant to be official. I said I would try.

I called Dad up and passed him the message. He gave a sad chuckle. 'What is there to talk about?'

I said I didn't know but Mr Lim had requested the call.

A long pause as he seemed to consider it.

'Ok,' he sighed.

I conveyed the message back to Chin Tong. But the call didn't happen that night, probably because Mr Lim got back late to KL from his constituency in Johor.

The next day, Friday, four days after Dad resigned, a flurry of activity began. Panic was setting in that the government that had been so hard-won was slipping away. Every side was trying to figure out how to take power.

While both the rebels and Pakatan were manoeuvring to gather their numbers, Dad came up with another idea. The country was facing a deadly health crisis with the Covid-19 virus spreading all around the world. Far from being confined to China, by late February it had reached Europe. Italy in particular was seeing thousands of infections and hundreds of deaths. Already it was making inroads in Southeast Asia, including Malaysia where the first cases—and deaths—were being reported.

He reasoned that it was not the time to be politicking. Malaysians, including politicians, had to come together to fight the deadly virus. As a doctor he knew that viruses do not recognize political affiliations, that anyone could be susceptible to it if nothing was done to protect them. An unstable government and the current wrangling for power certainly did not help. He proposed instead a 'unity government', one where handpicked individuals from any party would form the government and govern without regard to party loyalties, at least for the duration of the pandemic.

To me, already sick of the relentless politicking, it seemed like a good idea. Ever since winning the elections and forming the government, Pakatan Harapan had been attacked not just by the Opposition but also by pundits and lay critics. The Opposition chose to attack it on racial and religious grounds, claiming that Dad's appointment of Lim Guan Eng as Finance Minister and Tommy Thomas as Attorney General meant that he favoured minorities over the majority Malays, a wild accusation considering that Dad had always championed Malay rights and had even been accused of being a supremacist. At the same time, some of Pakatan's Ministers seemed to be either making mistakes, underperforming or in some cases, not performing at all. To add to their woes, PKR was mired in ever more public internal fights, particularly between Team Anwar Ibrahim and Team Azmin Ali. There was every reason for the public to be fed up with these political antics.

At that time when nobody knew who was going to actually govern, I had jokingly proposed forming a new party called PARFUM, the Party of Really Fed-Up Malaysians. It was open to all except those who stank. Applicants for membership had to pass a smell test. I posted it on my Facebook page and received lots of supportive comments, even from overseas friends. Perhaps it encapsulated what every Malaysian was feeling then: what was going on in government was foul.

Pakatan Harapan component parties did not react warmly to Dad's idea. DAP countered that in our system of parliamentary democracy modelled on Westminster, governments can only be formed by political parties, not individual Members of Parliament. Voters also ticked their ballot papers for the political parties, not individuals who, although some may be much-loved and charismatic, campaigned under the manifestos of the parties they belonged to. Some worried about who exactly would be invited to join the government. I listened incredulously as speculations that people like Najib or Zahid, the very people Dad had worked so hard to depose, would be asked to join it.

Nevertheless, Pakatan had also run out of ideas. The days were ticking by. To return to governing, numbers were crucial. Whichever side that aimed to rule had to prove they had a majority of the 222 members of Parliament and had to convince the King that their candidate for Prime Minister commanded their confidence. By the middle of that confusing week, nobody really knew who had the majority.

That Friday I received calls from Pakatan representatives asking me to arrange a meeting between Dad and their leadership. I suppose they thought I was neutral enough, had no axe to grind, nothing to lose if I helped. But I knew it was not going to be easy. Dad was annoyed that nobody would support his idea of the unity government. They had dropped him in favour of Anwar as Prime Minister without so much as a by-your-leave.

Still, after a flurry of calls and texts back and forth all day, Dad agreed to meet them on Friday night after dinner. Having helped to set it up, I decided I was not going to miss it.

At first it was only to be a meeting of a select few, Lim Guan Eng and Mat Sabu principally. Anwar was not coming but would only send his representative in the form of Saifuddin Nasution, a long-time Anwarist. But as it neared evening, I received a message that Anwar would be attending himself.

Guan Eng arrived first with Betty, his wife, who went to sit at the dining table with Mum. I led him and Chin Tong to sit in the living room to wait for Dad who was upstairs. A few minutes later Mat Sabu arrived, followed by Anwar accompanied by Saifuddin Nasution. Not long after Sallehudin Ayub and Senator Husam Musa of Amanah also turned up, as well as Anthony Loke of DAP and Syed Saddiq, the loyal head of Bersatu's youth wing Armada, all with faces serious with worry.

Dad came and sat down, his face stern. Anwar sat on one side of him while Guan Eng on the other. The others sat on any seat they could find facing them.

Having run out of chairs near enough to the main protagonists (or was it antagonists?), I sat on the floor facing all of them and placed my phone on the coffee table in front of Dad. Somehow, I felt the moment needed to be recorded. Either nobody noticed or if they did, they didn't object.

Dad began by once again, going over his decision to resign.

'At the (Pakatan Harapan Presidential Council) meeting,' he said, 'there was no request that Anwar should join (the government) or that I should fix a date . . . nobody raised the matter . . . in the end they said that I fix the date, there is no compulsion for me to name the date.

'So, I told myself, when the time comes, I will resign. It may be after APEC; it may be before APEC. But give me time. That's the same plea I made to Muhyiddin, give me time. I went to the (Bersatu) Majlis Tertinggi meeting. I told them what is happening, and I said, give me time. Let's not push now. Please don't apply pressure on me, don't force me. I appealed to them not to force me.

'But in the end this Zahid Mat Arip, he banged the table. I tell you, he banged the table, people supported him. It means they have no confidence in me. I am supposed to be their leader. But they followed this man.'

He continued, 'I said why can't you wait? Oh, they can't. If we wait, then somebody will not back me. I said, what kind of support is this when you say that if I don't do it now, they will not support me?

'All in all, I find that all these pledges, support, nice words, and all that don't mean anything.'

I watched Dad's face as he voiced his disappointment. He explained the Agong had been very worried about the situation and that was why he agreed to the Agong's verification process, meeting every MP and asking them who they supported for PM.

'What can I do if I have no majority? That's it. And my own party doesn't support me, you see? Instead, they are basically supporting UMNO . . . and that man will come back as the government.'

Dad's logic was that if Bersatu teamed up with UMNO, being the bigger party UMNO will dominate. And the first thing they will do is let Najib's and Zahid's court cases as well as any other corruption trials involving UMNO politicians be dismissed.

There was no disagreement on that. But persuading Dad to take the helm again was another matter.

For over two hours, they went back and forth over the numbers. Guan Eng, Anwar and the rest tried to convince Dad that if he returned as their leader, they would have the numbers to form the government.

But there should be no talk of a unity government. Instead, it had to be again a Pakatan Harapan government.

'How can the losers take over the government?' Guan Eng asked, when it was Pakatan Harapan that had won the people's mandate to govern. This was the central question but how to regain the government was a matter of debate. Dad was convinced that he would have had enough MPs supporting him if Pakatan had not abandoned him and named Anwar as their PM candidate. The others said that they thought he had resigned as Chair of Pakatan Harapan and therefore had taken himself off consideration as PM.

It went on and on like this, the argument circling and circling and finding no agreed end. The leaders were convinced that if Dad returned, they could convince some of those who had left or were uncertain to return. Much depended on the support of the Sabah and Sarawak parties. They were sure that they could get more than the 112 MPs needed. But, just as in 2018, they recognized that Dad was crucial.

I watched the faces of these men, men who had had a brief taste of power and who had lost it through the treachery of their former colleagues. It wasn't just the fault of those who crossed to the other side, it was also theirs for not seeing the danger signs and not doing enough to stem the wounds. The public cannot have confidence in political parties that cannot avoid washing their dirty linen in broad daylight for all to see. Indeed, there did not seem to be any attempt at resolving any of the issues, to find any compromise at all.

Like many ordinary Malaysians, I had watched in despair as the exhilaration of the win in 2018 quickly dissipated in the wake of incompetence on the part of some and infighting. Just after the victory, a foreign journalist had asked me if Dad would be able to manage this new coalition. In all confidence I had replied that he should be able to since he had experience in managing coalitions for twenty-two years.

I forgot that the previous coalition not only all belonged to the same side, but Dad led the dominant party then, UMNO. In Pakatan Harapan, Dad was leading a coalition made of parties that had disparate ideologies, even if they all united against Barisan Nasional. Furthermore, he was not in the strongest position, being Chair of a new small party. Pakatan Harapan could not have won the 14th General Elections without him because voters had doubts about the leadership abilities of the other party leaders and believed that only he had the experience to run the government. But once they were in, they had to climb a very steep learning curve. It was one thing to be in the Opposition where you did not have to deal with the realities of administration, it's quite another to actually have to make it work. In addition, Dad could only choose Ministers from the names given to him by the respective parties and some proved to be total duds.

The night wore on as the leaders discussed how to save their government even though the deadline to present the Agong with their numbers was less than twelve hours away. By the end of the evening, Dad agreed to lead them again under two conditions: they had to ensure that they did have the majority of MPs by the next morning and they had to agree that he would not appoint to the Cabinet two people he deemed radioactive: Guan Eng and Anwar. One of the complaints of the group that left the coalition was that Guan Eng as Finance Minister had made policies that did not favour Malays, and although Dad had tried to persuade them that he could discuss with Guan Eng on the folly of some of his policies, they refused to accept it. After much debate, Guan Eng, his face red, agreed. 'I'm doing it for the country, Tun,' he said, softly.

Anwar however proved a harder nut to crack. For twenty years, he had gone through jail time and trial after trial that kept him away from active politics except for brief periods. He had sat out the 2018 elections in hospital where he was being treated while his wife and eldest daughter Nurul Izzah had won their respective seats. The understanding before the elections was that one of them would make way for him once he finished his sentence, or better still, received a Royal pardon.

The pardon was given soon after Pakatan formed the new government but neither Dr Wan Azizah nor her daughter seemed willing to give up their seat. After scrambling to find an MP who was prepared to sacrifice themselves for their leader, it fell to a novice Danyal Balagopal Abdullah who had won the Port Dickson seat in the 2018 general elections. I have often wondered what he felt at being asked to vacate the seat only four months after having fought so hard to win it. Even in my small role in the campaign, the eleven days of hustling had exhausted me, what more an actual candidate. Regardless, Danyal made way for his boss, who won with a bigger majority despite a smaller turnout.

With Anwar back in Parliament, he was now eligible to join the Cabinet and therefore move closer to the Prime Ministerial post. But one person stood in his way: his wife. As Deputy Prime Minister, she was the highest-ranking woman in the Malaysian government. Concurrently she was the Minister for Women, Family and Community Development. Although she could never be called a feminist of even the mildest stripe, women's groups were pleased that a woman was so near the top of the power totem pole. But would she make way for her husband, as good Muslim wives are expected to do?

In an interview with Anwar Ibrahim after he was pardoned, the famed TV journalist Christine Amanpour asked him what his plans were. He said he would join the government after his wife stepped away from her constituency and Cabinet position. To which Amanpour asked, 'But why should she? Just because she's your wife?' Feminists everywhere watched gleefully as he struggled to reply.

Amanpour or not, Wan Azizah showed no signs of stepping aside from her Cabinet post for her husband. There were rumours that she was afraid to do so, in case Dad would not automatically appoint him to replace her. On the other hand, the very idea of having a husband and wife in the Cabinet was unpalatable to many. Either she had to go, or her spouse had to bide his time.

With the Cabinet unravelled when Dad resigned however, there was now an opportunity for Anwar to join it without his wife. For two days it seemed he had achieved his dream to finally, after two decades, become Prime Minister. But reality sunk in very quickly. There were not enough MPs who would accept him as their leader; the very possibility had made some of them leave, causing the Pakatan government to fall. He had no choice but to agree that Dad had to once again be their candidate for PM.

But Dad's condition, that Anwar be left out of the Cabinet, was difficult to swallow. Dad was frank about his reasons. None of it was personal but he had gauged that much of the unhappiness within the coalition had arisen from doubts about Anwar's leadership. Even though Dad had been bitterly disappointed by Muhyiddin and Azmin's betrayal, it did not mean that Anwar had to be automatically included in the Cabinet and in line for the premiership.

Anwar was wedged tight between his ambition and the realization that the government needed to be saved. If they failed to persuade a majority of MPs to rally behind Dad, there would be no Pakatan government and a Cabinet post for Anwar, let alone the Deputy Prime Minister position, would be moot. Pride needed to take a backseat.

It was well into the night when the meeting ended. The party leaders had achieved one goal, to get Dad to return to lead them. But they had to accede to his conditions. By the next morning they had to perform two tasks: they needed to gather the pledges of more than 112 MPs to support Dad as their PM. And they had to persuade their own party members that neither Guan Eng nor Anwar were going to be in the new Cabinet if they succeeded. It was not going to be easy.

Throughout that tense night, I had swung from despair to hope, however thinly it had been. But the words of one person underscored the gravity of the situation for me personally. Senator Husam Musa from Amanah, a soft-spoken gentle man, turned to me as they were all preparing to leave. 'You know, if we lose tomorrow, I will just go back to my village and my quiet life. But you and your family . . . if Najib returns to power, he will come after you with a vengeance.'

Those words haunted me for weeks.

Epilogue

The Apple and the Tree

When apples drop from their parent tree, they may not fall far but that doesn't mean they will one day grow into an exact copy of what they were born from. A lot of DNA may be the same but cross-pollination from other similar species of apple or even other trees may result in a new version of the parent, with perhaps more extensive branches, brighter or differently-coloured flowers, even fruit that tastes different. The original tree can't control what their fruit will become, only try and provide the shelter and environment that might influence their progeny's growth.

I know that I'm the apple that has not strayed far from the tree and that is only natural. In my middle age, I have seen that, while my train may have taken a far more circuitous route than my dad's, there are many elements that I recognize as being similar as his. Dad is famous for his work ethic and discipline. I have grown up believing myself to be lazy and have worked to overcome it almost all my life. Of late, especially having returned to studies at this mature age, I have discovered a capacity for discipline I never knew I had. Without it, I could not have coped with living on my own, commuting every week and finishing all my reading and assignments on time.

I have long known that Dad has little patience with people who are slow to think. As a child, I would dissolve into tears whenever

Dad decided to present a Maths problem for us to solve. He would do this at mealtimes, just when I wanted to focus on eating rather than calculating, which I thought was unfair. As I grew up, I sometimes exhibited the same impatience but at least I knew to reserve it for the appropriate times. Perhaps that was Mum's DNA coming through.

Mum is sociable and loves to have conversations with anybody. Dad, on the other hand, does not like small talk. He doesn't mind having to speak at meetings and conferences but becomes quiet and shy at purely social gatherings. I am a combination of both; I will talk when I need to but am often uncomfortable asking people about themselves at parties in case it sounds intrusive. I know a lot of people but keep a very few trusted friends around me. This trust becomes a necessity in the position I found myself in for twenty-four years.

I know that many people are fascinated by those who are close enough to power to be presumed to be intimately acquainted with it. In that intimacy, they may be either varnished or tainted by it. Outsiders see the glamour of the proximity to power most of all. Somehow those elevated ones seem to have smoother skin, slimmer wrists and ankles, shinier hair and shoes than the average citizen. Indeed, the nearness and almost perpetual access to inner sanctums give the lives of these families a seemingly enviable glisten. Power has a centrifugal force; everything revolves around it. As long as you're in the orbit, you get to enjoy all the perks—the plush living quarters, the front seats, the ability to have every craving and whim catered to, if you so wish. Then there's the inevitable deference given to you by staff for the simple virtue of having the family name. If you're the sort who basks in this obsequiousness, you might actually find it enjoyable, although I should add that deference is not always the same as respect. That respect can only be earned by how well you treat the people who are employed to serve your power source in office.

There have been seven Prime Ministers in our country's history and none of their offspring had any say in their fathers' careers. Some of them have had excellent careers in their own field and most have kept a low profile. But I took a different course. Arguably, because I never planned it, I chose to be a public figure in my own right, beginning during Dad's first time in office. And he was there for a very long time.

This book talks about how that relationship affected everything I did. But in answer to the question of what it really, personally, felt like to be the PM's daughter, there is only one answer I can most honestly give: it all depends on how you were brought up.

I can only speak for myself and not for any other politicians' daughters. But I do believe that how you present yourself as your politician parent's child depends so much on the values they brought you up in. Politics is a regular dinner table topic in some families, and children grow up with the expectation that it will always be a part of their life. Some families expect their children to participate in elections and legislating while others don't, especially not of daughters. Politics was just your Dad's job, like any other job, and you would no more partake in it than you would if he were a doctor or teacher.

From my childhood, my parents emphasized the values of hard work and service as the only routes to success. They would snort in derision if we wanted to take part in newspaper competitions, where you had to write a slogan to enter, or participate in raffles where luck would be the main thing you needed to win the prize. For them, there was no easy way to get anything in life. Education was paramount; there was no way around it. You went to school and finished it at degree level. After that, you can do what you want. My parents sat on that fence between pushing us just enough but without the hard-driven ambition of some Asian families. We did not have to be top in everything, but we also could never get away with just scraping by.

Although they never told us what we should choose for our careers, they also never talked about political office as a choice. If we wanted to join politics—and this was before Dad had any position beyond a Parliamentary seat—we had to take the same route he had: get a degree, work and then get into politics for only one reason, to help people. Dad's work with poor people who needed medical care was what motivated him, besides his experience during British colonial times and the Japanese occupation. He left government service because he knew he could not be active in politics as a civil servant.

Our parents also drilled into us that our name had no currency, that using it was the worst way to get anything. We had to prove—in fact, doubly prove—we were capable of being good at everything we did, whether it was writing as I did in my first job at Berita Publishing, or in finance and business as my brothers did. We were told in no uncertain terms that we could not expect a leg-up from Dad in anything we wanted to do.

Just as nobody, including me, could have predicted my evolution as an activist when I led the Malaysian AIDS Council, few foretold at the beginning what my column, 'Musings', would become. Originally my editor June Wong had wanted me to write as a mother and wife, about home and family, since I had at the time a very young daughter. But as time went on, the column grew out of that limited brief and went on to talk about anything that was bugging me that week, whether it was an injustice towards women or young people, or discrimination against people living with HIV or what I had read or observed overseas that I felt had relevance to our own country. I kept it going every fortnight almost without fail for more than twenty-five years except for the year I took a sabbatical out of frustration with the pressure my editors sometimes imposed on me to tone down my comments. Today it is a monthly column in the *Sunday Star*, unfortunately behind a paywall as the newspaper tries to compete with the many online portals that have cropped up in the past decade.

Along the way, 'Musings' has attracted attention, even controversy, been censored a number of times principally during Najib's tenure as Prime Minister, and has been compiled into three books, *In Liberal Doses* (1997), *Telling It Straight* (2012) and *Dancing on Thin Ice* (2014). Once I was asked to go to court as a witness in Lim Guan Eng's trial against the then Chief Minister of Melaka, Rahim Thamby Chik, because I had written an indignant piece about the case. I don't think I helped much really, but it was the first time I met Lim in person.

As I have said many times, I never set out to write to or for a particular audience. I simply wrote what I thought about the issues I cared about, which were women's rights, children, education and health. As I grew in my activism work, I learnt that human rights and social justice issues overlaid everything that was wrong in our country and tried to suggest ways they could be put right. My word limit of about a thousand words, later shortened to 800, meant that I had to discipline myself to write in a straightforward style, occasionally sardonic, that I think people found easy to read.

But being so public and forthright with my views, as well as my activism on behalf of people vulnerable to HIV, meant that I became a target for criticism from many quarters. In fact, I was a sitting duck. While Dad was in office, the Opposition, especially the more conservative sector, saw me as a suitable surrogate for any flames they wanted to throw at Dad, knowing that there was little I could do about them. I was accused of promoting immoral behaviour by advocating for safe sex, using condoms. By extension, I must have also been brought up by an immoral father, the one who was then holding the reins of power. Then, as now with the Covid pandemic, they had little interest in science and worked themselves into a frenzy trying to show that the entire country would go to pot if any of my proposals for HIV prevention were allowed to be implemented. All I could do was to rely on the facts and explain it all patiently over and over again.

In a country that is so used to binary concepts—with us or against us—I think I confused people a lot. I am the daughter of a man that many love to hate. Therefore, I must surely be the Devil's spawn, must surely have the same genes that make the man so confident that he is right. Yet I talked about human rights, even those of the people that erstwhile liberals tended to ignore or neglect. There I was, daughter of the most elite among the elite, hanging out with transexual sex workers and drug users, for God's sake! And not just spending time with them but actually championing them as equals to everyone else in the country. I have been called a 'liberal', a dirty word in Malaysia. Some people may have taken the title of my first book literally.

On the other hand, I am patently not a rebellious daughter, going against a father publicly. Whatever disagreements my father and I had, and yes, we had some, we duked them out privately. Sometimes there was no middle ground at which we could meet and there would be long silences until one or the other decides to break the ice and act as if nothing had happened. But outwardly I would be nothing but loyal. I would not necessarily defend Dad on anything because I knew he needed no help in that, but I would refuse to say anything against him.

It would often surprise me why some people never thought that was good enough. To those who would excoriate me for not criticizing my dad publicly for something he said or did, I wanted to ask if that was something they would do to their own father. Perhaps they would. But too few people have been in my shoes, for as long as I have, to truly know what they would actually do in the same situation. It is something you can only imagine in theory but brought up as I have, always respectful of older people in that time-honoured Asian way, it is not something anyone would realistically do. Yes, there have been times when I have dreaded reading headlines, times when I have not wanted to talk to anybody, times when I walk around assuming everyone is hostile. But there has been nothing to do but to swallow it all and keep going.

This is not to say that it is fun to see criticisms of Dad, especially in these free-for-all social media days. If I want to spoil my day, I'll go read the comments on certain online portals and as unfair as I might find many of them, they still grate. Sometimes they do hurt. In fact, they probably cause me more grief than they do him. He's still my father ultimately; I would not be here if it were not for him.

This is why I don't spend much time on social media anymore. I have a life outside of it, a life where I do mundane things like grocery shopping or pay utility bills and see no need to live all of it online. If I do have something to say, I might say it on Facebook or Twitter. But otherwise, I have far too full a life to have time to share it with the entire world.

I've also noticed that negative comments, especially of the rudest sort, is an industry in itself, one that requires no more effort than to repeat what someone else has said, with the addition of a few more choice words. I have friends who disagree with me on many things, including about politics, but they give me substantive arguments delivered in civil dialogue. Those are much more likely to make me think about my positions and possibly change my mind. The types of comments I often see online are not about changing my mind; I suspect some people might be horrified if I agreed with them. It's merely about using me as target practice because they know I'm not going to entertain them, much less make police reports.

I did take some comments seriously enough to file a defamation case against ISMA once, took them to court and won a public apology from them. But in their usual shakily 'Islamic' way, they twisted the verdict to make it sound as if they won. The lesson I learnt? Never deal with dishonest people.

I grew up with the idea that people are inherently good. Despite many disappointments especially from people who wear the mantle of religion, I still believe that. The values I grew up with remain the same. I cannot tell the whitest of lies without an uncomfortable pricking deep within my soul. I do not steal except from my husband's bag of crisps. Hypocrisy makes my toes curl.

It is these values that have defined Dad when he was in office and when he was not. In other words, he is the same person regardless of what his station in life is. Similarly, with me, I am the same whether I am the PM's daughter or not.

The tracks we rode on may have wound around different hills and dipped into varied valleys. But in the end, we arrived at the same station.

Acknowledgments

Writing a book from start to finish is a scary business, especially if it relies so much on memory as this one does. For its initiation and completion, I have had many shepherds who pushed, pulled and nudged me along in the right direction.

Having never written an entire book before, I had to first go and learn how. Bernard Chauly was the first to tell me about the creative writing courses at the University of East Anglia and Li Shan Chan, an alumnus of the Masters in Biography and Creative Non-Fiction programme helped me through the intricacies of crafting the right application. I have to thank my tutors Dr Helen Smith, Professor Kathryn Hughes, Professor Jean McNeil and Mr Ian Thompson for their wise guidance to a nervous student. The Non-Fiction Masters class of 2018/2019—Amber, Cailey, Caroline, Caroline, Elli, Jairus, Jon, Katrina, Katie, Liz, Pyae, Rosa, Shantelle and Vik—were the most supportive group of classmates I could have ever hoped for. Thanks for your feedback, your insights and most of all your friendship that made my UEA experience so much better than I thought it would be. I'm also grateful to another UEA alumnus, Tash Aw, who time and again bolstered my confidence in writing my dissertation as well as this book.

Long before I was approached to write this book, I had already started writing the essays that formed its basis. My coursemates on the Curtis Brown online memoir course helped me shape my initial chapter into a fuller more personal story. Their suggestions were all much appreciated.

June Ho of RiteOnCourse was the angel who told Nora Nazerene Abu Bakar at Penguin Random House SEAsia about me and set this project on its path to publication.

Pyae Mo Thet War, Rose Ismail, Zainah Anwar, Ivy Josiah, Vivienne Lee, Aishah Ali, Ambiga Sreenevasan, Karim Raslan and Keith Leong read my draft chapters and gave lots of helpful advice and memory jolts.

I am eternally grateful to my colleagues at Sisters in Islam, Musawah and Zafigo.com for their patience and understanding when I took time off to study and then to finish this book.

All my love goes to my husband Tara and my daughters Ineza and Shasha who encouraged me to fulfil my dream of going back to university to study creative writing. It was truly the best 60th birthday present.

Finally, I have to thank my parents for giving me a life so full of stories I couldn't even put them all in this book.